Introduction to Software Design with Java

Martin P. Robillard

Introduction to Software Design with Java

 Springer

Martin P. Robillard
School of Computer Science
McGill University
Montreal, Québec, Canada

© 2017 Circlecreativestudio/iStock

ISBN 978-3-030-24093-6   ISBN 978-3-030-24094-3   (eBook)
https://doi.org/10.1007/978-3-030-24094-3

This Springer imprint is published by the registered company Springer Nature Switzerland AG
The registered company address is: Gewerbestrasse 11, 6330 Cham, Switzerland

Preface

This book is inspired by well over a decade of teaching software design at McGill University. At first, my focus was to explain the software design know-how available from high-quality references. Soon, however, I realized that the main challenge of teaching software design lay elsewhere. Communicating *how* to apply a design technique or use a programming language mechanism was relatively easy. The real struggle was to convey in which *context* we want to use a certain design technique, and *why*. To do this, I needed to explain what is going on in a software developer's head. Over time, my lectures came to be more about exploring the space of alternative design decisions one can make in a given context.

The goal of this book is to help readers learn software design by discovering the *experience* of the design process. I share my experience of designing software through a narrative that introduces each element of design know-how in context, and explores alternative solutions in that context. The narrative is supported by hundreds of code fragments and design diagrams.

My hope is that this book can serve as an effective resource and guide for learning software design. However, I do not believe that it is possible to develop significant design skills solely by reading a book. In my own learning process, I have benefited hugely from reading other people's code, regularly writing code, and relentlessly refactoring existing code to experiment with alternative design solutions. For this reason, this book places a lot of emphasis on coding and experimentation as a necessary complement to reading the text. To support this aspect of the learning process, I provide a companion website with practice problems, and three example applications that capture numerous design decisions. An orientation through these example applications is provided in a section called "Code Exploration", at the end of each chapter.

As its title indicates, this book provides an introduction to software design using the Java language. The code used throughout the book, as well as the example applications, are in Java (version 8). My use of the Java language, however, is a means to communicate design ideas, and not the topic of the book. I aimed to cover design concepts and techniques that are applicable in a host of technologies. Many concepts (such as encapsulation), will be generally relevant in any technology. Others (such as inheritance) will be paradigm-specific, but usable in multiple programming languages. For both general and paradigm-specific information, it should be possible to adapt the examples to other languages relatively easily. In a few cases, the material needs to address a Java-specific mechanism with implications on design (e.g., cloning). In such cases, I make sure to present the mechanism as one implementation of a more general technique.

This book is targeted at readers who have a minimum of programming experience and want to move from writing small programs and scripts to tackling the development of larger systems. This audience naturally includes students in university-level computer science and software engineering programs. However, I kept the prerequisites to specific computing concepts to a minimum, so the content is also accessible to programmers without a primary training in computing. In a similar vein, understanding the code fragments requires only a bare minimum knowledge of the language, such as would be taught in an introductory programming course. Information about Java that is crucial to understand the text is provided in an appendix, more advanced features are introduced and explained as necessary, and I make a minimum of references to specific elements of the language's class library. My hope is thus that the book can be useful to almost anyone who wants to write clean, well-designed software.

Organization of the Book

The first chapter is a general introduction to software design. The subsequent chapters provide a progressive coverage of design concepts and techniques presented as a continuous narrative anchored in specific design problems. In addition to the main content, the book includes different features to orient readers and help use the book as a launchpad for further exploration and learning.

- **Chapter Overview:** At the beginning of each chapter, a callout lists the concepts and principles, programming mechanisms, design techniques, and patterns and antipatterns covered in the chapter.
- **Design Context:** Following the overview, a paragraph titled "Design Context" introduces the design problems that are used as running examples in the chapter. It is thus not necessary to read all previous chapters to understand the code discussed in a given chapter.
- **Diagrams:** Each chapter includes numerous diagrams that illustrate design ideas. Although they are provided to illustrate the ideas in the text, the diagrams are also realistic illustrations of diagrams that can be used in practice as part of design discussions.
- **Code Fragments:** Each chapter includes many code fragments. The code generally follows the conventions presented in Appendix B, with occasional concessions made to make the code more compact. A complete version of the code fragments can be downloaded from the companion website (see below).
- **Insights:** In each chapter, the main numbered sections are followed by an unnumbered section titled "Insights". This section forms an actionable summary of

the key information and advice provided in the chapter. It is meant as a sort of catalog of applicable design knowledge, and assumes the material in the chapter has been mostly assimilated. The insights are in bullet points to be easily perused.

- **Code Exploration:** Following the "Insights" section is a section titled "Code Exploration" that provides a discussion of software design in practice. To facilitate good flow and avoid getting lost in details, the design contexts discussed in the main chapters are kept as simple as possible. As a result, some interesting aspects of the software design experience do get lost in the simplification. The code exploration activity supported by this section is the opportunity to consider how some of the topics presented in the chapter manifest themselves in reality. The "Code Exploration" section points to specific parts of the code of the example applications. Before reading the text in the Code Exploration section, I recommend reviewing the code referenced and trying to understand it as much as possible. The example applications discussed in the "Code Exploration" section are described in Appendix C. They include JetUML, the application used to create all the diagrams in the book.

- **Further Reading:** The Further Reading section provides pointers to references that complement the material presented in the chapter.

- **Companion Website** Additional resources for this book are available in the repository `https://github.com/prmr/DesignBook`. The material in the repository includes a complete and commented version of the code that appears in the chapter content, as well as practice exercises and their solutions.

- **Example Applications** The three Java applications described in Appendix C were developed following many of the principles and techniques described in the book, and are provided as an accessible basis for additional study and exploration.

Acknowledgments

I am most grateful to Mathieu Nassif, who carried out a detailed technical review of the entire manuscript, providing me with hundreds of corrections, suggestions, and interesting points for discussion. I warmly thank Jin Guo for reviewing most of chapters and testing some of the material in her own teaching, and Kaylee Kutschera, Brigitte Pientka, and Clark Verbrugge for feedback on various parts of the manuscript. I am also thankful to Ralf Gerstner, the executive editor in charge of computer science at Springer, for believing in the project from the start and for seeing it through with his usual diligence and professionalism.

Martin P. Robillard
April 2019

Contents

Chapter 1
Introduction

In 1988, a fascinating little piece of code hits the limelight. That year, one of the winners of the annual International Obfuscated C Code Contest features a program that writes out to the terminal console the text of an eighteenth-century poem titled "The Twelve Days of Christmas". Figure 1.1 shows the first three verses of the text, as they appear on the output console when executing the code. This poem is particular in that its text has a regular structure. Text with such a structure is amenable to being constructed by software in a way that goes beyond printing hard-coded data. With a poem like "The Twelve Days of Christmas", there was thus opportunity for creating a clear and compact solution for displaying a poem on the console. However, as promised by the name of the contest where it was featured, the program is anything but clear. If fact, its inner workings are unfathomable. Figure 1.2 reproduces the complete code of the program.

```
On the first day of Christmas my true love gave to me
a partridge in a pear tree.

On the second day of Christmas my true love gave to me
two turtle doves
and a partridge in a pear tree.

On the third day of Christmas my true love gave to me
three French hens, two turtle doves
and a partridge in a pear tree.
...
```

Fig. 1.1 Partial output of "The Twelve Days of Christmas" program of Figure 1.2

In a way, this quirky piece of computer science trivia illustrates the impact of a lack of self-evident structure in software. Here we have a programming problem with trivial requirements: the functionality of interest requires no argument and produces a single, unchangeable output. Yet, the code to support this functionality

© Springer Nature Switzerland AG 2019
M. P. Robillard, *Introduction to Software Design with Java*,
https://doi.org/10.1007/978-3-030-24094-3_1

```
main(t,_,a ) char* a;{return!0<t?t<3?main(-79,-13,a+main(-87,
1-_,main(-86, 0,a+1 )+a)):1,t<_?main( t+1, _, a ):3,main(-94,
-27+t, a )&&t == 2 ?_<13 ? main ( 2, _+1,"%s %d %d\n" ):9:16:
t<0?t<-72?main( _, t, "@n'+,#'/*{}w+/w#cdnr/+,{}r/*de}+,/*{*+\
,/w{%+,/w#q#n+,/#{l,+,/n{n+,/+#n+,/#;#q#n+,/+k#;*+,/'r :'d*'\
3,}{w+K w'K:'+}e#';dq#'l q#'+d'K#!/+k#;q#'r}eKK#}w'r}eKK{nl]\
'/#;#q#n'){)#}w'){){nl]'/+#n';d}rw' i;# ){nl]!/n{n#'; r{#w'r\
 nc{nl]'/#{l,+'K {rw' iK{;[{nl]'/w#q#n'wk nw' iwk{KK{nl]!/w{\
%'l##w#' i; :{nl]'/*{q#'ld;r'}{nlwb!/*de}'c ;;{nl'-{}rw']'/+,\
}##'*}#nc,',#nw]'/+kd'+e}+;#'rdq#w! nr'/ ') }+}{rl#'{n' ')# \
}'+}##(!!/"):t<-50?_==*a?putchar(31[a]):main(-65,_,a+1):main
((*a == '/')+t, _,a+1):0<t?main ( 2, 2 , "%s"):*a=='/'||main
(0,main(-61,*a,"!ek;dc i@bK'(q)-[w]*%n+r3#l,{}:\nuwloca-O;m\
 .vpbks,fxntdCeghiry"),a+1);}
```

Fig. 1.2 Source code of the 1988 "The Twelve Days of Christmas" C program by Ian Phillips. This code compiles normally and executing it will produce the output illustrated in Figure 1.1. © 1988, Landon Curt Noll and Larry Bassel. Reproduced with permission.

cannot be understood by a normal human being. What is the problem with that, one might ask?

Software needs to change, and for software to change, at least one person must be involved at some point. Software needs to change for a variety of reasons, from fixing bugs to adapting the code to an evolving world. For example, many of the "gifts" referred to in the poem are European birds (e.g., partridge, turtle doves, French hens). Contemporary software development best practices include the *localization* of software applications, namely, the option to tailor a software application to account for region-specific characteristics. It would thus be nice to adapt the code of the application to replace the name of European birds to some that readers could relate to based on their own region (for example, to replace "partridge" with "turkey" for North American users). To modify a piece of code, however, one must understand its structure, and this structure must, to a certain extent, accommodate the change. In the case of "The Twelve Days of Christmas", any ambition to ever change the code is hopeless.

The example of "The Twelve Days of Christmas" is facetious for sake of illustration. Because this code was obfuscated on purpose, it would be comforting if we could discount it as irrelevant. Unfortunately, because writing messy code is often the path of least resistance in the complex social, technological, and economic reality of modern software development, badly designed code is not hard to find. For example, in a famous high-profile case where automotive software was determined by the courts to be responsible for a fatal accident, the experts who reviewed the software likened its structure to that of a bowl of spaghetti. Whether code is cryptic purposefully or accidentally, the result is similar: it is hard to understand and change without introducing errors.

To explore the contrast, let us design a version of the program where the structure is evident. Consistently with the rest of the code in this book, the program is in Java. First, we can tackle the issue of producing the first line of a verse:

```java
static String[] DAYS = {"first", "second", ..., "twelfth"};

static String firstLine(int day)
{
  return "On the " + DAYS[day] +
    " day of Christmas my true love sent to me:\n";
}
```

This code is clear because the function is short, it abstracts an obvious concept (the creation of the first line), and the only parameterization involved maps directly to the problem domain (changing the day).

The second sub-problem is to create the list of gifts for a given day. In this case we can leverage the inherent recursion in the poem's structure to organize the code in a function that creates a list of gifts by adding the last gift to a smaller list of gifts:

```java
static String[] GIFTS = { "a partridge in a pear tree",
                          "two turtle doves", ... };

static String allGifts(int day)
{
  if( day == 0 ) { return "and " + GIFTS[0]; }
  else { return GIFTS[day] + "\n" + allGifts(day-1); }
}
```

The allGifts function provides a classic implementation of a recursive algorithm. In this case, the code's structure is explicit because it trivially realizes a foundational strategy in computing.

At this point the only thing left it to put the poem together by assembling the twelve verses. Here the only small issue is that in the first verse, we do not add the conjunction "and" in front of "a partridge". No matter how small a program, it can be difficult to completely avoid annoying corner cases.

```java
static String poem()
{
  String poem = firstLine(0) + GIFTS[0] + "\n\n";
  for( int day = 1; day < 12; day++ )
  { poem += firstLine(day) + allGifts(day) + "\n\n"; }
  return poem;
}
```

At a glance, we see the overall structure of the code: a special case for the first verse, then an iteration through the remaining eleven verses, where each verse is created by concatenating the output of two functions: one to create the first line, and the other to create the list of gifts.

1.1 Defining Software Design

Software design is a mysterious activity. For many software development projects, if you ask for "the design" for the software system, you may get a blank look. The "design" is not necessarily something you can retrieve and look at. Similarly, very few people walk around with the title of "software designer". In that sense, designing software is not like designing furniture or clothing.

There are many definitions of software design, each with a different focus. The word "design" is also both a verb and a noun, which adds to the ambiguity because it can thus refer to both a process ("to design") and the outcome of this process ("a design"). My working definition of software design (the process) is *the construction of abstractions of data and computation and the organization of these abstractions into a working software application*. At first this may sound overly restrictive, but when we consider everything that the term "abstraction" can mean (variables, classes, objects, etc.), we see that we are afforded quite a bit of flexibility for interpreting what software design means.

In practice, the design process is essentially one of decision making. Should we use a list or a stack? What services should this interface offer? Where should this error be handled? Considering design as decision making leads to the concept of a *design space*. A design space can be imagined as an *n*-dimensional geometric space where each dimension corresponds to a design quality attribute. Typical design quality attributes for software include understandability, reusability, and ease of implementation. Within such a design space, each specific design decision (or coherent set of decisions) corresponds to a coordinate in the space that represents the consequence of the decision. Figure 1.3 illustrates the idea with two dimensions. In practice, any design decision is likely to be good in some dimension, but less good in other dimensions, something we call a *design trade-off*.

Two sub-spaces of the design space that are useful to consider are the space of *possible solutions*, and the space of *acceptable solutions*. Note that the theoretically optimal solution, which best satisfies all dimensions at the same time, is unlikely to be possible. All this to say that design is a decision process for which there is rarely a single "right answer", only solutions that are better or worse in some dimensions (including some solutions that are pretty bad in most dimensions).

The concept of a design space may make it look like selecting a design decision is a systematic, almost mathematical process. Unfortunately, this is not the case. Where the analogy breaks down is that a geometric space is completely defined, whereas the reality of software design is rife with uncertainty. First, not all possible decisions are known, and in complex situations there may be an infinity of them. Second, estimating to what extent a design decision fulfills a given quality attribute (e.g., understandability) is a very approximate process. Consequently, there is no standard formula for arriving at a point in the design space. In most realistic software development contexts, it will not be the case that to design and implement a software requirement, we can follow a pre-determined set of steps. This revelation can be unsettling at first. How can we learn about design, if there is no recipe to learn? Design is a highly *heuristic* process: it consists of iterative problem-solving guided by experience, general principles, and design techniques. In fact, the heuristic nature of the software design process is what makes it an exciting creative activity.

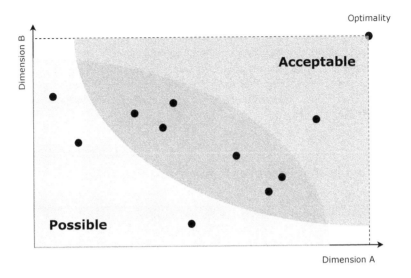

Fig. 1.3 An illustration of the concept of a design space

The quality attributes that constitute the dimensions of the design space also correspond to the general goals of design. One of the most important goals for software design is to reduce the complexity of software, which means making it easier to understand. Cleanly-designed code that is easy to understand is less error-prone and easier to modify. Messy code obscures the important decisions of its original developers. When developers ignore existing design constraints, they risk modifying code in a way that does not agree with the original structure, and thereby introduce errors and generally degrade the quality of the code. The problem of modifying code in a way that does not respect the original structure has been called "ignorant surgery" (see Further Reading).

In general, the relative importance of design goals depends on the context in which a piece of software is being designed. A *design context* is a specific set of requirements and constraints within a domain in which a design solution must be found and integrated. For example, because of economic or contractual reasons, it may be required to design a particular piece of software to maximize its reusability. Or, if a piece of code is intended to be integrated into safety-critical applications, it may be more important to prioritize robustness (i.e., resilience to errors). In this book, I give a lot of importance to the understandability quality attribute. I try to emphasize designs where the code itself reveals the underlying design decisions and the *intent* behind these design decisions. The idea of having design decisions be self-evident in code is a property I call *sustainability*.

If we consider that the design process is a series of decisions-making activities about software abstractions, then it follows that a good definition for "a design" or "the design" is the collection of these decisions. This definition for a design artifact is sufficiently general to avoid dictating the medium in which the design is captured. In formal software development settings, this could be an official standardized design document. In less formal contexts, design decisions could be stored in the code, diagrams, or various documentation pages associated with the project. In the extreme, design decisions could exist only in the head of the developers who made them. Because people tend to forget or misremember things, this latter approach is best kept to a minimum. Section 1.3 provides an overview of how design knowledge can be captured.

1.2 Design in the Software Development Process

Design is only one of the many activities that take place during the development of a software system. There is an abundant literature on different process models for software development. A process model describes (and sometimes prescribes) how the different steps required to create a system are organized. Different process models offer different ways of doing things for different reasons. In the early days of the software engineering discipline it was believed that a "planning-heavy" process, exemplified by the waterfall software process model, was the desirable way to build high-quality software. However, in the mid-1990s this belief was challenged by a movement towards a more organic approach to software development, also called *agile development*. In practice, ideas about how to best develop software keep evolving, and in the end the important things are to have a development process in the first place, and for that process to be well-adapted to the type of system being developed and the organization that develops it. For example, the process used by an organization to develop a prototype for a video game would probably be different from the process used to develop banking or aeronautical software.

The issue of devising, adapting, or even following a software development process is not the main focus of this book. However, even when beginning to learn about software design, it is useful to have a general idea of software development processes, if only to stay oriented in the wide and buzzword-laden realm of technology.

One concept of the software development process literature that is closely relevant to software design is the idea of a software development *practice*. A practice is a well-understood way of doing something to achieve a certain benefit. An example of a practice many programmers are familiar with is *version control* (the use of software tools to keep track of changes to software development artifacts). Another example of software development practice is *pair programming* (writing code as a team of two in front of a single computer). In this book I refer to a number of software development practices that directly support good design, including the use of *coding conventions* (see Appendix B) and *refactoring* (see below).

Another concept of software development processes that is directly relevant to software design is that of the *iteration*. As discussed in Section 1.1, when searching for a design solution, it is common practice to iterate over various alternatives. However, iterations also take place at a more macroscopic level in software development, in the sense that the design of the system may be periodically extended, reviewed, and/or improved. In some cases, the design can even be improved without any change to the observable behavior of the system. Improving the design of code without changing its functionality is the software development practice known as *refactoring*. There are various reasons why refactoring can become necessary or desirable. One reason is simply that the original developer did not really get it right, and after working with the code for a while it becomes obvious that a different design would be better. Another reason is that we might want to add modules and features that do not integrate well with the existing design, so we first refactor the design to prepare it so that it better supports the later addition of new code. A third reason is to reduce accumulated design weaknesses. As part of maintaining the code (e.g., to fix bugs), developers occasionally implement "quick and dirty" solutions that do not align properly with the existing design. This phenomenon is known as accumulating *technical debt*. By not investing the effort necessary to code a clean solution, the team effectively borrows development effort from the future. If allowed to accumulate, too much technical debt can threaten the viability of the project, just like the risk of bankruptcy incurred by excessive borrowing in the financial sense. When technical debt is incurred in a project, refactoring is a way to pay it back, and good software development teams will periodically refactor their code. Thus, software design is in continual evolution.

1.3 Capturing Design Knowledge

A design (or design solution) is a collection of decisions, each of which is the result of a search process through a design space for a particular design problem, or context. This definition naturally leads to the question of what a design decision looks like. Informally, we could say that a design decision is a statement about how to do a particular thing, ideally coupled with the reason for this statement. A simple example would be, "We will store the list of appointments in a linked list because we will mostly be performing additions to the list". For this decision to even exist, it has to be in at least one developer's brain at some point. We thus have a first medium for storing design decisions: a person's brain. For small projects, this could be sufficient. However, given the ephemerality of human memory, it can often be worthwhile to record important design decisions externally. This opens up the question of how to capture design knowledge. This fundamental question has been the subject of debate and academic and industry research for decades. Entire books have been written on the topic. Given that the present book is not one of them, the following is a concise summary of the options for externalizing design knowledge:

- **Source code (including identifiers and comments):** Many design decisions can be encoded directly in the source code. The example above, of selecting a linked list as a data structure, would be one example. The advantage of source code is that it is a formal language whose rules are checked by the compiler. Unfortunately, source code is not a good substrate for capturing the *rationale* of design decisions. For this purpose, code comments can be of some assistance.
- **Design documents (including general-purpose diagrams):** Design decisions can be captured in documents specifically aimed at capturing such design decisions. There exists a wide variety of formats for documents about software, from standardized design documents to blog posts. Design documents may also include diagrams, which are another way to represent design decisions.
- **Discussion platforms and version control systems:** Design information can be "recorded" in mailing lists and comments stored in other software development tools, such as issue management systems and version control systems.
- **Specialized Models:** In certain software development projects, developers use formal models to specify many aspects of the software. These models can then be automatically converted into code in a programming language. Such an approach is called *generative programming* or *model-driven development* (MDD). In model-driven development, the models serve as design documents. As a software construction approach, model-driven design and development is outside the scope of this book.

Because the level of design abstraction covered by this book remains close to the source code, many of the design decisions discussed will be at least partly reflected in the code. Subsequent chapters will also contain many diagrams and accompanying text that document design decisions.

The Unified Modeling Language

There will often be situations where we need to discuss design problems and solutions that are cumbersome, inconvenient, or simply too complex to describe using either source code or natural language. For this purpose we can use a specialized *modeling language*. This situation is not limited to software. For example, describing instrumental music in plain language is near-impossible: instead, we use musical notation.

Historically, many different modeling languages and notations have been developed for representing, at an abstract level, various aspects of a software system. This disparity was, however, an obstacle to adoption because of the overhead involved in interpreting models expressed in an unfamiliar notation. Thankfully, in the mid-1990s the main software modeling notations were merged into a single one, the Unified Modeling Language (UML), which was subsequently adopted as a standard by the International Organization for Standardization (ISO).

The UML is a modeling language organized in terms of different types of diagrams intended to illustrate different aspects of software. Examples of design information than can be neatly captured in the UML include relationships between classes (e.g., A inherits from B), changes in the state of an object (e.g., the `list` object goes from "Empty" to "Non-Empty" when the first element is added), and sequences of calls dispatched on objects (e.g., `a.m1()` results in a call to `b.m2()`).

Not all development teams use the UML. However, those who do use it in different ways for different reasons. For example, UML can be used to produce formal design documentation in waterfall-type development processes. Others use the UML to describe enough of the software to be able to automatically generate the code from the models, following the idea of generative programming. In this book, I use the UML simply for *sketching* design ideas. The diagrams included in this book are not expected to be automatically transformable into code. I also use the smallest subset of the modeling language necessary, and introduce the notation progressively.

An important thing to remember about UML diagrams is that they are *models*. This means that they are not intended to capture every single little detail of a solution. Ideally, a UML diagram should focus on illustrating a *single main idea* and only include the relevant information. In UML diagramming it is a common practice to leave out the parts of a system and details that are not directly relevant to the point being illustrated.

1.4 Sharing Design Know-How

Capturing knowledge about the design of a particular system is one thing, but how do we capture general know-how about the design process? Software design is influenced by the skills and experience of the designer, and this type of heuristic knowledge is not easy to synthesize and package for dissemination. In earlier days, organized approaches to disseminate design know-how centered around comprehensive *design methods*, which prescribed a sequence of steps and the use of specialized charts and other instruments. Such approaches peaked in the 1980s, and were replaced with adaptations suited to object-oriented programming, a paradigm that was then quickly gaining adoption. Comprehensive object-oriented design methods themselves peaked in the mid-1990s. At that time, it was being observed that some elements of design solutions tended to recur between many object-oriented applications.

Design Patterns

The idea of reusing elements of object-oriented design was captured in the concept of a *design pattern* in the book *Design Patterns: Elements of Reusable Object-Oriented Software* [6]. This book, often referred to as the "Gang of Four" book from the author list, is one of the most influential software design books in existence. Following the concept of an architectural pattern originally proposed by an architect named Christopher Alexander, the book describes 23 patterns for addressing common software design problems. Since then, countless other patterns have been documented. The idea to capture abstract design solutions that address specific problems was a breakthrough for software engineering, because it provided a practical way to convey design know-how and experience without the requirement to adopt a comprehensive design method. To this day, design patterns and close variants of the concept have been a dominant way to capture design know-how. There currently exist countless design catalogs for different programming languages, in the form of books and websites.

According to the original Gang of Four book, a pattern has four essential elements:

> The *pattern name* is a handle we can use to describe a design problem, its solutions, and consequences in a word or two. Naming a pattern immediately increases our design vocabulary. It lets us design at a higher level of abstraction. Having a vocabulary for patterns lets us talk about them with our colleagues, in our documentation, and to ourselves...
>
> The *problem* describes when to apply the pattern. It explains the problem and its context...
>
> The *solution* describes the elements that make up the design, their relationships, responsibilities, and collaborations. The solution doesn't describe a particular concrete design or implementation, because a pattern is like a template...
>
> The *consequences* are the results and trade-offs of applying the pattern... [6]

In this book I present a subset of the original patterns by integrating them in the flow of the material when they become relevant. I do not reproduce the structured description that can be easily found in other pattern catalogs. I instead use a lightweight description for a pattern that focuses on the link between the problem and solution, and I include a discussion of important design decisions related to the pattern. I also prefer to refer to the problem as the *context* for applying a pattern, because design problems can sometimes be difficult to isolate. Finally, I will sometimes express the solution embodied by a pattern as a UML diagram that captures the name of the *abstract elements* of the pattern. Because these elements are abstract, I prefer to refer to them as a *solution template* rather than a solution. A typical task when attempting to apply a design pattern in a context is to map the abstract elements of the solution template to concrete design elements in the code. In the text, the name of design patterns are set in SMALL CAPS FONT. This is to indicate that a term refers to a well-defined design concept, as opposed to a general use of the term. For example, one design pattern is called the "Strategy" pattern. Instead of continuously referring to it as the "Strategy design pattern", I will refer to it as the STRATEGY, which will distinguish it from the concept of a *strategy* as a general problem-solving approach.

Because solution templates for design patterns can easily be looked up in any number of resources, the most important skill to develop with respect to design patterns is to know where to apply them. For this reason, my coverage of design patterns emphasizes the rationale for using a pattern and a discussion of its strengths and weaknesses in different contexts, and de-emphasizes the focus on solution templates. One potential pitfall when first learning about design patterns is to get over-enthusiastic and try to apply them everywhere. Like all other elements of design solutions, a particular instance of a design pattern will occupy a specific point in

the design space, with attendant benefits and drawbacks. If I can make one generalization about the use of design patterns, it is that employing one tends to make
an overall design more flexible. Sometimes, this flexibility is exactly what we need.
Other times, it is overkill and leads to unnecessary structures and clutter in the code.
In other words, using a particular design pattern in a particular way in a given context is a design decision which, like most other design decisions, should be critically
assessed.

Design Antipatterns

An interesting take on the idea of a design pattern is that of a design *antipattern*. Just
as it can be observed that some design solution elements recur between applications,
it is also the case that recognizable flaws can be abstracted from many similar cases
and catalogued. This influential idea took hold around the turn of the millennium
in a popular book on refactoring, which documents 22 antipatterns as motivation
to refactor the corresponding code [5]. Typical antipatterns include problems such
as DUPLICATED CODE†, LONG METHOD†, and others that will be covered in this book.
For reasons similar to design patterns, antipatterns are set in SMALL CAPS†, but are
followed by a dagger symbol to distinguish them from actual patterns. Design antipatterns are also known as *code smells*, or *bad smells* (in code), to convey the idea
of a symptom that something is not quite right.

Insights

This chapter introduced software design and placed it in the general context of software development projects.

- The verb "to design" refers to the process we follow when we design software,
  and the noun "a design" refers to the outcome of this process;
- The process of software design is the construction of abstractions of data and
  computation and the organization of these abstractions into a working software
  application;
- There is rarely a single "right answer" to a design problem, only solutions that
  are better or worse in some dimensions;
- A design artifact is an external representation of one or more design decisions;
- Design is only one of many activities that take place during the development of a
  software system. Software development follows a process that can vary from organization to organization, and vary from planning-heavy to agile. Development
  processes typically involve iterations;
- A software development practice is a well-understood way of doing something to
  achieve a certain benefit. Examples include version control, coding conventions,
  and refactoring;

- Design knowledge can be captured in source code comments, specialized documents, discussion forums, and models;
- The Unified Modeling Language, or UML, is a modeling language organized in terms of different types of diagrams. Using UML can be an effective way to illustrate different aspects of software without getting caught up in details;
- A design pattern captures an abstract design solution that is applicable in a common design context. The description of a design pattern includes a name, a description of the design problem or context it addresses, a solution template, and a discussion of the consequences of applying the pattern;
- A design antipattern is an abstract description of a common design flaw.

Further Reading

The paper "Software Aging" by David L. Parnas [12] introduces the term "ignorant surgery" and provides a compelling motivation for the benefits of maintaining good design in software. Parnas is one of the early contributors to the software engineering discipline. Chapter 1 of the book *Clean Code: A Handbook of Agile Software Craftmanship* by Robert C. Martin [7] discusses the various ills of bad or "messy" code. My short paper titled "Sustainable Software Design" discusses in more detail what it means for design decisions to be self-evident [14].

Chapter 1 of the book *UML Distilled, 3rd Edition* by Martin Fowler [5] provides a more comprehensive introduction to the UML. Fowler distinguishes between three modes for using the UML: as sketches for design, as a blueprint for creating an application, and as source code that can be executed. Sketching is the mode employed in this book.

The original book on design patterns is *Design Patterns: Elements of Reusable Object-Oriented Software* by Erich Gamma, Richard Helm, Ralph Johnson, and John Vlissides [6]. This book is often referred to as the "Gang of Four" book. Because it predates the UML, the notation it uses for capturing software designs may feel a bit foreign. Nevertheless, it is a timeless reference work.

The book *Refactoring: Improving the Design of Existing Code*, also by Martin Fowler [3] is the main reference on the practice of refactoring. It introduces the idea of design antipatterns (which are called "code smells" in the book). Robert C. Martin also includes a list of bad smells in Chapter 17 of *Clean Code*, cited above.

Chapter 2
Encapsulation

This chapter covers:

> **Concepts and Principles:** Encapsulation, information hiding, abstraction, immutability, interface, reference sharing, escaping references;
> **Programming Mechanisms:** Typing, enumerated types, scopes, access modifiers, assertions;
> **Design Techniques:** Class definition, object diagrams, immutable wrappers, reference copying, copy constructors, design by contract;
> **Patterns and Antipatterns:** PRIMITIVE OBSESSION†, INAPPROPRIATE INTIMACY†.

An essential technique in software design is to decompose a system into distinct, manageable abstractions. However, there is little value in decomposing a piece of software into several parts if each part depends on all the other parts in a tangled mess of interactions. For a decomposition to be useful, the resulting abstractions have to be well isolated from each other. For good design, an idea that should be inseparable from that of software abstraction is *encapsulation*.

Design Context

We start our exploration of software design by considering how to effectively represent a deck of playing cards in code. This representation would be necessary for most computer card games, for example the Solitaire game used as an example application. In the common card deck used as a running example, there are 52 distinct cards and any given card can be completely defined by its *suit* (Hearts ♡, Spades ♠, Diamonds ♢, Clubs ♣) and its *rank* (Ace, 2, 3, ..., 10, Jack, Queen, King). A software structure to represent a deck of cards should therefore be able to represent any sequence of any number of distinct cards between 0 and 52.

© Springer Nature Switzerland AG 2019
M. P. Robillard, *Introduction to Software Design with Java*,
https://doi.org/10.1007/978-3-030-24094-3_2

2.1 Encapsulation and Information Hiding

The idea of *encapsulation* is to enclose something as if it were in a capsule. For example, we can think of a nut, which is encapsulated in its shell. The shell, or capsule, serves as protection. In software design we encapsulate both data and computation to limit the number of contact points between different parts of the code. Encapsulation has several benefits: it makes it easier to understand a piece of code in isolation, it makes the use of the isolated part by the rest of the code less error-prone, and it makes it easier to change one part of the code without breaking anything. In software design, the equivalent of a shell is the general concept of an *interface*

Encapsulation in software design is related to the principle of *information hiding*, which has been around since the early 1970s. The idea of information hiding is for encapsulated structures to only reveal the minimum amount of information that is necessary to use them, and hide the rest. A typical example of information hiding is an implementation of a stack abstract data type (ADT) whose interface only provides `push` and `pop` operations. This minimal interface allows *client code* to make full use of the stack structure, but low-level design decisions on how to store elements in the stack remain hidden from the code that uses the stack. In this book, I use the term *client code* to refer to any code that refers to an abstraction (e.g., the stack ADT) that is not part of the definition of this abstraction.

Although encapsulation and information hiding are very general principles for software design, there exist specific techniques we can use to help ensure our code respects these principles. The rest of this chapter presents some of these techniques.

2.2 Encoding Abstractions as Types

As our first design task, we will define the abstractions that are necessary to represent a deck of cards. Here, by "defining", I mean to decide what the abstractions represent, and what they will look like in terms of source code. In the case of a deck of cards, the first part of the process is straightforward, because the concepts we need to represent in code (a deck of cards, a playing card) are well-defined in the real world. This will not always be the case.

Essentially, a deck of cards is simply an ordered collection of playing cards. We could thus use any standard data structure to represent this collection (an array, a list, etc.). However, what would such a collection hold? What is a card? In the code, we can represent a playing card in many different ways. For example, using a single integer between 0 and 51 where the value of the integer somehow represents the card according to a given convention (e.g., clubs have numbers 0–12 in increasing rank, hearts 13–25, etc.):

```
int card = 13;        // 13 = The ace of Hearts
int suit = card / 13  // 1 = Hearts
int rank = card % 13; // 0 = Ace
```

This would also require us to have similar conventions to represent suits and ranks, as illustrated on the second and third lines.[1] To avoid having to continually divide and multiply numbers that represent cards to switch between suits, we could also represent a card as a pair of values, the first one encoding the suit, and the second one encoding the rank (or vice-versa):

```
int[] card = {1,0}; // The Ace of Hearts
```

While we are at it, we could even decide to represent a card using a combination of six Boolean values. Although terrible, this design decision is technically possible to implement: it is an example of a decision that is possible, but not acceptable (see Section 1.1). As it turns out, all three options above actually have major drawbacks.

First, *the representation of a card does not map to the corresponding domain concept.* To facilitate code understanding and help avoid programming errors, the representation of values should ideally be tied to the concept they represent. For example, the general type `int` maps to the concept of an integer (a type of number), not that of a playing card. We could define a variable of type `int` intended to store a playing card, and unwittingly put a value that represents a different entity in it (e.g., the number of cards in the deck). This will not be noticed as an error by the compiler, yet it is likely to lead to intense confusion when executing the code.

Second, *the representation of a card is coupled to its implementation.* If our design decision is that cards should be represented as integers, any location in the code that must store a value that represents a card will refer to an integer. Changing this encoding to something else (e.g., the two-element array discussed above) will require discovering and changing every single location where an `int` variable is used to store a card, and all the code that works with cards as integers.

Third, *it is easy to corrupt a variable that stores a value that represents a card.* In Java a variable of type `int` can take 2^{32} distinct values. To represent a playing card we only need a tiny subset of these (52). Consequently, the overwhelming majority of values we can store in an `int` variable ($2^{32} - 52$) does not represent any valid information. This opens the door very wide to errors. This problem would have been even worse had we decided to use a two-element array of type `int`, which supports $2^{33} + 1$ values.[2]

Clearly, we can do better. It is generally a bad idea to try to shoehorn domain concepts into basic general types like `int`, `String`, and so on. Ideally, these types should only be used to hold values that are proper values of the type. For instance, the `int` type should only be used to hold actual integers (and perhaps very similar concepts, such as currency). Similarly, `String`s should be used only to hold sequences of characters meant to represent text or text-like information, as opposed to being some encoding of some other concept (e.g., `"AceOfClubs"`). The tendency to use primitive types to represent other abstractions is a common problem in software design that has been captured by the antipattern PRIMITIVE OBSESSION†.

To apply the principle of information hiding, we instead organize our code to *hide* the decision of how exactly we represent a card. We hide this decision behind

---

[1] The modulo operator (%) returns the remainder of the integer division.

[2] The additional value comes from the fact that array-typed variables can also be null.

an interface specifically tied with the concept of a card. In programming languages with a strong support for types, such as Java, this is typically accomplished through the use of types. In our case, to properly represent a card in code, we define our own type `Card` as a Java class:

```
class Card {}
```

As we will see below, the use of a specific type to represent a card will allow us to hide the decision of how we represent a card internally. However, although we now have a class `Card`, we still need to decide how to represent a card within the class. All options are back on the table. We could do simply:

```
class Card
{
  int aCard; // 0-51 encodes the card
}
```

This class defines a single instance variable `aCard` of type `int`. The name of the instance variable includes the prefix `a` as part of a coding convention detailed in Appendix B. Client code can refer to this variable through dereference, for example:[3]

```
Card card = new Card();
card.aCard = 28;
```

Although using a class somewhat links the value a bit better to the domain concept of a card, the other problems are still present. First, it is still possible to corrupt the representation of a card. Second, the decision to represent this value as an `int` is not exactly hidden, given that client code would be accessing the variable directly through a dereference of the instance variable. Let us then tackle the issue of representing the card internally. The next section handles the issue of hiding this decision.

Two key observations can help us arrive at a better way to encode a card. First, the value of a playing card is completely and exactly defined in terms of two subconcepts: its suit (e.g., clubs) and its rank (e.g., ace). So, we can take the process of decomposition one step further, and define abstractions for ranks and suits. Following the same logic as above, primitive values are not a good match for encoding these abstractions, so we prefer to use a dedicated type. However, here the second important observation comes into play: the rank of a playing card can only be one of 13 distinct values, which are known in advance and can be enumerated. In the case of suits, the number of values is even smaller (four). The best tool at our disposal to encode such abstractions is the *enumerated type*:

```
enum Suit
{ CLUBS, DIAMONDS, SPADES, HEARTS }
```

In Java, enumerated types are a special kind of class declaration. The identifiers listed in the declaration of the enumerated type are globally available constants (i.e.,

---

[3] Technically, this code only compiles if placed in a method declared in a class that is in the same package as class `Card`. This detail is not important here. Section 2.3 explains where class members can be accessed in the code.

static fields, see Section A.3 in the appendix). These constants store a unique reference to an object of the class that corresponds to the enumerated value. For example,

```
Suit suit1 = Suit.CLUBS;
Suit suit2 = Suit.CLUBS;
boolean same = suit1 == suit2; // same == true
```

Enumerated types are a perfect fit in our situation. They meet all our design requirements, because variables of type Suit and Rank are directly tied to their corresponding concept of rank and suit, and variables of these types can only take values that are meaningful for the type.[4] Enumerated types are a simple yet effective feature for creating or implementing robust designs. They help avoid PRIMITIVE OBSESSION† and generally make the code clearer and less error-prone.

The code below completes our definition of class Card as a combination of a rank and a suit value. It assumes that each enumerated type is defined in its own file.

```
enum Suit { CLUBS, DIAMONDS, SPADES, HEARTS }
enum Rank { ACE, TWO, ..., QUEEN, KING }

class Card
{
  Suit aSuit;
  Rank aRank;
}
```

Now that we have a reasonable type to represent a playing card in the code, we can return to the issue of representing a deck of cards, and follow the same line of thinking. Because a deck is just a collection of cards, we could represent a deck of cards as a List of Cards:

```
List<Card> deck = new ArrayList<>();
```

However, the disadvantages of this approach are the same as the disadvantages of representing a playing card as an **int** value:

- A list of cards is not strongly tied to the concept of a deck. It could represent any list of cards, e.g., the cards in one of the piles created while playing Solitaire, the cards discarded as part of the game, etc.
- Using a list of cards ties the representation of a deck in the program with its implementation. If we decide later to replace the list by, say, an array, we would have to change all the corresponding source code locations.[5]
- The structure can easily be corrupted: A simple deck of cards can hold a maximum of 52 cards, without duplicates. A list allows one to put any number of cards in the structure, including duplicates.

---

[4] With the unfortunate exception of **null**. See Section 4.5.

[5] Disturbingly, replacing the list by a Stack on the right-hand side of the assignment in the listing would actually work because in Java Stack is a subtype of List. In Chapter 7 I explain why this is disturbing.

A better way to approach the representation of a deck of cards in our code is to also define a proper type for it:

```
class Deck
{
  List<Card> aCards = new ArrayList<>();
}
```

Although it may seem redundant to define a new class to hold just one instance of an ArrayList, this decision helps avoid many of the problems discussed above. The new type Deck specializes the list and ties it directly to its corresponding domain concept. It also becomes possible to hide the decision of how the cards are stored. The remainder of this chapter presents the details of how to achieve this hiding in practice.

2.3 Scopes and Visibility Restrictions

Encoding abstractions as types is only the first step in the process of encapsulation. Once we have types we feel are good abstractions for our design, we need to ensure that these types are effective in hiding information from client code. At this point we have determined that four types are necessary to represent a deck of cards in code: Deck, Card, Rank, and Suit. Each of these types defines a set of possible values and a set of operations on these values. We now turn to the problem of specifying the values these types can take and the operations on these types so as to achieve good encapsulation of both the values and computation.

In Java and most other object-oriented languages, an *object* is a mechanism to group variables together and access their values through the process of dereferencing (see Section A.2 in the appendix). Without encapsulation, any variable that forms part of an object can be accessed indiscriminately. For example, given the following code:

```
class Deck
{
  public List<Card> aCards = new ArrayList<>();
}

class Card
{
  public Rank aRank = null;
  public Suit aSuit = null;
}
```

we could use our objects as follows:[6]

```
Deck deck = new Deck();
deck.aCards.add(new Card());
deck.aCards.add(new Card());
deck.aCards.get(1).aRank = deck.aCards.get(0).aRank;
System.out.println(deck.aCards.get(0).aSuit.toString());
```

Because of the complete lack of encapsulation, we can make unprincipled use of the internal implementation of our types. Without major effort, this kind of code almost invariably leads to bugs, simply because the number of ways to misuse the structures greatly exceeds the number of ways to use them properly. For example, although it may not be immediately apparent, the code above, when executed, raises a `NullPointerException`. With good encapsulation, it should be near-impossible to misuse one of our types.

The idea of encapsulation is to hide the internal implementation of an abstraction behind an interface that tightly controls how an abstraction can be used. Designing good abstractions and good interfaces for these abstractions are tandem tasks that underlie most of software design. Designing good interfaces can be tricky and requires a combination of different mechanisms and techniques. We start with one of the simplest, *access modifiers*. Access modifiers are Java keywords that control what parts of the code can *see*, or *access*, certain program elements (e.g., classes, fields, methods). The idea of restricting access to fields is very similar to that of visibility and *scope* for local variables. In most programming languages, a *scope* is a lexical region that acts as a sort of boundary for variables. In Java, scopes are defined using curly braces. The following code fragment:

```
public static void main(String[] args)
{
    { int a = 0; }
    { int b = a; }
}
```

has a compilation error because in the second assignment, the reference to a cannot be resolved because, according to Java scoping rules, it is not visible in the second scope. In this tiny example, the scoping restriction may look like a limitation. However, it is actually a powerful feature. To understand what happens in the second statement, we only need to track down references to variables that are in scope (as opposed to every code location). We can do the same with classes.

In Java, it is possible to control the visibility of classes and class members (and in particular fields) through the use of access modifiers. In this chapter, I only focus on the distinction between the **public** and **private** access modifiers.[7] Members marked **public** are visible anywhere in the code. In the example above, because the field aCards of class Deck is **public**, the variable aCards of any object of type

---

[6] This code is not defined in any method because its exact location does not matter. For example, the code could be placed in a main method

[7] The other two are **protected** and "default" (absence of a modifier). Members with default visibility are accessible by code in classes declared in the same package. The **protected** modifier is discussed in Chapter 7.

Deck is visible from any code that has a reference to the object. In contrast, members
marked **private** are only visible within the scope of the class, namely, between the
left curly brace that begins the declaration of the class body and the last right curly
brace of the class declaration.

A general principle for achieving good encapsulation is to use the narrowest possible scope for class members. Thus, instance variables should almost always be
private. Also, **public** methods should reveal as little as possible about implementation decisions meant to be encapsulated. A revised design for class Card that
respects this guideline is as follows:

```
public class Card
{
  private Rank aRank;
  private Suit aSuit;

  public Card(Rank pRank, Suit pSuit)
  {
    aRank = pRank;
    aSuit = pSuit;
  }

  public Rank getRank() { return aRank; }
  public Suit getSuit() { return aSuit; }
}
```

This class properly encapsulates the representation of a playing card because
client code cannot interact in any way with the internal representation of a card.
In fact, with this design it is possible to change the representation of the card to
use a single field of type **int**, or an enumerated type (say, PlayingCard), without
requiring *any* change to the client code.

As a mechanism for software design, access modifiers serve a dual purpose. First,
they express the *intent* of the developer about how certain structures are meant to be
used. Second, they support the automatic enforcement of the stated intent through
compilation. In an ideal design, the intent of the developer should be clear, or at
least not egregiously ambiguous.

2.4 Object Diagrams

Object diagrams are a type of UML diagram (see Section 1.3) that represent an existing graph of objects (i.e., class instances). Whenever a **new** statement is executed,
an object is created and a reference to this object is returned and can be passed
around. It can often be useful to visually represent the resulting graph of objects and
their inter-dependent references, especially when groups of objects are structured or
organized in sophisticated ways, or when relations between objects are especially
important.

I introduce a slight enhancement to official UML object diagrams, so as to provide a representation of an object's fields and values that resembles the kind of

data-structure diagrams often used in introductory computer science classes. In an object diagram, a rectangle represents an object, with its name and type indicated as `name:type`. Both name and type information are optional, but in general it is useful to have at least one of the two. By convention, in UML diagrams the name of objects (as opposed to classes) are underlined. Objects can contain *fields*, which are just like fields in a Java program. Fields can contain a value of a primitive type or a value of a reference type (see Section A.1 in the Appendix). In the latter case, the value is represented as a directed arrow to the object. Let us consider the diagram of Figure 2.1:

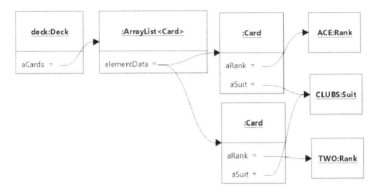

Fig. 2.1 Example object diagram that shows a detailed model of the object graph that represents a deck of cards

This diagram models an instance of the `Deck` class named `deck`. It would have been fine to omit this name and simply indicate `:Deck` in the rectangle, as in the case of `ArrayList<Card>`, which is anonymous. This `deck` has a field `aCards` whose current value is a reference to an `ArrayList<Card>` object. The `ArrayList<Card>` object's `elementData` field references two `Card` instances. Here, because `ArrayList` is a library type, it is necessary to have knowledge of the source code of the library to accurately model objects of this class. However, for a design sketch, using the actual name is not critical. To model internal properties of library types without looking up all their implementation details, it is often sufficient simply to make up evocative names. For example, the diagram would be just as informative if the field had been named `data` or `elements`.

   Through modeling, we can skip over some details. In reality, in an instance of `ArrayList` the `elementData` field refers to an array of `Object`-typed cells that contain the actual data. This information is not useful here, and we link directly to the contained data. It is also worth noting how the list refers to two cards, and not three or four or 52. Another important point about object diagrams is that they represent a *snapshot* in the execution of a program. Here it was at the point where the list had two cards. An alternative explanation is that we did not think it was useful to include all 52 cards to make the point that a deck is a list of cards. The two `Card` instances, however, are modeled in full detail. The values of enumerated types are distinguished by name, as they should be, and the enumerated value `Suit.CLUBS` is *shared* between two cards. I will cover reference sharing in more detail in Chapter 4.

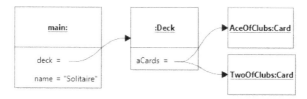

Fig. 2.2 Example object diagram that shows a simplified model of the object graph that represents a deck of cards

The second example diagram (Figure 2.2) illustrates some of the additional modeling simplifications we can do, when appropriate. First, I added an untyped object named `main`. This "object" is actually a trick intended to represent a method body. Object diagrams do not have an explicit notation to represent code statements that form the body of a method declaration. However, this can be achieved through untyped objects by observing that, from the point of view of the diagram, an object and a method body are simply collections of variables (instance variables in the first case, local variables in the second). A second difference is that the `Deck` object is now anonymous, and the name `deck` is used to represent the *variable* in which a reference to an object (any object) is stored, as opposed to a specific object. Third, the `main` method contains a `name` variable that stores a string. In Java, strings are technically instances of reference type `String`. To be strictly accurate, we should thus represent a string value as a reference to an instance of class `String` that has a reference to an array of **char** values, each with one letter. That level of detail would be both superfluous and annoying, so we just show the string literal. A fourth important difference is that the `ArrayList` has been abstracted away. In this diagram, we see that a deck somehow keeps track of a number of cards, but how these are stored internally is not represented. The cards could be in an array, a list, whatever. Although in some cases (such as in the next section) the details may be important, it is often the case that details of internal data structures are superfluous. Finally, and this may be a bit of a stretch, the value of the `Card` instances are represented artificially by using an evocative name for the objects, instead of modeling the field values. This does not mean that these `Card` instances do not have the `aRank` and `aSuit` fields, it just means this detail has been elided from the diagram.

2.5 Escaping References

The use of the visibility restrictions for fields using the **private** keyword provides
a basic level of encapsulation, but it by no means ensures an iron-clad protection of
internal structures. We explore this problem by returning to the issue of storing an
aggregation of Card objects within an instance of a Deck object. Let us assume we
decided to implement a Deck as a list of cards using Java's ArrayList type.[8]

```java
public class Deck
{
  private List<Card> aCards = new ArrayList<>();

  public Deck()
  {
    /* Add all 52 cards to the deck */
    /* Suffle the cards */
  }

  public Card draw() { return aCards.remove(0); }
}
```

So far, the only way to use an instance of Deck from code outside the class is
to *draw* (i.e., remove) a card from the deck: there are no other members (methods
or fields) that could be referenced outside the class. The class is thus very well
encapsulated, but also very limited it the services it can offer. Let us assume the
client code needs to inspect the content of the deck. We could simply add a "getter"
method to the class:

```java
public class Deck
{
  private List<Card> aCards = new ArrayList<>();

  public List<Card> getCards() { return aCards; }
}
```

Unfortunately, this solution solves the problem of providing access to the content
of the deck at a great cost: it allows a reference to the private internal list of cards to
escape the scope of the class, thus granting access to internal elements of the class
from outside the class. For example:

```java
Deck deck = new Deck();
List<Card> cards = deck.getCards();
cards.add(new Card(Rank.ACE, Suit.HEARTS));
```

Here, the reference to the list of cards held within an instance of Deck *escaped*
into the scope of the client code, which can then use it to mess things up, for example
by adding an additional ace of hearts.

Clearly, declaring fields private is insufficient to ensure good encapsulation. If a
class is well encapsulated, it should not be possible to change the data stored by an

---

[8] It may appear that Stack could be a better choice, but I prefer to avoid this type because its
implementation is victim of a design flaw discussed in Chapter 7.

object without going through one of its methods. In turn, to achieve this encapsulation quality, it is also necessary to prevent references to internal structures to escape the scope of the class. There are three main ways in which a reference to a private structure can escape the scope of its class: returning a reference to an internal object, storing an external reference internally, or leaking references through shared structures.[9]

Returning a reference to an internal object

This problem is demonstrated above through the use of the getter method. It is not a good idea to automatically supply getters and setters for each field because, as in this case, it may result in a degradation of encapsulation. Figure 2.3 shows the effect of this escape.

Fig. 2.3 Effect of leaking references outside the class scope

Although an object is a collection of variables, in the context of design, these variables correspond to an abstraction. Having a class that is mostly accessed through getters and setters points to a design weakness, because the abstraction the object represents is not effective. This problem is also known as the INAPPROPRIATE INTIMACY† antipattern, because its symptom is that classes "spend too much time delving in each others' private parts" [3]. To the extent possible, objects should interact with each other using methods that involve abstractions above individual instance variables. In the case of the Deck class, this means prohibiting access to the internal list of cards, which constitutes a "private part".

Storing an external reference internally

The problem with returning a reference to an internal object is that this reference becomes shared by the client code. A similar problem is to introduce this sharing by using a reference to an external object to initialize the internal state of another object.

---

[9] A fourth, more indirect, way is to use metaprogramming. See Section 5.4.

For example, if we have a "setter" method for the content of the deck:

```
public class Deck
{
  private List<Card> aCards = new ArrayList<>();

  public void setCards(List<Card> pCards) { aCards =  pCards; }
}
```

the reference will already be "escaped" as soon as it is assigned to the field:

```
List<Card> cards = new ArrayList<>();
Deck deck = new Deck();
deck.setCards(cards);
cards.add(new Card(Rank.ACE, Suit.HEARTS));
```

Here, we can corrupt the state of the deck from the scope of the client code, for example by adding an ace of hearts. From an object graph perspective, the outcome of this code is similar to the one caused by leaking a reference through a getter method, as illustrated in Figure 2.3.

A similar version of this problem is to set the content of the deck from a constructor, as opposed to a setter method:

```
public class Deck
{
  private List<Card> aCards = new ArrayList<>();

  public Deck(List<Card> pCards) { aCards =  pCards; }
}
```

Although the leak uses a different type of programming language element (constructor vs. setter method), the result is identical.

Leaking references through shared structures

The issue of escaping references is complex because references can escape through any number of shared structures, which may not always be obvious. Although a bit contrived, the following example shows how this could come about:

```
public class Deck
{
  private List<Card> aCards = new ArrayList<>();

  public void collect(List<List<Card>> pAllCards)
  { pAllCards.add(aCards); }
}
```

with the corresponding client code:

```
List<List<Card>> allCards = new ArrayList<>();
Deck deck = new Deck();
deck.collect(allCards);
List<Card> cards = allCards.get(0);
cards.add(new Card(Rank.ACE, Suit.HEARTS));
```

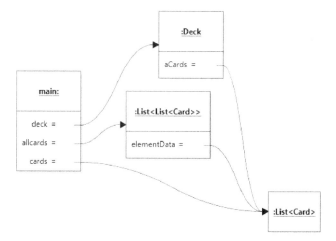

Fig. 2.4 Effect of leaking references through a shared structure

Figure 2.4 illustrates the result. Unfortunately, automatically detecting escaping references is a difficult program analysis problem, and there currently does not exist any production tool that can accomplish it for Java. Preventing the escape of references from the class scope is currently a manual process that relies on rigourous programming and code inspection practices. Section 2.7 introduces techniques for exposing some carefully selected information encapsulated by an object, without leaking references to internal structures.

2.6 Immutability

One of the major design insights of this chapter is that to ensure good encapsulation, it should not be possible to modify the internal state of an object without going through its methods. Section 2.5 discussed the issue of escaping references, and how they threaten encapsulation. There is, however, one situation where leaking a reference to an internal object is harmless: when the object is immutable (i.e., impossible to change). Let us consider the following code:

```
class Person
{
  private String aName;
  public Person(String pName) { aName = pName; }
  public String getName() { return aName; }
}
```

```
public class Client
{
  public static void main(String[] args)
  {
    Person person = new Person("Anonymous");
    String name = person.getName();
  }
}
```

The implementation of class Person clearly violates the advice given in Section 2.5 (of not returning references held in private fields), since Person.getName() returns a reference to the value of an instance variable. We can also represent this situation with an object diagram (Figure 2.5):

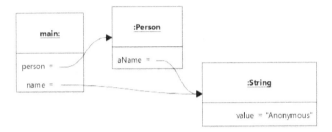

Fig. 2.5 Illustration of a shared reference to a String instance

However, a crucial notice in the reference documentation of the String library type changes things considerably:

> Strings are constant; their values cannot be changed after they are created. [...] Because String objects are immutable they can be shared.

Because it is not possible to change the data encapsulated by a String instance after its creation, sharing a reference to a String that forms the internal data encapsulated by an other object is harmless, because it will not be possible to change the object using the reference. This applies to any immutable object.

Objects are *immutable* if their class provides no way to change the internal state of the object after initialization. By extension, I call a class that yields immutable objects an *immutable class*.[10] Unfortunately, in Java and most other programming languages, there is no mechanism to guarantee that a class yields immutable objects. For the designer of a class, the only way to ensure immutability is to carefully design the class to prevent any modification (e.g., by providing no setter methods, leaking no reference, etc.). When relying on library classes (such as String), unless we are willing to personally inspect the source code of the class, we have to trust the documentation. Generally speaking, immutable objects have many advantages.

---

[10] This is a slight abuse of language because, technically speaking, it makes no sense for a class to be immutable. However, *immutable class* is a more convenient term than *class that yields immutable objects*.

In the context of this chapter, the immediate benefit is to support sharing information encapsulated in an object without breaking encapsulation. Chapter 4 provides
additional insights that can help with the design of immutable classes. For now, it is
sufficient to say that immutability is a desirable design property in many cases.

Let us conclude this brief introduction to immutability by defining class `Card` to
be immutable. First, we rely on our two enumerated types `Rank` and `Suit` which
we assume to be immutable.[11] With the following declaration, class `Card` will be
immutable:

```
public class Card
{
  private Rank aRank;
  private Suit aSuit;

  public Card(Rank pRank, Suit pSuit)
  {
    aRank = pRank;
    aSuit = pSuit;
  }

  public Rank getRank() { return aRank; }
  public Suit getSuit() { return aSuit; }
}
```

In this definition of the class, the only way to set the values of the two instance
variables is through the constructor call which, by definition, is only executed once
for each object. The fields are private, so they cannot be accessed from outside the
class. There are only two methods. Although they are public, neither mutates (i.e.,
changes) the state of the object. Finally, although the methods return a reference
to the content of a field, the type of these fields is immutable, so it will not be
possible to change the state of the referenced objects in any case. The class is thus
immutable.[12]

2.7 Exposing Internal Data

In many cases the objects of the classes we define will need to expose part of the
information they encapsulate to other objects. How can we do this without breaking
encapsulation? As often in software design, there are different options, each with its
strengths and weaknesses. For sake of discussion, let us consider that we want to
design our `Deck` class so that it is possible to find out what cards are in a deck.

---

[11] Simple enumerated types, which only enumerate values, are immutable. Although it is technically possible to define enumerated types that are *not* immutable, this is not a good idea. See
Chapter 4.

[12] To make the immutability of the class even more explicit, the keyword **final** could be placed in
front of the **class** keyword, as well as before the type of both fields. The use of **final** instance
variables is introduced in Chapter 4, and the use of **final** classes is introduced in Chapter 7.

```
public class Deck
{
  private List<Card> aCards = new ArrayList<>();
}
```

As discussed above, adding a getter method that simply returns aCards is out of the question, as this allows code outside the class Deck to modify the internal representation of a Deck instance.

Extended interface

One solution is to extend the interface of the class to include access methods that only return references to immutable objects. In our case, we could accomplish this goal by adding two methods to the Deck class:

```
public int size() { return aCards.size(); }
public Card getCard(int pIndex) { return aCards.get(pIndex); }
```

If class Card is immutable, this solution fulfills its mandate. However, it is somewhat inelegant if client code typically needs to access all the cards in the deck. In such a situation, the code would become cluttered with calls to size() and for loops going over all indexes. Code might also need to be written to check that the argument to getCard is not out of bounds, and so on.

Returning Copies

Another option, which mimics returning a reference to the field aCards without breaking encapsulation, is to return a *copy* of the list stored in aCards. Thus, we could add a new method:

```
public List<Card> getCards()
{ return new ArrayList<>(aCards); }
```

This code relies on the behavior of the constructor ArrayList(Collection), which creates a new ArrayList and initializes this list with all the elements in the collection, in the same order. Thus, a client would receive a reference to a different list of cards, with the same cards, as illustrated in Figure 2.6.

Assuming Card is immutable, we have a valid solution to expose the content of a Deck to clients. Figure 2.6 shows the result of executing:

```
public static void main(String[] args)
{ List<Card> cards = deck.getCards(); }
```

We see that it is not possible to change the internal state of Deck from a reference to its cards. There are different ways to implement this idea. For example, the library class Collection.unmodifiableList(List) returns an unmodifiable wrapper around the argument, which in our case would achieve a similar result, so we could do:

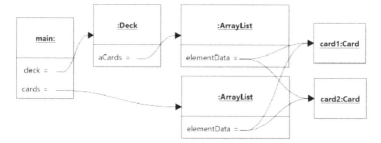

Fig. 2.6 Reference to a copy of a list of cards

```
public List<Card> getCards()
{ return Collections.unmodifiableList(aCards); }
```

There are other strategies for returning a copy of a data structure or a wrapper for it. Ultimately, the details of the implementation do not matter as much as the central idea, which is to return a different object that has all the same information as the internal structure we wish to keep encapsulated.

Although it looks like a simple idea, copying objects is actually a tricky topic, because it requires deciding how deep to copy the object graph. So far, we assumed that Card objects were immutable, so it was sufficient to perform a shallow copy. A shallow copy of a list is a copy of the list with shared references to the elements in the original list (i.e., the elements are not copied). But what if Card instances were mutable? In this case the above solution would not offer good encapsulation, because it would become possible to change the state of a deck without going through its interface, e.g.,

```
public static void main(String[] args)
{
  Deck deck = new Deck();
  deck.getCards().get(0).setSuit(Suit.HEARTS);
}
```

With mutable Card instances, to implement the copying solution correctly, we need to go one step further and copy all cards when we copy the list of cards encapsulated within a Deck instance. In turn, this introduces a new requirement, namely, to find a clean way to copy card objects.

A common technique for copying objects is to use a *copy constructor*. The idea is to design a constructor that takes as argument an object of the same class, and (usually) to copy matching field values:

```
public Card(Card pCard)
{
  aRank = pCard.aRank;
  aSuit = pCard.aSuit;
}
```

In fact, the code above, where we use **new** `ArrayList<>(aCards)`, is an example of a copy constructor for `ArrayList`. To perform a deep(er) copy of our list of cards now becomes a bit more involved;

```
public List<Card> getCards()
{
  ArrayList<Card> result = new ArrayList<>();
  for( Card card : aCards )
  {
    result.add(new Card(card));
  }
  return result;
}
```

However, this extended solution ensures that encapsulation would be preserved even with mutable `Card` objects. Java provides other mechanisms for copying objects, including its *cloning* mechanism (see Section 6.6), metaprogramming (see Section 5.4) and its *serialization* mechanism (not covered in the book).

Advanced Techniques

Copying objects is only one of many strategies for exposing information internal to an object while maintaining encapsulation. Other strategies will be covered later in the book. These include iterators (see Section 3.5) and streams (see Section 9.6).

2.8 Design by Contract

One of the benefits of encapsulation is to make it difficult or impossible for client code to corrupt the value of a variable. Following the principles and guidelines presented in this chapter helps us achieve this goal. Let us consider the following implementation of class `Card` (which assumes `Rank` and `Suit` are plain enumerated types):

```
public class Card
{
  private Rank aRank;
  private Suit aSuit;

  public Card(Rank pRank, Suit pSuit)
  {
    aRank = pRank;
    aSuit = pSuit;
  }

  public Rank getRank() { return aRank; }
  public Suit getSuit() { return aSuit; }
}
```

The encapsulation provided by this class is very good, but there remains a crack in the "shell" it provides: it is possible to create a new card with a null reference:

```
Card card = new Card(null, Suit.CLUBS);
```

For most use cases where a representation of a playing card is required, this would be incorrect. At least, I am not aware of any card game that involves a "null of clubs". We thus corrupted the variable. Section 4.5 provides an extended discussion of the issue of null references. For now, an important point is that the interface to the class is ambiguous: it is not clear whether client code should not use `null` as an argument to the constructor, or whether it should simply be careful not to use a card for which either the rank or suit is null. Ambiguity of this nature can very easily destroy the quality of a design, render code incomprehensible, and upset developers using it.

Observing that the problem comes from the ambiguity about what is or should be a legal value for the arguments of the `Card` constructor, one natural solution is to define interface elements such as method signatures so that the ambiguity is minimized or eliminated. The idea of *design by contract* is to follow a principled approach to the specification of interfaces. Although in practice, method signatures already specify much of what is needed in an interface, they also leave room for ambiguity, as was shown by the example above. Diligent programmers can help eliminate ambiguities by stating the precise range of allowed values in a method's documentation. This is certainly better than nothing. However, design by contract goes further and provides a formal framework for reasoning about complete interface information. There is a lot to say about design by contract, so to keep things tractable this section only provides an overview of a simplified version of the approach.

The main idea of design by contract is for method signatures (and related documentation) to provide a sort of contract between the client (the caller method) and the server (the method being called). This contract takes the form of a set of *preconditions* and a set of *postconditions*. A precondition is a predicate that must be true when a method starts executing. The predicate typically involves the value of the method's arguments, including the state of the target object upon which the method is called. Similarly, postconditions are predicates that must be true when the execution of the method is completed.[13] Given preconditions and postconditions, the contract is basically that the method can only be expected to conform to the postconditions if the caller conforms to the preconditions. If a client calls a method without respecting the preconditions, the behavior of the method is undefined. In practice, design by contract is a great way to force us to think about all possible ways to use a method.

In the example applications (see Appendix C) I follow a lightweight version of design by contract where preconditions are specified using Java statements in the comments using the Javadoc `@pre` tag and postconditions are specified using the tag `@post`.

---

[13] The complete approach also involves the concept of *invariants*. In theory, invariants are predicates that are expected to remain true at all times. In the practice of design by contract, it is sufficient for invariants to be true at all method entry and exit points.

```
/**
 * @pre pRank != null && pSuit != null
 */
public Card(Rank pRank, Suit pSuit) { ... }
```

It is possible to make pre- and postconditions (and any other predicates) *checkable* in Java using the **assert** statement:

```
public Card(Rank pRank, Suit pSuit)
{
   assert pRank != null && pSuit != null;
   aRank = pRank; aSuit = pSuit;
}
```

The **assert** statement evaluates the predicate in the statement and raises an AssertionError if the predicate evaluates to false.[14]

Correctly implemented, design by contract helps prevent the tedious idiom of *defensive programming* where corner cases (such as null references) are checked for everywhere in the code. Additionally, the technique supports rapid *blame assignment* while debugging: If a precondition check fails, the client (caller method) is to blame. If a postcondition check fails, the actual method being called is to blame. More generally, **assert** statements are a simple yet powerful tool to increase code quality and they can be used anywhere, not just for pre- and postconditions. Whenever an assertion check fails, we know exactly where the problem is, and we can thus save hours of debugging time.

A final note about design by contract is that the addition of preconditions to a method's interface actually relieves us of the requirement to handle the condition. So the code below is not properly designed because it *both* states that null references are not a valid input *and* handles them in a consistent way (by raising an exception). If a method checks for a certain type of input (like null references) and produces a well-defined behavior as the result, then this is part of the method's interface specification. When designing method interfaces, it is important to decide whether the method will be in charge of rejecting illegal values, or whether these will simply be specified as invalid. These are two different design choices.

```
/**
 * @pre pRank != null && pSuit != null
 */
public Card(Rank pRank, Suit pSuit)
{
   if( pRank != null || pSuit != null )
   { throw new IllegalArgumentException(); }
   ...
}
```

---

[14] Assertion checking is disabled by default in Java, so to use this properly it is necessary to add −ea (enable assertions) as a VM parameter when running Java programs.

Insights

This chapter focused on how to follow the principles of encapsulation and information hiding when defining classes.

- Use classes to define how domain concepts are represented in code, as opposed to encoding instances of these concepts as values of primitive types (an antipattern called PRIMITIVE OBSESSION†);
- Use enumerated types to represent a value in a collection of a small number of elements that can be enumerated (e.g., card suits, months of the year, etc.);
- Hide the internal implementation of an abstraction behind an interface that tightly controls how an abstraction can be used. Declare fields of a class `private`, unless you have a strong reason not to. Similarly, declare any method `private` if it should not be explicitly part of the type's interface;
- Ensure that the design of your classes prevents any code from modifying the data stored in an object of the class without using a method of the class. In particular, be careful to avoid leaking references to private fields of the class that refer to mutable objects;
- To provide information about the internal data in an object without violating encapsulation, two strategies include extending the interface of the class or returning copies of internal objects;
- Object diagrams can help explain or clarify the structure of complex object graphs, or how references are shared;
- Make classes immutable if possible. In Java, it is only possible to ensure that a class is immutable through careful design and inspection;
- Use design by contract to avoid ambiguity in method signatures, and therefore to avoid the possibility that client code will misuse an instance of a class.

Code Exploration

The code examples for this chapter illustrate design decisions related to defining abstractions, encapsulation and class interface design.

`Cell` in Minesweeper

The first thing we notice when reading the code of class `Cell` is the use of a private enumerated type. Indeed, `CellInteractionStatus` is meant to be used only within the scope of `Cell`. The reason for this decision is that `CellInteractionStatus` captures a combination of two dimensions: whether a cell is revealed or not, and whether a cell is marked or not. However, storing this information in two Boolean fields is risky, since the logic of the game makes it impossible to have a cell that is *both* revealed *and* marked. For this reason, I decided to encode these two dimensions as a value of an enumerated type to make the offending combination impossible. However, because there is little risk in allowing client code to query for the *revealed/hidden* and *marked/unmarked* dimensions individually, I provide the information through Boolean getter methods instead of returning a value of the enumerated type, which I felt was less intuitive.

The second thing to notice about the implementation of `Cell` is that it is not immutable: instances of this class are intended to represent cells in a minefield. Although it would be possible to change the design so that the *mined* attribute is set in the constructor and never changed, the rules of the game dictate that it should be possible to mark/unmark a cell, or to reveal it. This requirement makes it awkward to implement a solution with immutable cell objects.

Finally, no part of the interface of `Cell` provides information about any neighbours of the cell. However, when implementing a game of Minesweeper, it is necessary to know how many of the neighbours of a cell hide a mine. Would it not be elegant to be able to write code such as `cell.getNeighbours()`? Perhaps. However, this would also muddle the definition of the information represented by the `Cell` abstraction. In the present design, the responsibility of an instance of `Cell` is limited to retaining and processing information about a single cell, in isolation from the rest of the minefield.

`Position` in Minesweeper

At first glance, class `Position` looks exceedingly simple: a row–column pair of integer coordinates. Why bother? Would it not be simpler to just use pairs of integers? Is this not excessive effort to avoid a case of PRIMITIVE OBSESSION†? The answers to these questions are not to be found in the definition of the class itself, but rather by looking at all the places in the code where `Position` is used: dozens. The problem with pairs of integers is that it is very easy to flip them by mistake, make off-by-one errors, etc. In the present design, the client code *never needs to initialize positions*. Class `Minefield` contains a method `getAllPositions()` which allows client code to iterate over all positions without ever having to specify initialization or termination values. How the iteration works will be covered in Chapter 3. Because an instance of `Position` represents a *single* position in a minefield, it makes sense to have this class be immutable.

`Dimension` in JetUML

In JetUML, class `Dimension` provides another example of "little abstraction", similar to `Position` in Minesweeper. The idea of encoding the concept of a "dimension" explicitly is twofold: to avoid the possibility of invalid dimensions (e.g., with negative values), and to prevent errors caused by flipping the width and the height. Of course, these have to be provided in the right order in a constructor call, but once a `Dimension` object is created, the risk of flipping the two values is eliminated.

`Card` in Solitaire

This chapter has used the creation of a deck of cards as a running example, so it is worth pointing out class `Card` in the Solitaire project. This class is an example of a non-trivial immutable class. However, a lot of the code in the class implements more advanced features that I will return to in Chapter 4, including the static members and the private constructor. Ignoring these, however, it should be possible to determine, by inspection, that the class is immutable, because there is no way to change the value of the `aRank` and `aSuit` fields outside of the constructor. Another noteworthy feature of this class is the use of inner enumerated types. The two enumerated types could alternatively be defined as top-level types in their own files. However, locating them within the definition of class `Card` strengthens the relation between the two, and emphasizes that these abstractions only make sense in relation to one or more `Card` instances.

`Rectangle` in JetUML

Class `Rectangle` in JetUML is another example of an immutable class, but this time a much more sophisticated one. In addition to numerous query methods (e.g., `getX()`, `getHeight()`, `getCenter()`), the interface of the class also includes methods that create *new* `Rectangle` instances as derivatives of the implicit parameter. For instance, `translated(int, int)` returns a new instance of `Rectangle` that is a translated version of the implicit parameter. Note the subtle difference in naming: the method is called `translated` instead of `translate`, because `translate` would imply the translation of the implicit parameter. This approach is necessary because, being immutable, it is not possible to directly translate the implicit parameter. The pattern of "modifying" an immutable object by returning a modified version of the (unmodified) implicit parameter is not uncommon. The library class `String` provides many examples, such as `substring(int)`, which returns a new `String` instance that is a substring of the object on which the method is called. Given this roundabout way of obtaining modified rectangles, and the performance penalty involved in creating many new objects to have different rectangles, one can rightfully ask why not simply use mutable `Rectangle` instances. The main answer, at least in the context of JetUML, is one of program understanding. In Release 2.3, instances of `Rectangle` are used in over 50 different locations of the code. If a mutable `Rectangle` is passed around, keeping track of what physical rectangle this instance actually represents at any point in the execution of the application becomes extremely challenging.

Further Reading

Chapter 6 of the book *Software Architecture: A Comprehensive Framework and Guide for Practitioners* by Vogel et al. [17] provides a well-organized overview of the different general principles of software design, and how they are related. For a more historical perspective, the seminal paper on the principle of information hiding is Parnas's 1972 "On the Criteria to be Used in Decomposing Systems into Modules" [11]. The article contrasts two designs for a text processing system, and argues for the superiority of the design that realizes information hiding over a sequential processing decomposition.

The section titled "Enum Types" in the Java Tutorial [10] provides additional insights on how enumerated types work.

In the book *Effective Java* [1], Bloch calls copies of internal object encapsulated by a class "defensive copies" (Item 50).

The article "Applying Design by Contract", by Bertrand Meyer (the inventor of the technique), provides a more detailed presentation of the idea while remaining accessible [8].

Chapter 3
Types and Interfaces

This chapter covers:

Concepts and Principles: Interface, polymorphism, loose coupling, reusability, extensibility, separation of concerns, interface segregation;
Programming Mechanisms: Java interfaces, interface implementation;
Design Techniques: Decoupling behavior from implementation, interface-based behavior specification, class diagrams, function objects, iterators;
Patterns and Antipatterns: ITERATOR, STRATEGY, SWITCH STATEMENT†.

In the previous chapter we saw how to define well-encapsulated classes, but conveniently left out the question of how objects of these classes would interact. We now start facing this question. Interactions between objects are mediated through interfaces. The term "interface" is overloaded in programming: it can have different meanings depending on the context.

Design Context

Similarly to the previous chapter, the running examples in this chapter concern the design of a small class library to allow client code to instantiate and use a Deck and other collections of Card objects to support the development of different card games.

© Springer Nature Switzerland AG 2019
M. P. Robillard, *Introduction to Software Design with Java*,
https://doi.org/10.1007/978-3-030-24094-3_3

3.1 Decoupling Behavior from Implementation

An interface to a class consists of the methods of that class that are accessible (or visible) to another class. What methods are accessible depends on various language rules that take into account access modifiers and scopes. In this chapter I keep things simple and assume that the interface to a class is the set of its public methods. This is not strictly true, but for now we do not need additional distinctions. I will extend this definition in Chapter 7. Although the above definition of interface is expressed with respect to a class, it also makes sense to extend the definition to apply to objects. By extension, the interface to an object is the set of methods that can be called on the object. Which definition best applies will depend on the context. If we are thinking of a design solution in terms of class definitions, then the interface is that of the class. If we are thinking of a design solution in terms of a collection of instances of the class, then it is the object's interface that is relevant. I revisit this duality in the next chapter. For now, let us consider the following code:

```
public class Client
{
  private Deck aDeck = new Deck();
}

public class Deck
{
  public void shuffle() { ... }
  public Card draw() { ... }
  public boolean isEmpty() { ... }
}
```

The interface of class Deck consists of three methods. The code in other classes can interact with objects of class Deck by calling these and only these methods. Here we would say that the interface of class Deck is fused with the class definition. In other words, the interface of class Deck is just a consequence of how we defined class Deck: there is no way to get the three services that correspond to the three methods of the class, without interacting with an instance of class Deck. In our example, to shuffle the deck, client code will need to invoke method shuffle() of a field or local variable of type Deck: there is no other option.

There are, however, many situations were we want to decouple the interface of a class from its implementation. These are situations where we want to design the system so one part of the code can depend on the availability of some services, without being tied to the exact details of how these services are implemented. Given that we are designing a library that can be used to build different card games, we note that many card games require the user to draw cards,[1] but not necessarily from a standard deck of 52 cards. For example, some games might require drawing cards from an aggregation of multiple decks of cards, from a set of cards of only one suit,

---

[1] The term *draw* here refers to the domain of card games, where "drawing" a card means removing it from a pile. This is not to be confused with the action of depicting the card on a user interface component, for example.

from ordered sequences of cards, etc. Let us consider the following code that draws cards from a deck up to a required number.

```
public static List<Card> drawCards(Deck pDeck, int pNumber)
{
  List<Card> result = new ArrayList<>();

  for( int i = 0; i < pNumber && !pDeck.isEmpty(); i++ )
  { result.add(pDeck.draw()); }

  return result;
}
```

This method can only work if the source of cards is an instance of class `Deck`. This is a pity, because exactly the same code should work for any object that has two methods `draw()` and `isEmpty()` that perform the expected behavior. Here it would be useful to specify an abstraction of an interface without tying it to a specific class. This is where Java interfaces come in. In Java, interfaces provide a *specification* of the methods that it should be possible to invoke on the objects of a class. So we could define an abstraction `CardSource` as any object that supports a `draw()` and `isEmpty()` methods:

```
public interface CardSource
{
  /**
   * Returns a card from the source.
   *
   * @return The next available card.
   * @pre !isEmpty()
   */
  Card draw();

  /**
   * @return True if there is no card in the source.
   */
  boolean isEmpty();
}
```

This interface declaration lists two methods, and includes comments that describe the behavior of each method. Notice how the specification of `draw()` includes the precondition that the method can only be invoked if `isEmpty()` is false. This precondition is provided to support the use of design by contract (see Section 2.8), and takes into account the existing state of the object. Because interface method declarations are a specification and not an implementation, details of what the method is expected to perform are very important. With a method implementation, it could always be possible to inspect the code (if we have access to it) and infer the specification. This is not an ideal situation, but it is better than nothing. With interface methods, though, reverse-engineering what the method does is not possible. In Java terminology, methods that do not have an implementation are called *abstract methods*.[2] To tie a class with an interface, we use the `implements` keyword.

```
public class Deck implements CardSource {...}
```

The `implements` keyword has two related effects:

- It provides a formal guarantee that instances of the class type will have concrete implementations for all the methods in the interface type. This guarantee is enforced by the compiler.
- It creates a subtype relationship between the implementing class and the interface type: here we can now say that a `Deck` is a type of `CardSource`.

The subtype relation between a concrete class and an interface is what enables the use of *polymorphism*. In plain language, polymorphism is the ability to have different shapes. Here, `CardSource` is an abstraction that can present itself in different concrete shapes. Each concrete shape corresponds to a different implementation of the `CardSource` interface.

For polymorphism to be useful in code, it is important to remember that according to the rules of the Java type system, it is possible to assign a value to a variable if the value is of the same type *or a subtype* of the type of the variable. Because the interface implementation relation defines a subtype relation, references to objects of concrete classes declared to implement an interface can be assigned to variables declared to be of the interface type. For example, because class `Deck` declares to implement interface `CardSource`, we can assign a reference to an object of class `Deck` to a variable of type `CardSource`, as such:

```
CardSource source = new Deck();
```

Taking this idea further, this means we can make our implementation of the `drawCards` method much more reusable:

```
public static List<Card> drawCards(CardSource pSource, int pNumber)
{
  List<Card> result = new ArrayList<>();

  for( int i = 0; i < pNumber && !pSource.isEmpty(); i++ )
  { result.add(pSource.draw()); }

  return result;
}
```

Now, the method can operate on objects of any class that implements the `CardSource` interface.

Another illustration of the use of polymorphism is the use of concrete vs. abstract collection types in the Java Collections Framework.

```
List<String> list = new ArrayList<>();
```

---

[2] Prior to Java 8, all interface methods were automatically abstract. With Java 8, this is no longer true, because interfaces can include default methods, which have an implementation. Nevertheless, it remains a good practice to thoroughly document the expected behavior of interface methods.

Here `List` is an interface that specifies the obvious services (add, remove, etc.), and `ArrayList` is a concrete implementation of this service that implements the list using an array structure. But we can just as well replace `ArrayList` with `LinkedList` and the code will still compile. Even though the details of the list implementation differ between `ArrayList` and `LinkedList`, they both provide exactly the methods required by the `List` interface, so it is permissible to swap them. Polymorphism provides two useful benefits in software design:

- *Loose coupling*, because the code using a set of methods is not tied to a specific implementation of these methods.
- *Extensibility*, because we can easily add new implementations of an interface (new "shapes" in the polymorphic relation).

3.2 Specifying Behavior with Interfaces

Typical design questions related to interfaces include: *do I need a separate interface?* and *what should this interface specify?* There are no general answers to such questions, because in each case the task is to determine if interfaces can help us solve a design problem or realize a particular feature. One good illustration of both the purpose and usefulness of interfaces in Java is the `Comparable` interface.

One obvious task to be implemented in the `Deck` class is to shuffle a deck of cards. This can be realized trivially with the help of a library method.

```
public class Deck
{
  private List<Card> aCards = new ArrayList<>();

  public void shuffle() { Collections.shuffle(aCards); }
}
```

As its name describes, the library method `shuffle` randomly reorders the objects in the argument collection. This is an example of code reuse because it is possible to reuse the library method to reorder any kind of collection. Here reuse is easy because to shuffle a collection, we do not need to know anything about the items being shuffled.

But what if we want to reuse code to *sort* the cards in the deck? Sorting, like many classic computing problems, is supported by many existing high-quality implementations. In most realistic software development situations it would not be acceptable to hand-craft one's own sorting algorithm. The Java `Collections` class conveniently supplies us with a number of sorting functions. However, if we opportunistically try the following without further consideration:

```
List<Card> cards = ...;
Collections.sort(aCards);
```

we are rewarded with a moderately cryptic compilation error. This should not be surprising, though, because how exactly is a library method supposed to know how we want to sort our cards? Not only is it impossible for the designers of library methods to anticipate all the user-defined types that can be invented, but even for a given type like `Card`, different orderings are possible (e.g., by rank, then suit, or vice-versa).

The `Comparable<T>` interface helps solve this problem by defining a piece of behavior related specifically to the comparison of objects, in the form of a single `int` `compareTo(T)` method. The specification for this method is that it should return 0 if the implicit argument is the same as the explicit argument, a negative integer if it should come before, and a positive integer if it should come after. Given the existence of this interface, the internal implementation of `Collections.sort` can now rely on it to compare the objects it should sort. Conceptually, the internal code of the `sort` implementation looks a bit like this:

```
if( object1.compareTo(object2) > 0 ) ...
```

So from the point of view of the implementation of `sort`, it really does not matter what the object is, as long as it is comparable with another object. This is a great example of how interfaces and polymorphism support loose coupling: the code of `sort` depends on the minimum possible piece of functionality required from its argument objects. This is a good general insight on how to define interfaces. Ideally, they should capture the smallest cohesive "slice" of behavior that is expected to be used by client code. For this reason, many interfaces in Java are named with an adjective that ends in "able", a suffix that means "fit to be...". Besides `Comparable`, examples include `Iterable`, `Serializable` and `Cloneable`.

To make it possible for us to sort a list of cards, we therefore have to provide this *comparable* behavior and declare it with the **implements** keyword:

```
public class Card implements Comparable<Card>
{
  public int compareTo(Card pCard)
  { return aRank.ordinal() - pCard.aRank.ordinal(); }
}
```

This minimal implementation sorts cards by ascending rank, but leaves the order of suits undefined, which leads to unpredictability. A more useful implementation of the `Comparable` interface would provide a well-defined total ordering.

Because interfaces are types, the type checking mechanism that is part of the compilation process makes it possible to detect that a `List<Card>` object cannot be passed to `Collections.sort` unless the `Card` class declares to implement the `Comparable<Card>` interface. How this happens is outside the scope of this book because it requires a good understanding of the typing rules for Java generic types (see Section A.6 in the appendix).

Many other library types that have a so-called "natural" ordering implement the `Comparable` interface. This includes `String` (with alphabetical order) but also many other pervasive types. In particular, Java enumerated types implement `Comparable` by comparing instances of an enumerated type according to their ordinal value. With this knowledge in hand, we can observe that our implementation of `Card.compareTo`, above, actually re-implements reusable behavior provided by the enumerated types. We thus have an opportunity to simplify our code:

```
public class Card implements Comparable<Card>
{
  public int compareTo(Card pCard)
  { return aRank.compareTo(pCard.aRank); }
}
```

Using small interfaces encourages the respect of a software design principle called *separation of concerns*. The idea of separation of concerns is that one abstraction should map to a single "concern" (or area of interest) for developers. In designs that do a poor job at separation of concerns, we find concerns to be *tangled* within an abstraction (a method for example), and/or *scattered* across multiple different abstractions. Here the use of the `Comparable` interface is a good example of effective separation of concerns: the code to compare cards is entirely contained within a clearly defined and identified abstraction (the `compareTo` method), which does only one thing.

3.3 Class Diagrams

Designs where the important concerns revolve around the definition of types and relations between types can quickly become overwhelming to describe in code, and are more easily captured through a diagram. Class diagrams represent a *static*, or *compile-time*, view of a software system. They are useful to represent how types are defined and related, but are a poor vehicle for capturing any kind of *run-time* property of the code. Class diagrams are the type of UML diagrams that are the closest to the code. However, it is important to remember that the point of UML diagrams is not to be an exact translation of the code. As models, they are useful to capture the essence of one or more design decisions without having to include all the details.

Class diagram have an extensive associated notation. In a class diagram, there is typically more going on than in an object diagram, say. I will be using only a small subset of the notation in this book. The Further Reading section includes references for UML class diagrams. Figure 3.1 shows the main concepts used in the book. In the figure, all quotes are taken from *The Unified Modeling Language Reference Manual, 2nd edition* [15]. The interpretation of the concepts of aggregation, association, and dependency will become clearer as we progress through the chapters. For now, we can consider simply that these represent that two classes are somehow related. The concept of navigability, represented with an arrow head, models how code supports going from objects of one type to objects of another type. Navigability can be unidirectional (as shown), bidirectional, or unspecified.

Figure 3.2 shows an example of a class diagram that models some of the key relations between the design elements for a card game that we have seen so far. We can observe the following:

- The box that represents class `Card` *does not have fields* for `aRank` and `Suit` because these are represented as aggregations to `Rank` and `Suit` enumerated types,

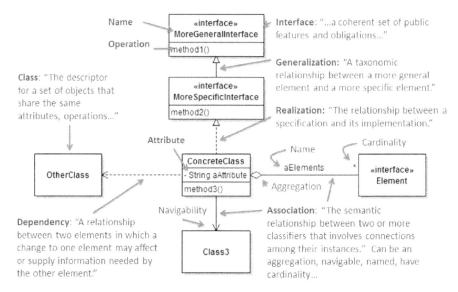

Fig. 3.1 Selected notation for class diagrams

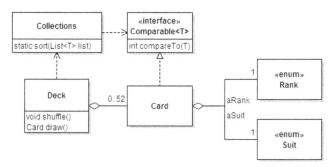

Fig. 3.2 Sample class diagram showing key decisions in the design of a `Deck` class

respectively. It is a modeling error to have *both* a field *and* an aggregation to represent a given field.

- The methods of class `Card` are not represented. Because they are just the constructor and accessors, I judged this to not be very insightful information. It would not be wrong to include them, but it would clutter the diagram.

- In the UML, there is no good way to indicate that a class *does not have* a certain member (field or method). To convey the information that `Card` does not have setters for the two fields, it would be necessary to include this using a note.

- Representing generic types is a bit problematic, because in some cases it makes more sense to represent the type parameter `Comparable<T>` and in some other cases it makes more sense to represent the type instance `Comparable<Card>`.

In this diagram I went with the type parameter because I wanted to show how `Collections` depends on `Comparable` in general.

- All UML tools have some sort of limitations one needs to get around. For simplicity, JetUML (see Appendix C) does not have different fonts to distinguish between static and non-static members. To indicate that a method is static in JetUML, we can simply add the keyword **static**.
- The model includes cardinalities to indicate, e.g., that a deck instance will aggregate between zero and 52 instances of `Card`.

3.4 Function Objects

A common case when using Java interfaces is that an interface represents only a subset of the complete interface of classes that implement it. This case is exemplified by `Comparable`: the complete implementation of `Card` comprises methods (e.g., `getSuit()` and `getRank()`) that add to the slice of behavior mandated by the interface. There are other situations, however, where it is convenient to define classes that specialize in implementing *only* the behavior required by a small interface with only one method.

To illustrate this point, let us continue with the problem of comparing cards. Implementing the `Comparable` interface allows instances of `Card` to compare themselves with other instances of `Card` using one strategy, for example, by comparing the card's rank, and using suits to break ties. What if we are designing a game where it makes sense to sort cards according to different strategies, and occasionally switch between them? One could tweak the code of `compareTo`, for instance by setting a flag in an instance of `Card` and switching the comparison strategy on this flag. However, harebrained schemes of this nature have many drawbacks. In our case, using such a flag instance variable:

- Would destroy the immutability of the `Card` class;
- Would degrade the neat separation of concerns between representing a card and knowledge of how the card should be sorted at a particular moment in the execution of the code.

In fact, the use of this kind of "switching" approach is often considered poor form, and this programming idiom is considered a design antipattern called SWITCH STATEMENT†.[3]

A more promising solution is to move the comparison code to a separate object. This solution is supported by the `Comparator<T>` interface. The most important method in this interface is `compare` (as opposed to `compareTo`).[4]

---

[3] There is evidence of the antipattern whether or not an actual **switch** statement is used, since the latter can be trivially emulated through **if–else** statements.

[4] As of Java 8, this interface provides a fairly intimidating list of methods. These are not important here. In Chapter 9 I revisit this interface to explain how we can leverage some of the additional methods.

```
int compare(T pObject1, T pObject2)
```

As for `Comparable`, `Comparator` is a generic type, so in the above declaration, `T` refers to a type parameter that must be instantiated (with type `Card` for example). Besides the slight name difference, the most notable difference is that the method takes two arguments instead of one. Indeed, its specification is very similar to that of `compareTo`, except that instead of comparing the implicit parameter (the **this** object) with an explicit parameter, it compares two explicit parameters with each other. Not surprisingly, library methods were also designed to work with this interface. For example: `Collections.sort`.

```
Collections.sort(List<T> list, Comparator<? super T> c)
```

This method can sort a list of objects that do not necessarily implement the `Comparable` interface, by taking as argument an object guaranteed to be able to compare two instances of the items in the list. One can now define a "rank first" comparator:

```
public class RankFirstComparator implements Comparator<Card>
{
   public int compare(Card pCard1, Card pCard2)
   { /* Comparison code */ }
}
```

and another "suit first" comparator:

```
public class SuitFirstComparator implements Comparator<Card>
{
   public int compare(Card pCard1, Card pCard2)
   { /* Comparison code */ }
}
```

and sort[5] with the desired comparator:

```
Collections.sort(aCards, new RankFirstComparator());
```

In this scenario, an instance of `Comparator` is simply an object that provides the implementation for a single method. In Java terminology, these are often referred to as *function objects*. Their interface typically maps one-to-one to that of an interface.

Although simple, the use of comparator objects (and, by extension, similar function objects) introduces many interesting design questions and trade-offs. First, if comparator classes are defined as standalone top-level Java classes, the code of their `compare` method will not have access to the private members of the objects they compare. In some cases the information available from getter methods is sufficient to implement the comparison, but in other cases implementing the `compare` method will require access to private members.

In such cases, one option to give comparator classes access to private members of the classes they compare is to declare the comparator classes as *nested classes* (see Section 4.10) of the class that defines the objects being compared:

---

[5] As of Java 8, method `sort` is also available on the `Collection` (no 's') interface. However, to preserve the symmetry with the use of the `Comparable<T>` interface, I retain this version.

```
public class Card
{
  static class CompareBySuitFirst implements Comparator<Card>
  {
    public int compare(Card pCard1, Card pCard2)
    { /* Comparison code */ }
  }
}
```

To client code the impact of this change in design would be minimal: the only difference is the additional qualification of the name of the comparator class:

```
Collections.sort(aCards, new Card.CompareBySuitFirst());
```

Another option is to define comparator classes as *anonymous classes*. In cases where the comparator is only referred to once, this makes a lot of sense:

```
public class Deck
{
  public void sort()
  {
    Collections.sort(aCards, new Comparator<Card>()
    {
      public int compare(Card pCard1, Card pCard2)
      { /* Comparison code */ }
    });
}
```

A third option is to use *lambda expressions*. Lambda expressions are a form of anonymous function. These and related mechanisms form the topic of Chapter 9. However, since it is possible to implement a very close equivalent to the code above using lambda expressions, I provide it here. The basic idea is based on the observation that to supply a comparator, not only do we not need to name a class because it is only an implementation of the Comparator interface, we also do not need to name the method, because it is only an implementation of compare. How this code actually works is explained in Chapter 9.

```
public class Deck
{
  public void sort()
  {
    Collections.sort(aCards, (card1, card2) ->
      card1.getRank().compareTo(card2.getRank()));
}
```

In the two examples above, we have brought back the problem of encapsulation, because the code in the anonymous class that implements the comparison is defined outside of the Card class. We can solve this with the help of a static *factory method*. I use the term "factory method" to denote any method whose primary role is to create and return an object.

```
public class Card
{
  public static Comparator<Card> createByRankComparator()
  {
    return new Comparator<Card>()
    {
      public int compare(Card pCard1, Card pCard2)
      { /* Comparison code */ }
    };
  }
}
```

A final question is whether a comparator should store data. For example, instead of having different comparators for sorting cards by rank and suit, we could define a `UniversalComparator` that has a field of an enumerated type that stores the desired type of comparison. Although this solution is workable, it can lead to code that is harder to understand, for reasons explained in Section 3.7 and further discussed in Chapter 4.

3.5 Iterators

A common requirement when designing data structures is to gain access to a collection of objects encapsulated by another object without violating encapsulation and information hiding. This problem was originally introduced in Section 2.7, where the solution proposed was to return copies of the internal data. For example, to return a copy of the list of cards encapsulated within a `Deck` instance. One issue with this solution is that it can subtly leak information about the way a structure is stored internally (or at least, give the impression that it leaks this information). For example, if we choose to return a deck's cards as a `List`:

```
public List<Card> getCards() {...}
```

code using the `Deck` may start relying on the operations defined on a list, or make the assumption that cards are internally stored in a list within a `Deck`. To achieve an even higher level of information hiding, it would be best to allow client code access to the internal objects of another object, without exposing anything about the internal structure of the encapsulating object. This design feature is supported by the concept of an *iterator*. The concept of iterator is very general, and it finds realizations in many programming languages.[6]

In Java, iterators are easy to use, but understanding how they work requires being aware of a careful coordination between at least three types of objects. Iterators are a good example of effective use of interfaces and polymorphism.

To support iteration we must first have a specification of what it means to iterate. As usual, this specification is captured in an interface, in this case the `Iterator`

---

[6] And in particular, Python. According to the official Python 3.7.0 tutorial "The use of iterators pervades and unifies Python."

interface. This interface defines two abstract methods: `hasNext()` and `next()`. So, according to the rules of subtyping, once a piece of code gains access to a reference to an object of any subtype of `Iterator`, the client code can iterate over it, independently of what the actual class of the object is. To enable iteration over the cards of a `Deck`, let us simply redefine the `getCards` method to return an iterator instead of a list:

```
public Iterator<Card> getCards() { ... }
```

This way, to print all the cards of a deck, we can do:

```
Iterator<Card> iterator = deck.getCards();
while( iterator.hasNext() )
{ System.out.println(iterator.next()); }
```

Although this design achieves our decoupling goal, we can generalize it to great effect. A first important insight is that in most software there will typically be many different types of objects that it would be useful to iterate over. Lists are an obvious example. In our case we have a `Deck`. In practice, the list of possibilities is infinite. The issue with the iterator system as we have it now, though, is that every class defines a different way to obtain an iterator. For class `List`, it is through the method `iterator()`. For our `Deck` class, it is through method `getCards()`. Although the behavior in both cases is identical (return an iterator), the *name* of the service is different. We can solve this issue with an interface. The `Iterable<T>` interface specifies the smallest "slice" of behavior necessary to make it possible to iterate over an object. To be able to polymorphically iterate over an object, the only thing we need from this object is that it supplies an iterator. So the only abstract method of the `Iterable` interface is `Iterator<T> iterator()`.

We can make our `Deck` class iterable by implementing the `Iterable<Card>` interface and renaming the `getCards()` method to `iterator()`:

```
public class Deck implements Iterable<Card>
{
  public Iterator<Card> iterator() { ... }
}
```

This way an instance of `Deck` can be supplied anywhere an `Iterable` interface type is expected. Figure 3.3 shows the main design elements of the iterator design so far.

Fig. 3.3 Class diagram for the design of an iterator

As it turns out, one of the main ways to use `Iterable` objects in Java is in enhanced **for** (a.k.a. *for each*) loops:

```
List<String> theList = ...;

for( String string : theList )
{ System.out.println(string); }
```

The above code is just syntactic sugar for:

```
List<String> theList = ...;

for(Iterator<String> iter = list.iterator(); iter.hasNext(); )
{
   String string = iter.next();
   System.out.println(string);
}
```

So to iterate over a deck, we can now do:

```
for( Card card : deck ) { System.out.println(card); }
```

The way the enhanced **for** loop works is that, under the covers, it expects the rightmost part of the loop head to be an instance of a class that is a subtype of `Iterable` (or an array type, which is a special case).

The final issue to solve to complete our iterator-based design for `Deck` is to find a way to return an instance of `Iterator` when the `iterator()` method is called. Although it would be possible to hand-craft our own user-defined class that implements the `Iterator<Card>` interface, here it is much easier to simply observe that the `List` contained within a `Deck` is also `Iterable`, and the `Iterator` it returns does everything that we want.

```
public class Deck implements Iterable<Card>
{
   private List<Card> aCards;

   public Iterator<Card> iterator() { return aCards.iterator(); }
}
```

Representing the implementation of the `Iterator` interface in the UML is not obvious given our reliance on an instance of an unknown concrete type. Although we know that the type returned by `List.iterator()` is some subtype of the `Iterator` interface, we do not know the name of the class that ultimately implements this interface. In fact, this may be an anonymous class, in which case, by definition, there is no name. So the fact to reckon with at this point is that we do not know the type. However, we cannot really write "Unknown" in a class in a class diagram, because this would indicate that the name of the class is known, and it is "Unknown", which is very confusing. For now, I will assume that the type is anonymous and indicate this fact with the UML *stereotype* (`<<anonymous>>`), leaving the name blank. In the UML, a stereotype is a variation on an element type, with the name of the variation placed in angle brackets.

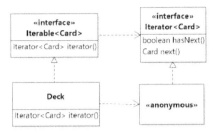

Fig. 3.4 Class diagram of the complete iterator design

3.6 The ITERATOR Design Pattern

The previous section introduced the use of iterators as a way to provide access to a collection of objects encapsulated within another object without violating the encapsulation and information hiding properties of this object. This solution is a common design pattern called, not surprisingly, the ITERATOR. The *context* for ITERATOR is to

> Provide a way to access the elements of an aggregate object sequentially without exposing its underlying representation. [6]

The *solution template* for ITERATOR can be best captured by the class diagram in Figure 3.5, which is simply an abstraction of the solution presented in Figure 3.4.

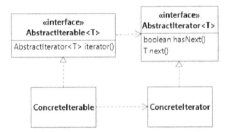

Fig. 3.5 Class diagram of the solution template for ITERATOR

An important difference to notice between the solution template in Figure 3.5 and its concrete realization in Figure 3.4 is that the solution template does not refer to the Java library interfaces `Iterable` and `Iterator`. Although they can be (and often are) supported by libraries, design patterns are abstract solution elements that can be realized in code independently of specific library implementations. For this reason, the solution template simply indicates that to instantiate `Iterator` in code, one needs a type to play the *role* of `AbstractIterable` and `AbstractIterator`, and similarly with their concrete implementation. This being said, in Java there are very few variants of ITERATOR. Because only subtypes of `Iterable` can be used in the enhanced **for** loop, there is a strong incentive to actually use `Iterable` as the `AbstractIterable`, which forces the use of `Iterator` as the `ConcreteIterator`. The remainder of the mapping is almost automatic, as the `ConcreteIterable` is whatever one wants to iterate over. How to create the `ConcreteIterator` is one design decision that yields more possibilities, but the most convenient option is often to simply return the iterator supplied by the data structure (e.g., `ArrayList.iterator()`). In some cases, it might be necessary to combine elements from various collections and iterate over them, or iterate in an order different from that of the collection holding the elements to iterate over. In such cases, the simplest option is often to create a new collection with the desired elements in the right order, and to return that collection's iterator.

3.7 The STRATEGY Design Pattern

One of the major benefits of interfaces and polymorphism is to promote flexible designs. One example of a flexible design enabled by interfaces is the use of a `Comparator` instance by the `Collections.sort(...)` method, as introduced in Section 3.4. The use of function objects such as comparators to customize the behavior of another part of the code (e.g., the sorting behavior) is recognized as one instance of a more general idea called the STRATEGY design pattern. The basic *context* for STRATEGY is to:

> Define a family of algorithms, encapsulate each one, and make them interchangeable. Strategy lets the algorithms vary independently from clients that use it. [6]

This is a very general definition, especially given that there is no agreed-upon definition for what a "family of algorithms" is. Fortunately, the *solution template* for STRATEGY provides a clarification for object-oriented code: algorithms in the same family implement the same interface.

Fig. 3.6 Solution template for STRATEGY

The STRATEGY looks exceedingly simple. In fact in many cases it can be indistinguishable from a basic use of polymorphism. I find it useful to think of a part of the design as an instance of STRATEGY when that part of the design is focused on allowing the switch between algorithms. One example, illustrated in Figure 3.7, is the use of different card comparators for a deck of cards. Another example is the implementation of different automatic playing strategies, as will be further discussed in the Code Exploration section.

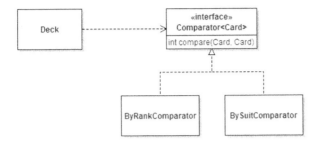

Fig. 3.7 Sample instantiation of a STRATEGY

Although nominally simple, in practice instantiating a STRATEGY requires thinking about many design questions:

- Does the `AbstractStrategy` need one or multiple methods to define the algorithm? Typically the answer is one, but in some cases it may be necessary to have more methods.
- Should the strategy method return anything or have a side-effect on the argument?
- Does a strategy need to store data?
- What should be the type of the return value and/or method parameters, as applicable? Ideally we want to choose these types to minimize coupling between a strategy and its clients.

Figure 3.7 shows an example instantiation of STRATEGY for the context of comparing cards. Here the design of the `AbstractStrategy` is already decided because we are reusing the `Comparator` interface. This strategy is purely functional as it does not have any side-effect and returns the result of applying the comparison algorithm. At this point it should become a bit clearer that implementing the `Comparator` interface as a `UniversalComparator` that holds a value to decide what kind of comparison to do, does not really respect the spirit of the STRATEGY because the actual strategy would be selected by changing the state of an object, as opposed to changing the concrete strategy object.

3.8 The Interface Segregation Principle

Throughout this chapter we saw the various benefits of defining specialized interfaces that specify a small and coherent slice of behavior that clients depend on.

This way code is not coupled with the details of an implementation, and only depends on the methods it actually requires. For example, code that processes cards can only depend on a `CardSource` interface with two methods, and can therefore be reusable with any class that can provide these methods. Similarly, the `Collections.sort(...)` method works because it can rely on just the fact that the items in the collection are `Comparable`. This idea is actually an instance of a general design principle called the Interface Segregation Principle (ISP). Simply put, the ISP states that *client code should not be forced to depend on interfaces it does not need.*

The idea of the ISP is easier to explain by presenting a situation where the principle is *not* respected. We can consider again the code in Section 3.1 where `drawCards` takes a `Deck` as argument:

```java
public static List<Card> drawCards(Deck pDeck, int pNumber)
{
  List<Card> result = new ArrayList<>();

  for( int i = 0; i < pNumber && !pDeck.isEmpty(); i++ )
  { result.add(pDeck.draw()); }

  return result;
}
```

In Section 3.1 I argued that this was a suboptimal design because it tied an interface with its implementation. Well, let us say we split the two by declaring an `IDeck` interface:

```java
public interface IDeck
{
  void shuffle();
  Card draw();
  boolean isEmpty();
}
```

```java
public class Deck implements IDeck...
```

which we rely on in `drawCards`:

```java
public static List<Card> drawCards(IDeck pDeck, int pNumber)
```

This effectively decouples interface from implementation, and supports the use of `drawCards` with non-`Deck` sources. However, this design is still suboptimal because it forces `drawCards` to statically depend on a method it does not need, namely, `shuffle`. What if we might want to draw cards from a source that cannot be shuffled? For this reason, the `CardSource` solution initially presented in Section 3.1 did respect the ISP, and only included methods `draw` and `isEmpty` in interface `CardSource`.

To push on this idea of ISP a bit, let us assume that there might be places in the code that only shuffle an object. To support this slice of behavior, we would define an interface `Shufflable` with a single method `shuffle()`. Figure 3.8 shows a maximally flexible separation of concerns for class `Deck`, with three different interfaces that capture three cohesive slices of behavior that are supported by class `Deck`, and three client code locations (represented by Client1-3) interested in different combinations of these services.

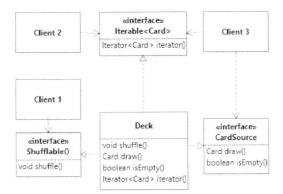

Fig. 3.8 Interface segregation in practice

This design has loose coupling, which is great. However, this loose coupling has one major disadvantage for cases where a client might be interested in more than one slice of behavior. This situation is represented in Figure 3.8 by Client 3, which needs to both iterate over an Iterable<Card> *and* draw some cards from the source. How can we express this combination, since in Java it is only possible to specify a single type for a variable? For example, if we pass an instance of CardSource to a method of interest and wish to iterate over the cards, we have to venture into inelegance:

```
public void displayCards(CardSource pSource)
{
  if( !pSource.isEmpty() )
  {
    pSource.draw();
    for( Card card : (Iterable<Card>) pSource) { ... }
  }
}
```

In fact this is not only inelegant, but also unsafe, because it could be possible to provide an argument to displayCards that is *not* a subtype of Iterable. A better solution to this issue is offered directly by the type system, in the form of subtyping. In Java, interfaces can be declared to extend each other, with the semantics that if A extends B, types that implement A must provide implementation for all the methods declared in B as well, transitively. By extending interfaces, we can more easily support combinations of services while respecting the ISP. In our scenario, if it is observed that a lot of the code that uses CardSource also uses Iterable<Card>, *but not the other way around*, then we can declare CardSource to be a subtype of Iterable<Card>, as illustrated in Figure 3.9.

In principle, the same reasoning could apply in the reverse situation: if we notice that most code that uses Iterable<Card> also uses CardSource *but not the*

Fig. 3.9 Example of interface extension

other way around, it would make sense to declare `Iterable<Card>` to extend `CardSource`. In practice, however, this is not possible because `Iterable<T>` is a library type, which it is not possible to modify. For this reason, there are also large amounts of code that depend on it without depending on `CardSource`, rendering the situation a mere theoretical possibility. Finally, software designs can be hard to get right immediately. It may be the case that two segregated interfaces end up always being used together in the client code. In such a situation, it is possible that application of the ISP went a bit too far, and it might be worth considering fusing two interfaces back into one, by collecting all method declarations into a single interface.

Insights

This chapter focused on how to use interfaces and polymorphism to achieve extensibility and reuse.

- Use interface types to decouple a specification from its implementation if you plan to have different implementations of that specification as part of your design;
- Define interfaces so that each interface groups a cohesive set of methods that are likely to be used together;
- Organize interfaces as subtypes of each other to create flexible groupings of behavior;
- Use library interfaces, such as `Comparable`, to implement commonly expected behavior;
- Use class diagrams to explore or capture important design decisions that have to do with how classes relate to each other;
- Consider function objects as a potential way to implement a small piece of required functionality, such as a comparison algorithm. Function objects can often be specified as instances of anonymous classes, or as lambda expressions;

- Use iterators to expose a collection of objects encapsulated within another without violating the encapsulation and information hiding properties of this object. This idea is known as the ITERATOR design pattern;
- Consider using the STRATEGY pattern if part of your design requires supporting an interchangeable family of algorithms;
- Make sure that your code does not depend on interfaces it does not need: break up large interfaces into smaller ones if you find that many methods of a type are not used in certain code locations.

Code Exploration

Comparable Java Versions in JetUML

In JetUML, class `JavaVersion` provides an example of a `Comparable` subtype. `JavaVersion` is responsible for detecting and representing the version of the Java run-time environment available on a user's machine. Because Java changed version numbering schemes over the years, this simple requirement turns out to be a nightmare to implement, which explains the amount of code in this class. In any case, the declaration of the class includes the required `compare(JavaVersion)` method, which compares the different components of a Java version (major, minor, and security, respectively). This feature is then used in method `checkVersion()` of class `UMLEditor`. In this case, however, the use of `Comparable` is *not* polymorphic. The only place in the code where method `compare` is called is on a variable typed `JavaVersion`, not `Comparable`. For this reason, the design would have been the same without using the `Comparable` interface (and we could also have called the comparison method anything we like). However, making `JavaVersion` a subtype of `Comparable` is also not harmful, and there may be a marginal benefit in making it obvious that to compare two versions, one can use a standard idiom supported by a library type.

Strategy Pattern Meets Interface Segregation in Solitaire

The interface segregation principle can be an especially powerful design feature when combined with different design patterns. In Solitaire, the package `ai` provides an elaborate example of the STRATEGY pattern. Interface `PlayingStrategy` defines a method `computeNextMove` that is called by a `GameModel` instance when the player uses the "auto-play" feature. With the auto-play feature, the software makes a decision of how to play the next move in the game, as opposed to waiting for the user to play a move. Any class that implements `PlayingStrategy` can provide a decision-making behavior for making a move. The package contains two examples of strategies. The `NullPlayingStrategy` never does anything, and always returns a so-called "null move". This is not very interesting. The

GreedyPlayingStrategy selects the move with the most immediate impact on the
game. To implement a different strategy, for example one that uses probabilities in
the decision-making process, a developer simply needs to create a new class that implements PlayingStrategy and assign an instance of this class in the initialization
of field GameModel.aPlayingStrategy.

To decide how to make a move, a strategy object needs some information about
the game. This information is provided as a parameter to the strategy method. In
the design of the Solitaire project, all the information about the game is stored in
an instance of GameModel. This is a very important class, which declares accessor methods (e.g., getScore()), but also methods that can change the state of the
game (e.g., reset()). This means that, by passing an instance of GameModel to a
strategy object, the code of the strategy object would be able to modify the state of
the game. This is excessive coupling, because in the design the playing strategies are
only supposed to compute a move, not actually do the move. To make this constraint
clearer, I used the interface segregation principle as follows. Class GameModel implements an interface GameModelView that declares *only* the methods of GameModel
that provide information about the game without changing anything. The effect of
this decision is to have a type that "narrows" the interface of GameModel to only include query methods. I then declared the type of the parameter of computeMove to
be GameModelView. This way, although it is still actually an instance of GameModel
that is provided to strategy objects, the limited interface makes it clear that the code
of strategy objects is only meant to query the state of the game, not change it.

Further Reading

The definitions for the notation of the class diagram shown in Figure 3.1 are adapted
from *The Unified Modeling Language Reference Manual* [15], which is one of the
most comprehensive resources available on UML. Chapter 3 of *UML Distilled* [5]
provides a more concise overview of the notation and semantics for this type of diagram. The Gang of Four book [6] has the original, detailed treatment of the ITERATOR
and STRATEGY patterns.

Chapter 4
Object State

This chapter covers:

> **Concepts and Principles:** Concrete and abstract object states, object life cycle, object identity, object equality, object uniqueness, state space minimization;
>
> **Programming Mechanisms:** Null references, final variables, optional types, nested classes, closures;
>
> **Design Techniques:** State diagrams;
>
> **Patterns and Antipatterns:** SPECULATIVE GENERALITY†, TEMPORARY FIELD†, LONG METHOD†, NULL OBJECT, FLYWEIGHT, SINGLETON.

One of the most difficult things to reason about when looking at a program is state changes. Which operations can have a side-effect, on which path can data flow, what impacts what? This chapter clarifies what object state is and how we can manage to keep control over its state in a principled way.

Design Context

In this chapter, I continue the discussion of how to design abstractions to effectively represent a deck of cards in code (see the Design Context section of Chapter 3 for details).

4.1 The Static and Dynamic Perspectives of a Software System

There are different ways we can look at a software system. One way is in terms of the software elements declared in the source code and the relations between them. For

© Springer Nature Switzerland AG 2019
M. P. Robillard, *Introduction to Software Design with Java*,
https://doi.org/10.1007/978-3-030-24094-3_4

example, a `Deck` class declares a field `aCards` that is a list of `Card` instances. This is a *static* (or compile-time) perspective of the system. The static perspective is best represented by the source code or a class diagram. A different, but complementary, way to look at a system, is in terms of objects in a running software system. For example, at one point a `Deck` instance contains three cards, then one card is drawn, which leads to the instance of `Deck` containing two cards, etc. This is the *dynamic* (or *run-time*) perspective on the software. The dynamic perspective corresponds to the set of all values and references held by the variables in a program at different points in time. It is what we see in a debugger while stepping through the execution of the code. The dynamic perspective cannot easily be represented by any one diagram. Instead, we rely on object diagrams, state diagrams (introduced in this chapter), and sequence diagrams (introduced in Chapter 6). The static and dynamic perspectives are complementary in software design. Sometimes it is best to think of a problem and solution in static terms, sometimes in dynamic terms, and sometimes we really need both. This duality between the static and dynamic perspectives on a software system is akin to the wave-particle duality for representing the phenomenon of light in physics:

> It seems as though we must use sometimes the one theory and sometimes the other, while at times we may use either. [...] We have two contradictory pictures of reality; separately neither of them fully explains the phenomena of light, but together they do.
> —Albert Einstein and Leopold Infeld, "The Evolution of Physics"

To paraphrase for software design: It seems as though we must use sometimes the one perspective and sometimes the other, while at times we may use either. We have two *complementary* pictures of a software system; separately neither of them fully explains the phenomena of software, but together they do. This chapter focuses on understanding important *dynamic* properties of software.

4.2 Defining Object State

An important concept when thinking of a design in terms of run-time objects is that of *object state*. Informally, the state of an object refers to the particular pieces of information the object represents at a given moment. It is generally useful to distinguish between *concrete state* and *abstract state*. The concrete state of an object is the collection of values stored in the object's fields. For example, we can consider a `Player` object which, for now, only holds a score for the player in a scored game of Solitaire:

```
public class Player
{
   private int aScore = 0;
}
```

The cardinality of the set of possible concrete states for Player is 2^{32}, or about 4 billion states.[1] We usually refer to the set of possible states for a variable or object as its *state space*. As soon as objects have fields of reference types, the cardinality (or size) of the state space explodes dramatically. For example, the state space of a Deck instance includes all possible permutations of any number of cards in the deck, a number in the range of 2.2×10^{68}. This is an enormous number.[2] With class Player, adding an aName field of type String blows up the size of the state space to something that is only limited by the physical memory of the computing system. For this reason, when designing software, it is more practical to think in terms of abstract states.

In principle, an abstract state is an arbitrarily-defined subset of the concrete state space. For example, considering the simple version of Player without the aName field, "even score" could be an abstract state for a Player instance that groups the roughly 2^{31} states that represent a score that is an even number. Likewise, for an instance of the Deck class, the abstract state "three kings" could represent any possible configuration of the deck where exactly three cards of rank Rank.KING are present. These two examples illustrate the fact that because abstract states are *arbitrary* partitions of the state space, they can really be defined as anything, no matter how whimsical. It should however be evident that neither of these two example abstract states would be particularly useful to design a realistic software system. In practice, the software design task of state space partitioning is to define abstract states that correspond to characteristics that will help construct a clean solution. A more useful abstract state for Player would be "non-zero score", and one for Deck would be "empty" (no cards in the deck), which in both cases happen to correspond to a single concrete state. When the distinction is necessary, I use the term *meaningful* abstract state to indicate abstract states that capture states that impact how an object would be used. For example, because it is not possible to draw a card from an empty deck, the abstract state "Empty" is meaningful because it effectively eliminates one usage scenario for the object (to call method draw). In contrast, the abstract state "three kings" is not meaningful because, at least in a game of Solitaire, whether a deck contains three kings or not has no impact on the game play and is not related to any design or implementation decision. Unless otherwise noted, future references to the term *abstract state* assume that we are talking about meaningful abstract states.

A special case when thinking about object state is that some objects do not have any state. For example, function objects (see Section 3.4), often do not have any associated state. In this case, we talk about *stateless* objects. When the contrast is important, we can refer to objects that have state as *stateful* objects. Another property of objects that is related to their state is mutability (see Section 2.6). This chapter is concerned with objects that are both mutable and stateful. In the case of immutable objects, the boundary between statefulness and statelessness becomes blurry, because in practice they only have a single state.

---

[1] In Java a variable of type **int** is allocated 32 bits of storage.

[2] Computed as $\sum_{k=0}^{52} \frac{52!}{(52-k)!}$.

4.3 State Diagrams

UML state diagrams are useful to represent how objects can transition from one abstract state to another during their lifetime as a reaction to external events (typically, method calls). They represent a *dynamic* view of a software system. The annotated diagram in Figure 4.1 shows all the state diagram notation used in the book.

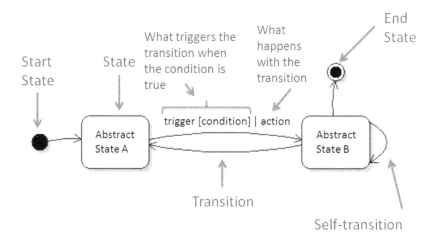

Fig. 4.1 State diagram notation

The example in Figure 4.2 illustrates both the notation and purpose of UML state diagrams. It models some of the important abstract states of an instance of a class `Deck` that represents a deck of 52 playing cards. Even this simple diagram captures key information about the design of the `Deck` class.

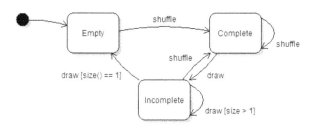

Fig. 4.2 State diagram for an instance of `Deck`

The abstract state "Empty" is annotated as the *start state*, which allows us to infer that the constructor returns a reference to a new `Deck` object with no cards in it.

In state diagrams, *absence of a transition* usually means that the absent transition is not possible (i.e., invalid) for that state. Here we can see that we cannot `draw` cards from an empty deck. Note that the transitions are annotated with names that correspond to methods of the class `Deck`. The only legal transition out of the "Empty" state is `shuffle` which brings the object in the "Complete" state. From this it can easily be inferred that "Complete" is a shorthand for "Complete and shuffled" (in this particular design).

The `shuffle` transition out of the "Complete" state illustrates the idea of *self-transitions*, namely, events that do not result in a change of abstract state. The only legal transition out of the "Complete" state is `draw`, which inevitably brings the deck object to an "Incomplete" state.

It is also possible to annotate transitions with an *action* that describes what happens as the result of the transition. The action that corresponds to the `draw` event is "remove card from the deck". The action information is optional and here I chose to leave it out of the diagram because it seemed redundant with the name of the event (considering that "to draw" is a synonym of "to remove" in the context of card games).

The two transitions out of the "Incomplete" state illustrate the importance of *conditions*, because here without the concept of a condition we would not be able to model the distinction between a `draw` event that leads to the "Empty" state, and a `draw` event that keeps the object in the "Incomplete" state. In this book, the language I use for modeling conditions does not need to follow a formal specification, but I nevertheless like to specify conditions using pseudo-code that is very close to what could be reasonably tested on an instance of the object. Here the conditions would assume the presence of a `size()` method in the `Deck` class.

Finally, this diagram does not include any *end state*. The end state model element is used to specify if an object *must* be in a certain state at the end of its lifetime. In Java, this means when all references to the object are eliminated, and the object becomes available for garbage collection. In many designs, objects can end their life (stop being used) in any state. In this latter case, the end state model element does not apply.

An important benefit of state diagrams is that they allow us to self-evaluate the impact of design decisions on the complexity of the abstract state space that must be considered when working with an object. Here the state space is very simple (three states) because of the decision to bundle the deck initialization code together with the shuffling code. Separating this behavior into distinct `initialize` and `shuffle` events, or including a `sort` event, leads to a much more complicated abstract state space for the object (see Figure 4.3 for an example).

Another important benefit of state diagrams is that they support systematically exploring the abstract behavior of an object of a given class. When modeling the state of an object, a good practice is to visit each state and consider each possible type of transition. This simple procedure is an excellent way to avoid overlooking certain paths through the code (e.g., shuffling an incomplete deck).

When getting started with modeling object states with state diagrams, one common tendency is to use the state diagram notation to model a type of "data flow"

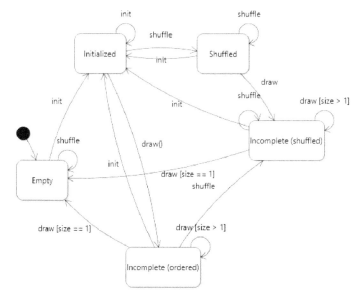

Fig. 4.3 State diagram for an instance of `Deck` where initialization and shuffling are separate operations

information, where states represent "processing", and arrows represent the flow of data between processing stages. This is an incorrect use of the notation.[3] A good tip for avoiding this pitfall is to think about the names of the states. If the names assigned to states include verbs or generally feel like they are describing actions (e.g. "draw card"), it is probably a sign that the diagram does not represent a good model of the state space.

Finally, it is worth noting that the concept of state diagram is very similar to that of *deterministic finite automata (DFA)*. This is not a coincidence, as both notations are intended to model some sort of stateful phenomenon. However, the purpose of each notation is different. DFAs are strict theoretical representations meant to fully and precisely describe computation models, whereas state diagrams involve communicating more abstract ideas about software to support software development activities such as software design, testing, and documentation. State diagrams can omit certain elements, but DFAs cannot.

4.4 Designing Object Life Cycles

As the result of method calls, a stateful and mutable object will transition between different abstract states. The state diagram model of an object can also be referred

---

[3] For which a better match is an activity diagram, which is, however, not covered in this book.

to as its *life cycle*, because it describes the "life" of an object, from its initialization to its abandonment and eventual destruction by the garbage collector. The idea of a life cycle is similar to that of humans, which are created (somehow), then go through various stages of life (childhood, adolescence, etc.). However, in contrast to humans and most types of biological organisms, where stages of life occur once in a given sequence, the life cycle of objects depends on their design, and can get very complex. Object life cycles can include actual cycles, different paths through the abstract state space, and dead ends. As the complexity of the class grows (in terms of number of abstract states), the life cycle of instances of the class can quickly become impossible to understand, even with the help of state diagrams. The contrast between Figure 4.2 and Figure 4.3 shows how quickly an object life cycle can gain in complexity, even as a consequence of a seemingly small design change.

Objects with a complex life cycle are difficult to use, difficult to test (see Chapter 5), and their design and implementation is error-prone. A good design principle to avoid objects with complex life cycles is thus to *minimize the state space of objects* to what is absolutely necessary for the object to conduct its business. In practice, this means designing the class so that it is both impossible to put the object in an invalid or useless state, and that there is no unnecessary state information.

Invalid and Useless States

Some states in the state space might simply be a consequence of how an object is designed or implemented, without there being any use for an object in that state in a given software system. For example, in a game of Solitaire, there is no use for an unshuffled deck of cards. A design where a fresh instance of `Deck` must be first initialized, then shuffled, introduces two abstract states, and all the consequent complexity visible in Figure 4.3, without any benefit. In some cases, eliminating some states from the life cycle of an object may seem like reducing the versatility of a class ("what if we need this one day?"). This is an argument that can be made in some situations. However, it is always important to consider the cost (in terms of software developer time spent understanding code, writing tests, and fixing bugs). Often, this kind of SPECULATIVE GENERALITY† is not worth the cost.

Unnecessary Stateful Information

Another common bad practice when designing objects is to "cache" stateful information in instance variables, typically for convenience, presumed performance efficiency, or both. This point is best illustrated with an example. Because this example is so simple, the argumentation may appear to be ridiculous. However, I have seen the problem it represents countless times in code.

The implementation of the `Deck` class we have been discussing so far stores cards in a list and provides a method `size()` to allow client code to determine the number of cards in a deck.

```java
public class Deck
{
  private List<Card> aCards = new ArrayList<>();

  public int size() { return aCards.size(); }
}
```

A developer with a keen eye for efficiency might observe that in a typical execution of the Solitaire application, method `size()` is called numerous times on an instance of `Deck` of the same size. For example, it may be possible to call `deck.size()` ten times and receive the same value, before `deck.draw()` is called (which changes the size of the deck). Every time, a call to `deck.size()` results in a "useless" call to `aCards.size()`! Instead, would it not be *much more efficient* to store the size directly in the deck, and return it?

```java
public class Deck
{
  private List<Card> aCards = new ArrayList<>();
  private int aSize = 0;

  public int size() { return aSize; }

  public Card draw()
  {
    aSize--;
    return aCards.remove(aCards.size());
  }
}
```

This design decision is an example of the classic computing trade-off between space and time: save a bit of time at the cost of a bit of extra memory. However, except in the case of genuine long-running operations (such as device input/output), the savings in terms of execution time and the cost in terms of memory tend to be insignificant, whereas the significant losers are the simplicity, elegance, and understandability of the code.

Similarly to a misplaced concern about performance, another common reason for storing redundant information in fields is convenience (e.g., when a value is difficult to obtain through other fields of an object). This case is more difficult to illustrate with simple code examples. The general principle, however, applies widely: to the extent possible, information should not be stored in an object unless it uniquely contributes to the intrinsic value represented by the object. A violation of this principle often constitutes an instance of the Temporary Field† antipattern.

4.5 Nullability

One aspect of most programming languages that gets in the way of designing clean state spaces and life cycles for objects is the possibility to assign the value **null** to a variable of a reference type. In Java (and many similar languages, such as C++), `null` is a special value that indicates, in a troublesome way, *the absence of value*. For example, if we assign `null` to a variable:

```
Card card = null;
```

we are in effect stating that the variable `card` is of a reference type `Card`, but that it refers to... nothing! This is a big problem because variables of reference types are intended to be dereferenced:

```
System.out.println(card.getRank());
```

Unfortunately, because, with a reference to nothing, there is nothing to dereference, the result is the dreaded `NullPointerException`, the obvious symptom of innumerable bugs in Java software. Generally speaking, the null reference is the ultimate anti-feature of the Java programming language, because of the harm that it causes. In fact, the inventor of the null reference, Tony Hoare, is reported to have stated his regret at implementing this feature (see Further Reading). In terms of low-level design, null references are a problem because of how difficult it is to think about all possible program paths that may lead to a null dereference. More generally, however, null references are a liability for software design because of their inherent ambiguity. Depending on the situation, a null reference in the state of an object could be interpreted to mean:

1. That a variable is correctly but temporarily un-initialized, but is expected to become initialized in a different abstract state for the object. For example, in class `Deck`, we could assign to the field `aCards` the value `null` until the deck is shuffled;
2. That a variable is incorrectly initialized because the programmer overlooked a path through the code where the variable had to be initialized;
3. That the value is a flag that correctly represents the absence of a useful value in the normal life cycle of an object;
4. That the value is some sort of other flag that must be interpreted in a special way.

To avoid unnecessarily enlarging and complicating the state space of an object with dangerous null references, a recommended best practice is to design classes so that null references are simply not used. How to realize this goal in practice depends on whether there is a need to model the absence of a value for a variable or not. The Minesweeper and Solitaire applications are two examples of code bases that do not use the null reference anywhere.

No Need to Model Absent Values

If it is possible to design a class to avoid any abstract state where a certain variable does not have a value, it is greatly desirable to design the class to forbid this eventuality. For example, "normal" playing cards *must* have a rank and a suit, so there is really no reason to allow null references for either instance variable.

```
public class Card
{
  private Rank aRank; // Should not be null
  private Suit aSuit; // Should not be null

  public Card(Rank pRank, Suit pSuit)
  {
    aRank = pRank;
    aSuit = pSuit;
  }
}
```

We can ensure that variables are not assigned a null reference by using either one of two approaches: *input validation*, or design by contract. With input validation, everywhere a variable can be assigned, we check whether the input value is a null reference and throw an exception if that is the case:

```
public Card(Rank pRank, Suit pSuit)
{
  if( pRank == null || pSuit == null)
  { throw new IllegalArgumentException(); }

  aRank = pRank;
  aSuit = pSuit;
}
```

With design by contract, we stipulate, using a precondition, that **null** is not a valid value for a variable and, optionally, check that the precondition is respected with an **assert** statement:

```
/**
 * @pre pRank != null && pSuit != null;
 */
public Card(Rank pRank, Suit pSuit)
{
  assert pRank != null && pSuit != null;
  aRank = pRank;
  aSuit = pSuit;
}
```

In either case, if the Card constructor is the only place where aRank and aSuit can be assigned, we have effectively ensured that the value stored in either variable will not be a null reference.

Modeling Absent Values

In many situations, the domain concept we are trying to model will require that we make a provision for the fact that there may not be a value. As an example, let us consider a variant of class Card where an instance can also represent a "joker". In many card games, a joker is a special card that has no rank and no suit. To flag a card as a joker, a simple approach is to add a aIsJoker field to its declaration:

```java
public class Card
{
  private Rank aRank;
  private Suit aSuit;
  private boolean aIsJoker;

  public boolean isJoker() { return aIsJoker; }
  public Rank getRank() { return aRank; }
  public Suit getSuit() { return aSuit; }
}
```

Here the logic to determine whether a card represents a joker is simple enough, but what should we do with its rank and suit? As usual, many options are possible. We can review three:

- *Null references:* We could just ignore the advice offered in this section and assign **null** to aRank and aSuit. This means it would be possible to call (for example) card.getRank().ordinal() on a joker, and get a NullPointerException. Not good.
- *Bogus values:* We could assign an arbitrary, meaningless value for the rank and suit of a joker (e.g., ace of clubs). However, this is both confusing and dangerous. A part of the code could erroneously request the rank of a joker, and receive the value Rank.ACE, which makes no sense. It is easy to imagine how tracking down this bug could be lengthy and annoying. Not good either.
- *Special values of an enumerated type:* We could add an INAPPLICABLE enumerated value to both Rank and Suit, and assign these values to the corresponding fields for instances of Card that represent jokers. In my opinion, this solution is slightly better than the two above, but it still has some clear weaknesses. First, it is a conceptual abuse of the idea of enumerated types, where each value is enumerated. Although technically that is what it is, conceptually INAPPLICABLE is not a valid value in the enumeration, but rather a flag that indicates that we do not have a value. Second, although we have four ranks and 13 suits, this solution will yield five and 14 enumerated values for each type, respectively. This discrepancy will muck up any code that relies on the ordinal values of these types (such as the initialization of a deck of cards), and introduce many opportunities for off-by-one errors.

Fortunately, there are better solutions for avoiding the use of null references to represent absent values.

Optional Types

One solution is to use the Optional<T> library type. The Optional type is a generic type that acts as a wrapper for an instance of type T, and which can be empty. To make a value of type T optional for a variable, we declare this variable to be of type Optional<T>. In our case:

```
public class Card
{
  private Optional<Rank> aRank;
  private Optional<Suit> aSuit;
}
```

To represent the absence of a value of the variable, we use the value returned by `Optional.empty()`. So, to create a constructor that instantiates a `Card` that represents a joker, we could have:

```
public class Card
{
  private Optional<Rank> aRank;
  private Optional<Suit> aSuit;

  public Card()
  {
    aRank = Optional.empty();
    aSuit = Optional.empty();
  }

  public boolean isJoker() { return !aRank.isPresent(); }
}
```

To create an instance of `Optional` that represents an actual value, we do `Optional.of(value)` if `value` is not (ever) expected to be null, and `Optional.ofNullable(value)` if `value` can be null (in which case `Optional.empty()` will be stored instead). To get the value wrapped by an instance of `Optional`, we call `get()`.

Using `Optional` in this way, we can both shed the dangerous use of null references and cleanly represent the absence of a value. The one main consequence, however, is that the two fields no longer have the types likely to be desired by the client code. While the client will probably be interested in working with values of type `Rank` and `Suit`, the fields of the class now store values of type `Optional<Rank>` and `Optional<Suit>`. To get around this issue, two main alternative are possible:

- *Change the interface of class* `Card` so that `getRank()` and `getSuit()` return `Optional<Rank>` and `Optional<Suit>`, respectively. This requires client code to call `get()` everywhere the actual instance is needed, which can be cumbersome.
- *Unwrap the optional within* `getRank()` *and* `getSuit()`, which preserves the interface but requires clients to ensure that they do not call the methods on a card that represents a joker (something that could be specified using design by contract, for example). This last solution is starting to look a lot like the use of null references, but it is technically safer, because calling `get()` on an empty instance of `Optional` will raise an exception immediately when the value is misused, as opposed to potentially propagating a null reference through the execution of the code.

The NULL OBJECT Design Pattern

There exists a second solution for avoiding the use of null references to represent absent values, which avoids the issue of unpacking wrapper objects. This solution uses a special object to represent the null value. For this reason, this idea is called the NULL OBJECT design pattern. Using a NULL OBJECT to represent a null value relies on polymorphism, so it is only applicable to situations where a type hierarchy is available. Because `Card` objects are not a subtype of any other user-defined type, we cannot use it to model a joker. To explore this solution, let us consider a different scenario, where a `CardSource` in client code could be unavailable. Let is consider that `CardSource` is an interface that defines methods `draw()` and `isEmpty()` and that it is implemented by the `Deck` class (see Section 3.1).

The main idea of NULL OBJECT is to create one special object to represent the absent value, and to test for absence using a polymorphic method call. Figure 4.4 captures the solution template as applied to the problem of handling potentially absent card sources.

Fig. 4.4 Class diagram showing the `CardSource` interface with support for the NULL OBJECT pattern

In this design, one method was added to the original `CardSource` interface to determine if we are dealing with the null object, and one class was added to represent the null object. As expected, `isNull()` returns **false** for objects of any concrete type except `NullCardSource`, and **true** for the instance of `NullCardSource`. Client code can then use this idiom to handle absent card sources:

```
CardSource source = new NullCardSource();
...
CardSource source = getSource();
if( source.isNull() ) {...}
```

With the features of Java 8, a NULL OBJECT solution can be implemented very efficiently by only modifying the interface at the root of the type hierarchy. First, we use a *default* method to avoid having to change all card source classes to implement `isNull` simply to return **true**. In Java, default methods are methods that have an implementation in the interface which is applicable to instances of all implementing types. To have a minimal impact on the rest of the code, we can also implement the NULL OBJECT as a constant in the interface by using an anonymous class.

```
public interface CardSource
{
  public static CardSource NULL = new CardSource()
    {
      public boolean isEmpty() { return true; }
      public Card draw() { assert !isEmpty(); return null; }
      public boolean isNull() { return true; }
    };

  Card draw();
  boolean isEmpty();
  default boolean isNull() { return false; }
}
```

With this solution, there is no longer a need for a separate `NullCardSource` class. Client code that must indicate an absent card source can simply use the reference available through `CardSource.NULL` instead. Because a `NULL CardSource` behaves just like any other card source, many special cases can be avoided. It is worth noting how this includes the call to `draw`: because calling `draw` on the `NULL` card source will automatically violate the precondition; the fact that we return a null reference afterwards is inconsequent. In fact, in an ideal application of the NULL OBJECT, a check method such as `isNull()` should not even be necessary. In our case, for example, because all client code that works with a card source must check for emptiness first, obtaining a `NULL` card source is indistinguishable from obtaining an empty one. For this reason, in practice it is very likely that we could dispense with the `isNull()` method altogether, and leverage polymorphism to its fullest to yield a simple and clean design without corner cases.

4.6 Final Fields and Variables

In Section 4.4, I argued that one useful principle to follow when designing a class is to try to keep the abstract state space for objects of the class to the minimum necessary for the objects of the class to provide the services expected of them. For example, a well-designed `Deck` class has three meaningful abstract states, not ten. Because object state is just an abstraction of the combination of values taken by the fields of an object, the way to realize the principle in practice is to limit the number of ways in which the field values can be updated. We already saw, in the previous section, how avoiding null references whenever possible can help us reach this goal. An even stricter constraint for keeping the abstract state space of objects nice and small, is to prevent changing the value of a field after initialization, so that the value of the field remains constant.

In Java, this constraint can be made explicit through the use of the **final** keyword placed in front of a variable declaration (which includes the declaration of instance variables). For example, if we declare the fields `aRank` and `aSuit` to be **final** in class `Card`:

```
public class Card
{
  private final Rank aRank;
  private final Suit aSuit;

  public Card( Rank pRank, Suit pSuit)
  {
    aRank = pRank;
    aSuit = pSuit;
  }
}
```

then the fields can be assigned a value *only once*, either in the initializer part of their declaration, or directly in the constructor (as in the example).[4] Attempting to reassign the value of the field anywhere else in the code leads to a compilation error. The `final` keyword thus goes a long way in limiting the state space of an object, since any field marked as `final` can only take a single value. In the case of class Card, making both aRank and aSuit `final` effectively renders objects of the class immutable, because there are no other fields.

An important thing to keep in mind with the use of the `final` keyword, however, is that for reference types, the value stored in a variable is a *reference* to an object. So, although it is not possible to reassign a `final` field, it is certainly possible to change the state of the object referenced (if the object is mutable). Let us illustrate this point by making field aCards of class Deck `final`:

```
public class Deck
{
  private final List<Card> aCards = new ArrayList<>();
}
```

A fresh instance of class Deck is shown in Figure 4.5.

Fig. 4.5 Instance of class Deck

Because field aCards is `final` (something not shown on the diagram), we can be sure that the reference held in the field will *always* refer to the one ArrayList named cardList on the diagram: it will not be possible for this arrow to "point" anywhere else. However, we can (and need to) change the state of cardList, for example to initialize it with all the cards. Thus, although final fields can be very helpful in restricting the state space of an object to make it easier to understand the behavior of the object at run-time, they do *not* make the referenced objects immutable.

---

[4] In practice, field initialization code (the right-hand side of the equal sign in a field declaration) gets executed as part of constructor call anyways.

The discussion above was concerned mainly with *instance* variables. However, local variables (including method parameters) can also be declared to be `final`. As opposed to fields, however, the case for making local variables final is much less clear since they are not long-lived.[5] There is one fairly technical special case where local variables must not be reassigned (see Section 4.10), but even then the variable does not need to be explicitly marked with the `final` keyword.[6] Personally, I occasionally declare a variable `final` to make my intent clear that the variable is not and should not be reassigned. This is only really useful for long and/or complex methods that may be a bit difficult to understand. Ideally, this should be a rare scenario, because well-designed methods are short and simple (and overly LONG METHOD† is a recognized antipattern).

4.7 Object Identity, Equality, and Uniqueness

Three important concepts to keep in mind when designing object life cycles are those of *identity*, *equality*, and *uniqueness*.

Identity refers to the fact that we are referring to a particular object, even if this object is not in a variable. In terms of programming environments, the identity of an object usually refers to its "memory location", or "reference/pointer to". However, in modern programming systems the memory management of objects is heavily abstracted, and for this reason it is best to simply think in terms of object identity. Most integrated development environments supply a convenient handle to represent an object's identity. For example, in the Eclipse debugger this is represented by the object id.

Fig. 4.6 Representation of object identity in the Eclipse debugger

In the small example of Figure 4.6 two `Card` objects are created, and consequently result in two distinct objects with two distinct identities, represented with internal object identifiers 21 and 22 (on the right, in the *Value* column). In the object diagram of Figure 4.7, the `main` method is represented as an object with two fields in place of local variables. The diagram shows how object identity corresponds to both object model elements and the references to these objects. If, for instance, a

---

[5] Local variables only exist for the duration of the execution of code in their scope.

[6] Since Java 8, local variables that are not reassigned are considered "effectively final" by the compiler.

reference to the `Card` object with id 21 is added to a list, there will be two locations that refer to a single shared identity.

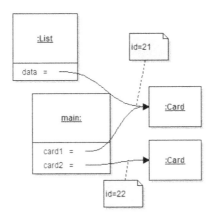

Fig. 4.7 Object identity example

The last statement in the `main` method in Figure 4.6, is a reminder that in Java, the `==` operator returns **true** if the two operands evaluate to the same value. In the case of values of reference types, "the same value" means referring to the same object (identity). So here the statement returns **false** because, although both cards represent an ace of clubs, they are references to different objects.

The situation above, where two different `Card` objects represent the ace of clubs, illustrates the concept of *object equality*. In the general case, *equality* between two objects must be programmer-defined because the meaning of equality cannot always be inferred from the design of the object's class. In very simple cases (like objects of class `Card`), one could say that two objects are equal if all their fields have the same value. However, for many objects of more complex classes, this would be too strict. For example, if some objects cache values or have non-deterministic or unspecified internal representations, they could be "equal" in the practical sense, without having *precisely* the same value for each field, transitively. For example, two instances of a set abstract data type (such as Java's `Set`) must be equal if they have the same elements, even if internally the order in which these elements are stored is different.

For this reason, Java provides a mechanism to allow programmers to specify what it means for two objects of a class to be equal. This specification is realized by *overriding* the `equals(Object)` method of the `Object` class. The default implementation of the `equals` method defines *equality* as *identity*. In other words, if the `equals` method is not redefined for a class, `a.equals(b)` is practically the same as `a == b`.[7] In many situations, like our example of playing cards, this is not what we need, and we must supply our own implementation of the `equals` method. Implementations of `equals` can usually follow this example as a template:

---

[7] Except in the case where `a == null`. The `==` operator will correctly compare null values, but if a is null, `a.equals(b)` will raise a `NullPointerException`.

```
public boolean equals(Object pObject)
{
  if( pObject == null )
  { return false; } // As required by the specification
  else if( pObject == this )
  { return true; } // Standard optimization
  else if( pObject.getClass() != getClass())
  { return false; }
  else
  {
    // Actual comparison code
    return aRank == ((Card)pObject).aRank &&
      ((Card)pObject).aSuit == aSuit;
  }
}
```

I will revisit some of the details of the overriding mechanism in Chapter 7. For now, it suffices to say that if the `equals` method is *redefined* in a class, calling `equals` on an object of this class will result in the redefined version being executed, and thus implement the custom definition of equality. In our case,

```
card1.equals(card2)
```

will return **true**.

A very important note when overriding `equals` in Java, is that any class that overrides `equals` must also override `hashCode()` so that the following constraint is respected:

> If two objects are equal according to the `equals(Object)` method, then calling the `hashCode` method on each of the two objects must produce the same integer result.
> —Reference documentation for `Object.equals`

This constraint is necessary because, among other things, many classes of the Collections framework rely interchangeably on equality testing and on an object's hash code for indexing objects in internal data structures.

A final consideration related to identity and equality is the concept of *uniqueness*. In our example code, we could rightfully wonder what is the point of tolerating duplicate objects that represent exactly the same card (e.g., ace of clubs). A sometimes useful property for the objects of a class is *uniqueness*. Objects of a class are unique if it is not possible for two distinct objects to be equal. If the objects of a class can be guaranteed to be unique, then we no longer need to define equality, because in this specific case, equality become equivalent to identity and we can compare objects using the `==` operator. Strict guarantees of uniqueness are almost impossible to achieve in Java due to mechanisms such as metaprogramming (see Section 5.4) and *serialization*.[8] However, in practice the use of two design patterns, presented below, and the conscious avoidance of metaprogramming and serialization, provide a good enough guarantee of uniqueness that can help simplify some designs.

---

[8] *Serialization* involves converting an object into a data structure that can be stored outside a running program, and then reconstructed later. The reconstruction of a serialized object almost invariably leads to a copy of the serialized object being created.

4.8 The FLYWEIGHT Design Pattern

The FLYWEIGHT pattern provides a way to cleanly manage collections of low-level immutable objects. Although often used to address performance concerns, FLYWEIGHT is also valuable to ensure the uniqueness of objects of a class.

The *context* for using FLYWEIGHT is when instances of a class are heavily shared in a software system. For example, `Card` objects in the Solitaire application are referenced in many different classes.

The idea that underlies the *solution template* is to manage the creation of objects of a certain class, called the *flyweight* class. Instances of the flyweight class are thus called flyweight objects. The crucial aspect of the FLYWEIGHT is to control the creation of flyweight objects through an *access method* that ensures that no duplicate objects (distinct but equal) ever exist. The three main components necessary to realize this constraint are:

1. A *private constructor* for the flyweight class, so clients cannot control the creation of objects of the class;
2. A static *flyweight store* that keeps a collection of flyweight instances;
3. A static *access method* that returns the unique flyweight object that corresponds to some identification key. The access method typically checks if the requested flyweight object already exists in the store, creates it if it does not already exist, and returns the unique object.

For example, we could decide to make the `Card` class a flyweight. Let us first consider the non-flyweight version:

```
public class Card
{
  private final Rank aRank;
  private final Suit aSuit;

  public Card(Rank pRank, Suit pSuit )
  {
    aRank = pRank;
    aSuit = pSuit; }

  /* Includes equals and hashCode implementations */
}
```

Instances of this class are clearly not flyweights, given that it is possible to use the constructor to create two instances that are distinct but equal:

```
Card card1 = new Card(Rank.ACE, Suit.CLUBS);
Card card2 = new Card(Rank.ACE, Suit.CLUBS);
System.out.println(String.format("Same?: %b; Equal?: %b",
  card1 == card2, card1.equals(card2)));
```

To implement step 1 of the solution template, we simply change **public** for **private** in front of the constructor. This prevents client code from creating new `Card` instances arbitrarily. Now we need to figure out a way for code outside of class Card to get instances of the class. Before tackling this question (step 3 in the solution template), let us create a store for flyweight Card instances (step 2 in the solution template). The two main decisions to make for realizing this step are choosing a data structure to hold the instances, and deciding where to locate this structure in the code. In our case, since playing cards can be completely indexed in terms of two keys (rank and suit), I will store them in a two-dimensional array. As to where this array should be located, an obvious choice is to hold it as a static field in class Card so that we can make it private and use methods of class Card to access it. The following code shows the definition of the flyweight store and an implementation of its initialization.

```java
public class Card
{
  private static final Card[][] CARDS =
    new Card[Suit.values().length][Rank.values().length];

  static
  {
    for( Suit suit : Suit.values() )
    {
      for( Rank rank : Rank.values() )
      {
        CARDS[suit.ordinal()][rank.ordinal()] =
          new Card(rank, suit);
      }
    }
  }
}
```

Because objects that represent playing cards are relatively small in number (52) and completely known in advance, I also chose to pre-initialize the flyweight store with a static initializer block.[9] This implementation is only one example of a FLY-WEIGHT implementation. Even for the same context (playing cards), many other alternatives are possible. For example, it would be possible to store flyweights in lists or hash tables.[10] With the current solution, accessing the collection with a correct index is guaranteed to produce the requested card. For example:

```java
CARDS[Suit.CLUBS.ordinal()][Rank.ACE.ordinal()];
```

will return the (assumed unique) instance of Card that represents the ace of clubs.

The code above is only correct if it is placed within the scope of class Card because CARDS is private. To grant access to cards to code outside the class, we need an access method. In our example the implementation of this method is trivial:

```java
public static Card get(Rank pRank, Suit pSuit)
{
  assert pRank != null && pSuit != null;
  return CARDS[pSuit.ordinal()][pRank.ordinal()];
}
```

---

[9] A block of code that executes once, when the class is first loaded in the run-time environment.

[10] The best choice is probably to use the EnumMap library type, but to get the point across with a minimum of explanation, the array-based solution is more accessible.

This method is static given that the flyweight store is static. This makes sense, because it would be bizarre to request a card instance through another card instance. For flyweight objects that represent playing cards, the use of the pair (rank, suit) as the identification key seems intuitive. In other cases, it is a bit less obvious what the identification key should be. For example, for an object of type `Person`, it could be a name, an identification number, etc. In any case, the identification cannot be an instance of the flyweight object itself. In our example with cards, such an approach would look like:

```
Card card = Card.get(someCard); // INVALID
```

This would mean that to obtain a flyweight object of class `Card`, it would be necessary to already have that object. Because the only way to get a flyweight object should be through its access method, this scheme leads to an infinite cycle, and is thus flawed.

An important concern when implementing the FLYWEIGHT pattern is whether to pre-initialize the flyweight store, or whether to do this lazily, by creating objects as they are requested through the access method. The answer is context-dependent. In general, in cases where there exists a small and finite set of flyweights, it may make sense to pre-initialize them (as in the example). In other cases, additional logic must be added to the access method to check if the object exists in the collection and, if not, create it based on the key. In this latter case, the access method needs to be able to access all the information it needs to create the flyweight instance that corresponds to the requested key. The following code shows the FLYWEIGHT-relevant portion of a version of the `Card` class where instances are lazily created:

```
public class Card
{
  private static final Card[][] CARDS =
    new Card[Suit.values().length][Rank.values().length];

  public static Card get(Rank pRank, Suit pSuit)
  {
    if( CARDS[pSuit.ordinal()][pRank.ordinal()] == null )
    {
      CARDS[pSuit.ordinal()][pRank.ordinal()] =
        new Card(pRank, pSuit);
    }

    return CARDS[pSuit.ordinal()][pRank.ordinal()];
  }
}
```

Finally it is also important to note that flyweight objects should be immutable to ensure that their uniqueness can be preserved, and that they can be shared and compared throughout the code.

4.9 The SINGLETON Design Pattern

The SINGLETON design pattern provides a principled way to ensure that there is only one instance of a given class at any point in the execution of the code. The *context* for this design pattern is the need to manage an instance that holds, in one place, a large or crucial amount of information that different parts of the code might be interested in. An example of a typical SINGLETON object, in the Solitaire application, is the instance that represents the aggregated state of the game: the deck of cards and the various piles of cards in the game in progress. The solution template for SINGLETON involves three elements:

1. A *private constructor* for the singleton class, so clients cannot create duplicate objects;
2. A *global variable* for holding a reference to the single instance of the singleton object.
3. An *accessor method*, usually called `instance()`, that returns the singleton instance.

In the Solitaire sample project, an object that encapsulates the aggregated state of the game, of class `GameModel`, is implemented as a singleton as such:

```
public class GameModel
{
  private static final GameModel INSTANCE = new GameModel();

  private GameModel() { ... }

  public static GameModel instance() { return INSTANCE; }
}
```

The SINGLETON pattern differs from FLYWEIGHT in that it attempts to guarantee that there is *a single instance of a class*, as opposed to *unique instances of a class*. Singleton objects are typically stateful and mutable, whereas flyweight objects should be immutable.

A typical mistake when implementing the SINGLETON pattern is to store a reference to an instance of the class in a static field called INSTANCE or something like it, without taking proper care to prevent client code from independently creating new objects. In this case, use of the "Singleton" name is harmfully misleading, because users of the code may rely on the fact that the class yields a single instance when in fact it does not.

The classic way to prevent instantiation is to make the class constructor private. However, in *Effective Java* [1], Bloch proposes a controversial trick, namely, to use an enumerated type ("Item 3: Enforce the singleton property with a private constructor or an enum type"). For example, to make a `GameModel` class a singleton, one could do:

```
public enum GameModel
{
    INSTANCE;

    public void initializeGame() {}
}
```

This technically works because the compiler will prevent the instantiation of enumerated types. Although this approach is represented as "preferred" in *Effective Java*, it is not without detractors. My conclusion is that this strategy is a trick that uses a programming mechanism (enumerated types) for an intent other that originally designed, and as such can be confusing. Here the type `GameModel` is not a finite set of values that represent different game models, which is what one would initially expect when seeing an **enum** designation. I thus recommend sticking to a private constructor to ensure the single instance constraint.

4.10 Objects of Nested Classes

A particular state management concern is introduced by the use of nested classes in Java. Nested classes can be divided into two broad categories: *static nested classes* and *inner classes*. In turn, there are two special categories of inner classes: *anonymous classes* and *local classes*. The distinction between each of these categories of classes is discussed below. Figure 4.8 summarizes the categories and their relations.

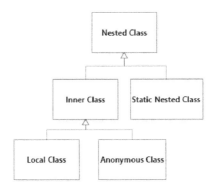

Fig. 4.8 Different categories of Java classes and relations between them. Note that the classifiers in the diagram represent the categories of classes, not source code classes.

Section 3.4 introduced the use of anonymous classes to implement function objects. As it turns out, inner classes can sometimes "secretly" maintain a reference to other objects. Because this can affect their state space and life cycle in important ways, it is important to know about this feature of the Java language.

Inner Classes

Let us start with inner classes. Inner classes are declared within another class, and used to provide additional behavior that involves an instance of the *enclosing* class, but which for some reason we do not want to integrate into the enclosing class. As an example, let us say we want the option to remember how many times a certain Deck instance was shuffled. As usual, there are different ways of doing this. To illustrate how inner classes work, we will define a Shuffler class as an inner class of Deck:

```
public class Deck
{
  public void shuffle() { ... }

  public Shuffler newShuffler() { return new Shuffler(); }

  public class Shuffler
  {
    private int aNumberOfShuffles = 0;

    private Shuffler() {}

    public void shuffle()
    { aNumberOfShuffles++; Deck.this.shuffle(); }

    public int getNumberOfShuffles()
    { return aNumberOfShuffles; }
  }
}
```

In this example, the first part of the declaration of class Shuffler looks pretty normal: we declare a class Shuffler with a field aNumberOfShuffles and a method shuffle(). However, things get interesting within the code of Shuffler-.shuffle(), where we observe the statement Deck.this.shuffle();. Instances of an inner class automatically get a reference to the corresponding instance of their enclosing class (called the *outer instance*). The outer instance for an inner class is the object that was the implicit parameter of the method where the instance of the inner class was created. This can be confusing at first, so let us run through an execution:

```
Deck deck = new Deck();
Shuffler shuffler = deck.newShuffler();
shuffler.shuffle();
```

The first line creates a new instance of Deck, as usual. The second line calls method newShuffler() on the instance of Deck referred to by variable deck. This method creates a new instance of Shuffler, whose outer instance will be the one referred to by deck. Within an inner class, the outer instance can be accessed through a qualified name that consists of the name of the class of the outer instance, followed by **this**. So, in our case, Deck.**this** refers to the outer instance of shuffler. On the third line, it is the method shuffle() of the Shuffler instance that is called, but when this method executes, it then calls the shuffle() method of class Deck on the `deck` instance using `Deck.this`. Figure 4.9 illustrates the scenario with an object diagram.

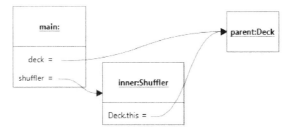

Fig. 4.9 Object graph for an inner class

With this design, the deck can be shuffled through the `shuffler` instance, which will remember how many times the method was invoked. It is also possible to shuffle the deck without going through the `shuffler` instance, in which case the field `aNumberOfShuffles` will not be incremented. The important point about this discussion, however, is that the concrete state space of inner classes *adds to* that of the outer instance. Although this can technically lead to mind-blowing complexity, it does not have to be so. In good design, the abstract state space of objects of inner classes should abstract the state of the outer instance. This is the case of the `Shuffler` class, for which the state of the outer instance does not influence how we would use the `Shuffler` instance.

Java also allows the declaration of **static** nested classes. The main difference between static nested classes and inner classes is that static nested classes are *not* linked to an outer instance. As such, they are mostly used for encapsulation and code organization.

Anonymous Classes

Just like inner classes, local and anonymous classes also have implicit access to additional state information through a reference to their outer instance. Because local classes are rarely used, this section focuses on anonymous classes. However, local classes work in a very similar way. Let us consider the following code for a factory method that creates a `Comparator<Deck>` instance that compares two decks in terms of the number of cards of a given rank that they have.

```
public class Deck
{
  public static Comparator<Deck> createByRankComparator(Rank pRank)
  {
    return new Comparator<Deck>()
    {
      public int compare(Deck pDeck1, Deck pDeck2)
      {
        return countCards(pDeck1, pRank) -
          countCards(pDeck2, pRank);
      }

      private int countCards(Deck pDeck, Rank pRank)
      { /* returns the number of cards in pDeck with pRank */ }
    };
  }
}
```

For example, in the code below, to see whether deck1 contains more kings than deck2, we could do:

```
Comparator<Deck> comp = Deck.createByRankComparator(Rank.KING);
boolean result = comp.compare(deck1,deck2) < 1;
```

This solution is an example of factory method used to create a function object of type Comparator, as explained in Section 3.4. The code is relatively unexciting, except perhaps for one intriguing observation. Upon closer inspection, it appears that the code of method compare *declared inside the anonymous class* has access to the parameter pRank of createByRankComparator, which is a *separate method in a separate class*. What could pRank possibly refer to when the code is running? Once the createByRankComparator method returns an object, this object has its own life cycle that is independent from that of the Deck object. Yet this is legal, compilable code, that actually works and does what we want.

Because referring to variables in the parent method from an anonymous class is such a useful programming idiom, it is supported by the language. To make this work, when the compiler creates the definition of the anonymous class, it also (invisibly) adds *fields* to the anonymous class, and copies references to each of the local variables referenced in the code of the anonymous class's method into a field. Thus, once an object of the anonymous class is created, the references to the local variables are now stored in fields of the same name in the anonymous class. The object diagram of Figure 4.10 illustrates this idea.

In this diagram the factory method is represented as a separate object with field pRank used to represent its parameter. This method returns a completely new object of an anonymous class. So that the compare method can still refer to the pRank parameter, a field pRank is created in the instance of the anonymous comparator, and the value of pRank is copied to it. A method definition together with references to its local environment variables is commonly called a *closure*. As the object diagram shows, it should be clear that closures can easily lead to shared references between object instances. To prevent unexpected behavior, Java prevents using variables that are reassigned within anonymous classes. In Java 7 and earlier, local variables ref-

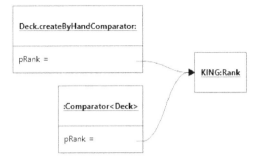

Fig. 4.10 Example of closure modeled by an object diagram

erenced in anonymous classes had to be declared `final`. With Java 8 the compiler can infer variables to be *effectively final* without the keyword.[11]

Insights

This chapter defined object state, argued that keeping track of all the different abstract states an object can go through can be difficult, and proposed a number of techniques for designing classes whose objects have simple and well-structured life cycles.

- For stateful classes, consider using state diagrams to reason systematically about the abstract states of the object of the classes and their life cycle;
- Try to minimize the number of meaningful abstract states for objects of a class: make sure it is not possible to put the object in invalid or useless states, and avoid storing information just for convenience or non-critical performance improvements;
- Avoid using null references to represent legal information in objects and variables; consider using optional types or the NULL OBJECT pattern to represent absent values, if necessary;
- Consider declaring instance variables `final` whenever possible;
- Be explicit about whether objects of a class should be unique or not;
- If objects are not designed to be unique, override the `equals` and `hashCode` methods; if objects should be unique, consider using the FLYWEIGHT pattern to enforce uniqueness;
- Consider using the SINGLETON pattern for classes that should yield only one instance of a stateful object;

---

[11] In Java, anonymous classes and lambda expressions are not closures in the strict sense because they cannot modify the variables they reference. However, because they are as close as we can get to closures in Java, I employ the term to refer to methods that capture some of the values in non-local variables, as in this case.

- Remember that additional data can be attached to instances of inner classes, either in the form of a reference to an instance of an outer class, or as copies of local variables bundled in a closure.

Code Exploration

`Minefield` in Minesweeper

In the Minesweeper application, class `Minefield` illustrates how the abstract state space of an object can actually be simpler than its equivalent in the application domain. Class `Minefield` has a *single* meaningful abstract state. As the code of the constructor shows, an instance of `Minefield` is completely initialized in the constructor, and there is no public method available to re-initialize the field. Thus, to create a "fresh" minefield according to the current design, client code would need to instantiate a new object. Looking at method `getStatus()`, one could challenge the assertion that the state only has one abstract state. Indeed, "status" is pretty much a synonym for "state", and the code of the method readily shows that the minefield can be one of NOT_CLEARED, CLEARED, or EXPLODED. So, how come these do not correspond to different abstract states? They could, of course, since abstract states are arbitrary. However, an important distinction for abstract states is that of *meaningful* abstract states. Looking at the interface of class `Minefield` (the list of its public methods), we see that every single method works in exactly the same way, independently of whether the field is cleared, not cleared, or exploded. So, from the perspective of clients of the `Minefield` class, there is no point in distinguishing between them, and we are left with a single abstract state.

`Card` in Solitaire

The implementation of class `Card` in the Solitaire application provides a complete illustration of the FLYWEIGHT pattern. The only additional feature is that the code includes *two* access methods for `Card` flyweights. One method takes as keys the rank and suit, as previously discussed. The second one uses a special string encoding that represents the card. Although this appears to violate the advice against PRIMITIVE OBSESSION† given in Section 2.2, this encoding is required for the special purpose of *serializing* a representation of the card.

`GameModel` in Solitaire

In the Solitaire application, class `GameModel` provides a typical example of an implementation of the SINGLETON design pattern. Two fields, `Tableau` and `Foundations`, represent entire collections of card stacks. Although the stack collections could have been declared directly in class GameModel, I used different types to avoid the GameModel class becoming too complex, and to have a way to partition the state space that would be directly represented in the code.

Move Anonymous Classes in Solitaire

Still in class GameModel, field aDiscard represents a specific type of move in the game, to discard a card from the deck. How this works with the rest of the code is the topic of a later chapter. However, the initialization of the field provides an example of how instances of anonymous classes retain a reference to their parent class. By instantiating an anonymous subtype of interface Move, the initialization of the field has to provide an implementation for the three methods of the interface. Part of the explanation is to be found in the code of method perform, which actually performs the discard move. In the code, we see references to three fields: aDiscard, aDeck, and aMoves. These are *not* fields of the anonymous class, but fields of its enclosing class, GameModel.

ApplicationResources in JetUML

Class ApplicationResources in JetUML provides a way to obtain the various text strings that appear in the application (for example, button and menu labels). Following the practice of string externalization, these strings are not hard coded, but stored in a separate configuration file. The class provides an example of the SINGLETON, but with a quirk: there is no instance() method, and instead the field storing the singleton instance is called RESOURCES and is public. In this case, I compromised on the strict implementation of SINGLETON, mostly for cosmetic reasons. The singleton instance is referred to in over 100 locations in the code. Instead of the cumbersome ApplicationResources.instance() reference, I relied on Java's static import mechanism to import the name of the instance field. Because it would not be very meaningful to refer to just INSTANCE, however, I named the field RESOURCES. This way, the singleton instance of class ApplicationResources can be referred to anywhere in the code with the name RESOURCES (assuming the mention **import static** ...ApplicationResources.RESOURCES; is present).

Further Reading

The Gang of Four book [6] has the original, detailed treatment of the FLYWEIGHT and SINGLETON patterns. Chapter 3 of *Refactoring: Improving the Design of Existing Code* [3] mentions the TEMPORARY FIELD† and LONG METHODS† antipatterns. The entry "Introduce Null Object" in Chapter 8 discusses the idea of NULL OBJECT.

Chapter 10 of *Java 8 in Action* [16] is entitled "Using Optional as a better alternative to null", and provides more details and examples on the use of the `Optional` type. This is also where I found the anecdote about Tony Hoare. Item 55 in *Effective Java* [1] provides useful insights on when and how to use optional types.

The API documentation for `Object.equals(Object)` and `Object.hashCode()` provide additional information on the meaning of equality in Java. The section on nested classes in the Java Tutorial [10] is a good reference.

Chapter 5
Unit Testing

This chapter covers:

Concepts and Principles: Unit testing, regression testing, quality attributes of unit tests, test suites, test coverage;

Programming Mechanisms: Unit testing frameworks, JUnit, metaprogramming, annotations;

Design Techniques: Test suite organization, use of test fixtures, testing with stubs, testing private structures, use of test coverage metrics, testing exceptional conditions;

Patterns and Antipatterns: DUPLICATED CODE†.

Unit testing is a practice wherein we automatically execute our code to check that it does what we think it should. With unit testing, we can build a possibly large collection of tests that can quickly be executed, for instance every time we change the code, to make sure everything that worked still does. Additionally, writing unit tests provides insights into the quality of a design. This chapter introduces mechanisms that facilitate unit testing (metaprogramming and type annotations) and presents basic techniques for designing unit tests and evaluating their quality.

Design Context

This chapter discusses the testing of code derived from design elements of the Solitaire example application. For simplicity, the examples are slightly adapted from the actual project code. The first examples focus on the simple library function `Math.abs(int)`, then a method of the `Suit` enumerated type. Subsequent examples revolve around `FoundationPile`, a class that represents one of the four "piles" where finished suits are accumulated in the game. The final design problem con-

© Springer Nature Switzerland AG 2019

M. P. Robillard, *Introduction to Software Design with Java*,

https://doi.org/10.1007/978-3-030-24094-3_5

cerns the partial testing of class `GameModel`, which encapsulates the entire aggregated state of a game of Solitaire in progress.

5.1 Introduction to Unit Testing

Software quality problems are often caused by programmers writing code that does not quite do what they expect, and the programmers remaining ignorant of this mismatch between expectations and reality. As a real example, one bug in JetUML made the directory structure disappear from the file chooser[1] when a user wanted to select the location where to export a file. The offending code statement was in a method in charge of deciding whether to accept a file for display in the file chooser or not:

```
public boolean accept(File pFile)
{
  return !pFile.isDirectory() &&
    (pFile.getName().endsWith("." + pFormat.toLowerCase()) ||
     pFile.getName().endsWith("." + pFormat.toUpperCase())));
}
```

At a quick glance, and with insufficient caffeine, this code looks reasonable: "if the file is not a directory and its name ends with a specified extension, in either lower or upper case, accept it". The idea of the last clause was to avoid exporting images to directories named, for example, `directory.jpg`. Unfortunately, focusing on this quirky possibility had obscured the much more obvious requirement that we *do* need to show directories in the file chooser. This kind of blind spot is typically how bugs appear. And they really do like to hide in compound conditional statements. Once exposed, the fix was trivial: remove the negation operator and replace the first and operator (`&&`) with an or operator (`||`).

One way to detect bugs, and to gain confidence that a part of the code does what we expect, is to *test* it. Testing is a software quality assurance technique that can take many forms. Given that this is an introductory book on software design, I focus on one specific testing approach called *unit testing*. The idea of unit testing is to test a small part of the code in isolation. This way, if a test fails, it is easy to know where to look for problems.

A *unit test* consists of one or more executions of a *unit under test* (UUT) with some input data and the comparison of the result of the execution against some oracle. A UUT is whatever piece of the code we wish to test in isolation. UUTs are often methods, but in some cases they can also be entire classes, initialization statements, or certain paths through the code. The term *oracle* designates the correct or expected result of the execution of a UUT.

---

[1] A graphical user interface component that allows the user to select a file by browsing a view of the file system.

For example, the statement: `Math.abs(5) == 5;` technically qualifies as a test. Here the UUT is the library method `Math.abs(int)`,[2] the input data is the integer literal 5, and the oracle is, in this case, also the value 5. The comparison of the result of executing the UUT with the oracle is also called an *assertion*. The name captures the idea that the role of the comparison is to "assert" that the result is what we expect.

When testing non-static methods, it is important to remember that the input data includes the *implicit argument* (the object that receives the method call). As a second example that involves an implicit argument, let us consider a version of the `Suit` enumerated type that includes an additional method `sameColorAs(Suit)`. In a standard deck of cards, the clubs and spades are "black" suits and the diamonds and hearts are "red" suits.

```java
public enum Suit
{
  CLUBS, DIAMONDS, SPADES, HEARTS;

  public boolean sameColorAs(Suit pSuit)
  {
    assert pSuit != null;
    return (ordinal() - pSuit.ordinal()) % 2 == 0;
  }
}
```

With this design we are not returning the color of a `Suit` instance, but rather, whether the suit is of the same color as some other `Suit` instance. In the case of a game where the color of a suit does not matter, only whether it is the same color as some other suit, this design decision makes a lot of sense. Following the principle of information hiding, we only provide the information that is absolutely needed. Returning to our example, something to note is that the code was written by a programmer who favors compact code over clarity of intent and robustness. To give ourselves confidence that this actually works despite the hackery, we can write a unit test for the method:

```java
public static void main(String[] args)
{
  boolean oracle = false;
  System.out.println(oracle == CLUBS.sameColorAs(HEARTS));
}
```

This example makes it clear that although method `sameColorAs` takes a single *explicit* argument, there are in fact two arguments to the UUT: the explicitly provided argument (`Suit.HEARTS`), and the implicit argument: `Suit.CLUBS`. According to the definition of a unit test provided above, this `main` method qualifies as a unit test: it includes a UUT (`Suit.sameColorAs`), some input data (`CLUBS` and `HEARTS`), an oracle (`false`), and an assertion that compares the result with the oracle. Executing the `main` method will tell us whether the test passes or not.

If we wanted to increase the number of inputs we test for `sameColorAs`, we could add additional pairs of suits. Because there are only four suits, we could actually test

---

[2] Function to compute the absolute value of an **int** value.

all possible inputs for `sameColorAs` with a mere 16 tests. This achievement, called
exhaustive testing, is almost never possible (see Section 5.9). Writing an exhaustive
test for `sameColorAs` will show that the method works correctly for all possible
inputs. This is fabulous, but only ephemerally so. Source code is not set in stone. To
continue with our scenario, let us say that a different programmer comes along later
and, because of some requirement change or other, reorders the suits as follows
without touching the `sameColorAs` method (perhaps because its implementation
looks fancy):

CLUBS, SPADES, DIAMONDS, HEARTS;

   In this case, running the test again will immediately reveal a bug introduced by
the fact that `sameColorAs` relies on an undocumented and unchecked assumption
about the order of enumerated values. This example illustrates the second major
benefit of unit tests: in addition to helping detect bugs in new code, they can also
check that tested behavior that used to meet some specific expectation still does
meet that expectation even after the code changes. Running tests to ensure what
was tested as correct still is (or for detecting new bugs caused by changes) is called
regression testing.

   An important thing to realize about unit testing is what it *cannot* do. Unit testing
cannot verify code to be correct! When a test passes, it only shows that the one
specific execution of the code that is being tested behaves as expected. There are
software engineering techniques designed to provide certain guarantees about all
possible code executions for a specific code element, but unit testing is not one of
them. Section 5.9 provides further justification for why testing is not a verification
technique.

5.2 Unit Testing Framework Fundamentals with JUnit

Although it is possible to test a system manually, unit testing is normally done automatically. Because in software development the way to automate anything is to
write code to do it, to automate software testing we also write code to test other
code. This task is typically supported by a *unit testing framework*.[3] Unit testing
frameworks automate a lot of the mundane parts of unit testing, including collecting
tests, running them, and reporting the results. In addition to tools to collect and run
tests and display the results, frameworks also include a set of constructs to allow
developers to write tests in a structured way and (if they so choose) efficiently. The
major constructs supported by testing frameworks are *test cases*, *test suites*, *test fixtures* and *assertions*. The dominant unit testing framework for Java is called *JUnit*. I
will introduce the basics of this framework sufficiently to illustrate all of the testing
techniques covered in this chapter. However, this chapter is not a tutorial on JU-

---

[3] The example with the `main` method in the previous section, although it qualifies as automation,
was only to illustrate a point, and should not be considered a reasonable way to test production
code.

nit, and the Further Reading section provides pointers to additional information and coaching on how to use JUnit.

In JUnit, a unit test maps to a method. The code below illustrates a series of simple unit tests with JUnit.

```java
public class AbsTest
{
  @Test
  public void testAbs_Positive()
  { assertEquals(5, Math.abs(5)); }

  @Test
  public void testAbs_Negative()
  { assertEquals(5, Math.abs(-5)); }

  @Test
  public void testAbs_Max()
  { assertEquals(Integer.MAX_VALUE,Math.abs(Integer.MIN_VALUE)); }
}
```

The @Test *annotation instance* indicates that the annotated method should be run as a unit test. Section 5.4 explains annotations in more detail. For now, it suffices to say it is a marker we put in the code to mark a method as a unit test. The definition of the @Test annotation is defined in the JUnit library.[4] The code example above shows a *test class* (see Section 5.3) that defines three tests, all intended to test the library method Math.abs(**int**).

To constitute proper tests, test methods should contain at least one execution of a unit under test. The way to automatically verify that the execution of a unit under test has the expected effect is to execute various calls to *assert methods*. Assert methods are different from the **assert** statement in Java. They are declared as static methods of the class org.junit.Assert and all they do is basically verify a predicate and, if the predicate is false, report a *test failure*. The JUnit framework includes a graphical user interface component called a *test runner*, which automatically scans some input code, detects all the tests in the input, executes them, and then reports whether the tests passed or failed. Figure 5.1 shows a screenshot of the result of executing all the tests in the test class TestAbs (above), using a version of the test runner available through the Eclipse integrated development environment. Notice how two tests passed but one test, testAbsMax, failed. Perhaps it seems surprising that the absolute value of Integer.MIN_VALUE is not, in fact, Integer.MAX_VALUE. This quirk is documented in the Javadoc header for the method:

> Note that if the argument is equal to the value of Integer.MIN_VALUE, the most negative representable int value, the result is that same value, which is negative.

The reason for this design choice is imposed by physical constraints: because one bit of information is used to encode 0, there is simply no space left available to encode the absolute value of Integer.MIN_VALUE in a 32-bit **int** type. In addition

---

[4] The JUnit library must be added to a project's class path before it can be used. This chapter is based on JUnit version 4.

to their bug detection potential, unit tests are a great way to surface important but otherwise obscure corner cases.

Fig. 5.1 Result of running JUnit using class `AbsTest` in the Eclipse IDE

5.3 Organizing Test Code

A collection of tests for a project is known as a *test suite*. By default, a project's test suite consists of all the unit tests for the production code in the project. However, for various reasons, it may be desirable to run only a subset of different tests at different times (for example, to focus on a specific feature, or save some time). Unit testing frameworks typically provide mechanisms to define arbitrary tests suites, or more generally, to run certain subsets of unit tests. As one example, JUnit provides a `@Suite` construct that allows a developer to list a number of test classes to be executed together. As another example, the JUnit plug-in for the Eclipse IDE allows users to execute the tests for only one package, or even a single test class. Because executing tests is a concern somewhat independent from the issue of designing them, the rest of the chapter focuses on writing the tests themselves.

A common question when building a suite of unit tests is how to organize our tests in a sensible manner. There are different approaches, but in Java a common idiom is to have one test class per project class, where the test class collects all the tests that test methods or other usage scenarios that involve the class. Furthermore, it is common practice to locate all the testing code in a different source folder with a package structure that mirrors the package structure of the production code. The rationale for this organization is that in Java classes with the same package name are in the same *package scope* independently of their location in a file system. This means that classes and methods in the test package can refer to non-public (but non-private) members of classes in the production code, while still being separated from the production code. The figure below illustrates this idea.

Fig. 5.2 Test suite organization for the JetUML example application

5.4 Metaprogramming

In the previous section, we saw that to mark a method as a test, we annotate it with the string `@Test`. The unit testing framework can then rely on this annotation to detect which methods are tests, and then proceed to execute these methods as part of the execution of the test runner. This general approach, employed by most unit testing frameworks, is a bit special in that in requires the code to manipulate other code. Specifically, the testing framework first scans the code to detect tests, and then executes the code, without having any explicit code for calls to test methods. This strategy is an illustration of a general programming feature called *metaprogramming*. The idea of metaprogramming is to write code that operates on a representation of a program's code. Although it may seem confusing at first, metaprogramming is simply a special case of general-purpose programming. When we write code, this code typically operates on data that represents various things in the world (playing cards, geometric shapes, bank records, etc.). With metaprogramming, this data happens to be pieces of software code (classes, methods, fields, etc.). Although metaprogramming is a programming feature, it is instrumental for testing, and can be used to implement many design ideas. In Java, metaprogramming is called *reflection*, and library support for metaprogramming features is available through the class `java.lang.Class` and the package `java.lang.reflect`.

Introspection

The most basic metaprogramming task is to obtain a reference to an object that represents a piece of code to learn about it, a procedure called *introspection*. In Java, the class `Class<T>` is the main access point for metaprogramming. For example, to obtain a reference to an object that represents the `Card` class of the Solitaire application, we do:

```
try
{
  String fullyQualifiedName = "cards.Card";
  Class<Card> cardClass =
    (Class<Card>) Class.forName(fullyQualifiedName);
}
catch(ClassNotFoundException e) { e.printStackTrace(); }
```

The call to `Class.forName` returns a reference to an instance of class `Class` that represents class `Card`, as illustrated in the object diagram of Figure 5.3.

Fig. 5.3 Instance of class `Class` that represents class `Card`

As is evident from the code above, calls to `forName` are brittle: there are many ways in which they can fail to work as expected. First, we notice that the call is enclosed in a **try**-**catch** block. Method `forName` declares the checked exception `ClassNotFoundException` and throws it whenever the argument does not correspond to the fully-qualified name of a class on the class path. This may seem easy to prevent in the example above, given the use of a string literal to specify the name of the argument to `forName`. However, any string can be supplied as argument to `Class.forName`, so the requested class name may not even be known at compile time, as in the example below:

```
public static void main(String[] args)
{
  try
  { Class<?> theClass = Class.forName(args[0]); }
  catch(ClassNotFoundException e) { e.printStackTrace(); }
}
```

For the same reason, we have to use a *type wildcard* as the instance of the type parameter in the type declaration of the variable that receives the reference supplied by `forName`. In the last example, the variable is declared as `Class<?>`. The exact functioning of the type wildcard is outside the scope of this book, but for now it suffices to say that it acts as a placeholder for any type. In the previous example, because we know exactly which type parameter is appropriate for class `Card`, we can use a downcast instead.

Besides the `forName` library method, Java offers two other ways to obtain a reference to an instance of class `Class` that are less brittle: *class literals*, and through an instance of the class of interest. Both strategies are illustrated in the code below:

```
Class<Card> cardClass1 = Card.class;
Card card = Card.get(Rank.ACE, Suit.CLUBS);
Class<?> cardClass2 = card.getClass();
System.out.println(cardClass1 == cardClass2);
```

The first line shows the use of class literals. In Java, a *class literal* is a literal expression that consists of the name of a class followed by the suffix `.class`, and that refers to a reference to an instance of class `Class` that represents the class named before the suffix. So, `Card.class` refers to the instance of class `Class` that represents class `Card`. Because, in the case of class literals, the argument `T` to the type parameter of `Class<T>` is guaranteed to be known at compile time, we can include it in the variable declaration. Class literals are the least brittle way to obtain a reference to an instance of class `Class`, but they require that we know the exact class to instrospect at compile time.

The final way to obtain an instance of class `Class` is through an instance of the class, as illustrated in the second and third lines of the code fragment. As will be explained in detail in Chapter 7, it is possible to call method `getClass()` on any object in a Java program, and the method will return a reference to an instance of class `Class` that represents the run-time type of the object. Because of polymorphism, this type is not known at compile time, so in this case also we have to use the type wildcard in the declaration of the variable.[5] However, because any call to `getClass()` is guaranteed to return a valid reference to an instance of `Class`, the method does not declare to throw an exception.

The last line in the code fragment illustrates a very important property of class `Class`: its instances are unique (see Section 4.7). If executed, the code should always print **true** on the console. Indeed, class `Class` has no accessible constructor, and its instances can be considered to be unique flyweight objects (see Section 4.8).

With metaprogramming, we can introspect any class, including class `Class`. This may at first seem contrived, but it is actually not a special case: class `Class` is just another class. The following code:

```
Class<Class> classClass = Class.class;
```

will produce the object graph illustrated in the diagram in Figure 5.4.

Fig. 5.4 Object graph for an instance of `Class.class`

---

[5] In this case it is possible to use a type bound, e.g., `Class<? `**extends**` Card>`.

Obtaining an instance of class `Class` is only the first step for instrospection. The interface to class `Class` provides numerous methods that can be called to obtain objects that represent the members of the class, its superclass, etc. As just one example of endless possibilities, the following code fragment prints the name of all the methods declared in class `String`. This example makes use of class `Method`, a library class intended to represent methods in Java code. Similar classes exist to represent constructors (`Constructor`) and fields (`Field`).

```
for( Method method :  String.class.getDeclaredMethods() )
{
  System.out.println(method.getName());
}
```

Program Manipulation

Obtaining information about a code base, or code introspection, only constitutes the most basic form of metaprogramming. However, in many cases we also want to actually manipulate the code of a program. Unlike more dynamic languages (such as Python or JavaScript), Java does not allow adding or removing members from classes (and objects, by extension). However, in Java it is possible to use metaprogramming features to change the accessibility of class members, set field values, create new instances of objects, and invoke methods. I only provide a small overview of the features most relevant to software testing and design in general. The API documentation of the relevant library classes will provide the catalog of possibilities.

Assuming that our implementation of class `Card` is a realization of the FLY-WEIGHT design pattern and has a private constructor, we will use metaprogramming to "cheat" the pattern and create a duplicate ace of clubs.

```
try
{
  Card card1 = Card.get(Rank.ACE, Suit.CLUBS);
  Constructor<Card> cardConstructor =
    Card.class.getDeclaredConstructor(Rank.class, Suit.class);
  cardConstructor.setAccessible(true);
  Card card2 = cardConstructor.newInstance(Rank.ACE, Suit.CLUBS);
  System.out.println(card1 == card2);
}
catch( ReflectiveOperationException e ) { e.printStackTrace(); }
```

In this example, the second statement obtains a reference to an instance of class `Constructor` that represents the (private) constructor of class `Card`. To make calls to this constructor *accessible* in a scope outside its class, the third statement changes the accessibility of the constructor, effectively bypassing the **private** keyword in the code. The fourth statement calls `newInstance` on the `Constructor` object. This call makes a new instance of the declaring class of the constructor *represented* by the `Constructor` instance, as opposed to a new instance of class `Constructor`. As this is class `Card`, and the constructor of this class requires two arguments of type `Rank` and `Suit`, we pass values of these types to the `newInstance` call. Because a lot of things can go wrong with a reflective constructor invocation, most of the methods in this example declare to throw checked exceptions of various types, the supertype of which is ReflectiveOperationException.

As a second example of metaprogramming that involves program manipulation, we use metaprogramming to turn a two of clubs into an ace of clubs. Although this just looks like a neat way to cheat at cards, it is also a technique that can be used to facilitate writing tests (see Section 5.7).

```java
try
{
  Card card = Card.get(Rank.TWO, Suit.CLUBS);
  Field rankField = Card.class.getDeclaredField("aRank");
  rankField.setAccessible(true);
  rankField.set(card, Rank.ACE);
  System.out.println(card);
}
catch( ReflectiveOperationException e ) { e.printStackTrace(); }
```

This code works similarly to the previous example, but with one notable difference. Because rankField represents a *field* of class Card, as opposed to an *instance* of the class, the call to set needs to know on *which instance* the field should be assigned a value. Thus, the first argument to set is the instance of Card on which we want to assign a new value to the field aRank, and the second argument is the actual value we want to assign.

Program Metadata

With metaprogramming, it is possible for code to operate not only on data that consists of code elements (e.g., classes, methods, fields), but also on metadata *about* these code elements. How meta can it really get? Very. In Java and similar languages, it is possible to attach additional information (i.e., meta-information) to code elements in the form of *annotations*. We have already seen one type of annotation: the use of @Test to indicate that a method is a unit test in JUnit.

To flag methods as tests for a unit testing framework, it would also have been possible to indicate this information in the comments, using some sort of convention. For example:

```java
public class AbsTest
{
  /* TEST */
  public void testAbsPositive()
  { assertEquals(5,Math.abs(5)); }
}
```

However, code comments constitute *unstructured* information meant to be consumed by humans, not code. Using code comments to encode metadata is error prone, because there is no effective way to check that required conventions are consistently respected. Instead, Java provides a system of *annotations* that can be attached to various code locations. In Java, an *annotation type* is declared similarly to an interface, for example:

```
public @interface Test {}
```

Then, *annotation instances* can be added to the code, in the form @Test. The main advantage of annotations in Java is that they are typed and checked by the compiler. The @Test annotation used to flag unit tests in JUnit is thus a type annotation provided by the JUnit library, and its use is checked by the compiler. For example, writing @test (with a lowercase 't') will result in a compilation error. Java annotations support many other features (see Further Reading), but their main usage scenario is to provide a way to add structured, type-checked metadata to some code elements, that can then be read by the compiler, development environments, unit testing frameworks, and similar tools. We will see other example applications of annotations later in the book. Because they are "officially" part of the code, information about annotations can also be accessed through metaprogramming.[6]

5.5 Structuring Tests

Writing unit tests for non-trivial classes is often a challenging creative process, not unlike writing production code. For this reason, there is no standard formula or template for writing the code of a unit test. In fact, browsing the test suites of different open-source projects will show that different communities follow different styles and use different testing techniques. This being said, certain basic principles are generally agreed upon, including that unit tests should be *fast, independent, repeatable, focused, and readable* [7].

- **Fasts.** Unit tests are intended to be run often, and in many cases within a programming-compilation-execution cycle. For this reason, whatever test suite is executed should be able to complete in the order of a few seconds. Otherwise, developers will be tempted to omit running them, and the tests will stop being useful. This means that unit tests should avoid long-running operations such as intensive device I/O and network access, and leave the testing of such functionality to tests other than unit tests. These could include, for example, *acceptance tests* or *integration tests*.
- **Independent.** Each unit test should be able to execute in isolation. This means that, for example, one test should not depend on the fact that another test executes before to leave an input object in a certain state. First, it is often desirable to execute only a single test. Second, just like code, test suites evolve, with new tests being added and (to a minimum extent) some tests being removed. Test independence facilitates test suite evolution. Finally, JUnit and similarly designed testing

---

[6] However, only annotation instances of annotation types marked with the @Retention-(value=RUNTIME) meta-annotation can be accessed in this way. See Further Reading for a reference to complementary information on annotations that covers meta-annotations.

frameworks provide no guarantee that tests will be executed in a predictable order. In practice, this means that each test should start with a fresh initialization of the state used as part of the test.

- **Repeatable.** The execution of unit tests should produce the same result in different environments (for example, when executed on different operating systems). This means that test oracles should not depend on environment-specific properties, such as display size, CPU speed, or system fonts.
- **Focused.** Tests should exercise and verify a slice of code execution behavior that is as narrow as reasonably possible. The rationale for this principle is that the point of unit tests is to help developers identify faults. If a unit test comprises 500 lines of code and tests a whole series of complex interactions between objects, it will not be easy to determine what went wrong if it fails. In contrast, a test that checks a single input on a single method call will make it easy to home in on a problem. Some have even argued that unit tests should comprise a single assertion [7]. My opinion is that in many cases this is too strict and can lead to inefficiencies. However, tests should ideally focus on testing *only one aspect* of *one unit under test*. If that unit under test is a method, we can refer to it as the *focal method* for the test.
- **Readable.** The structure and coding style of the test should make it easy to identify all the components of the test (unit under test, input data, oracle), as well as the rationale for the test. Are we testing the initialization of an object? A special case? A particular combination of values? Choosing an appropriate name for the test can often help in clarifying its rationale.

For example, let us write some unit tests for a method `canMoveTo` of a hypothetical class `FoundationPile` that could be part of the design of the Solitaire example application. The method should return **true** only if it is possible to move the input `pCard` to the top of the pile that an instance of the class represents. According to the rules of the game, this is only possible if the pile is empty and the input card is an ace, or if the input card is of the same suit as the top of the pile, and of a rank immediately above the top of the pile (e.g., you can only put a three of clubs on top of a two of clubs).

```
public class FoundationPile
{
  public boolean isEmpty() { ... }
  public Card peek()        { ... }
  public Card pop()         { ... }
  public void push(Card pCard) { ... }

  public boolean canMoveTo(Card pCard)
  {
    assert pCard != null;
    if( isEmpty() )
    {
      return pCard.getRank() == Rank.ACE;
    }
    else
    {
      return pCard.getSuit() == peek().getSuit() &&
        pCard.getRank().ordinal() ==
          peek().getRank().ordinal()+1;
    }
  }
}
```

As our first test, we will keep things small and only test for the case where the pile is empty:

```
public class TestFoundationPile
{
  @Test
  public void testCanMoveTo_Empty()
  {
    FoundationPile emptyPile = new FoundationPile();
    Card aceOfClubs = Card.get(Rank.ACE, Suit.CLUBS);
    Card threeOfClubs = Card.get(Rank.THREE, Suit.CLUBS);
    assertTrue(emptyPile.canMoveTo(aceOfClubs));
    assertFalse(emptyPile.canMoveTo(threeOfClubs));
  }
}
```

This test respects our five desired properties. It will execute with lightning speed, be independent from any other test that could exist, and is not affected by any environment properties. It is also focused, not only on a single method, but also on a specific input combination for the method. Finally, many properties of this test add to its readability. First, the *name of the test* encodes both the focal method and the input of interest. Second, the *names of the variables* describe their content. Finally, the assertion statements are self-evident. Reading the last line of the test, for example, we see clearly that calling canMoveTo with a three of clubs on an empty pile will return false, which is correct.

One issue with this test, however, is its *coverage*. The test only verifies a single path through the method, so many possible executions of the method remain untested. This issue will be further discussed in Section 5.9. For now, let us try to fix it by writing an additional test in the same class

```
@Test
public void testCanMoveTo_NotEmptyAndSameSuit()
{
  Card aceOfClubs = Card.get(Rank.ACE, Suit.CLUBS);
  Card twoOfClubs = Card.get(Rank.TWO, Suit.CLUBS);
  Card threeOfClubs = Card.get(Rank.THREE, Suit.CLUBS);
  FoundationPile pileWithOneCard = new FoundationPile();
  pileWithOneCard.push(aceOfClubs);
  assertTrue(pileWithOneCard.canMoveTo(twoOfClubs));
  assertFalse(pileWithOneCard.canMoveTo(threeOfClubs));
}
```

This test improves the test suite by adding to the coverage. However, we already note a lot of redundant code between the two tests, namely, the code to create an instance of FoundationPile, and the code to create cards. If we had, say, 20 tests, this would clearly look suboptimal. In test classes that group multiple test methods, it will often be convenient to define a number of "default" objects or values to be used as receiver objects, explicit parameters, and/or oracles. This practice avoids the duplication of setup code in each test method, which constitutes DUPLICATED CODE†. Baseline objects used for testing are often referred to as a *test fixture*, and declared as fields of a test class. However, for the reasons discussed above, and in particular because JUnit provides no ordering guarantee of any test execution, it is crucial to preserve test independence. This implies that no test method should rely on the fixture being left in a given state by another test. In most cases, this precludes the use of the test class constructor to initialize the fixture, because the constructor is only called once when the test class is instantiated by the framework. The workaround is to nominate a method of the test class to execute before any test method, and initialize all the required structures afresh. Conveniently, JUnit provides a feature to perform this method call without requiring the test code to include an explicit method call.

By using the @Before annotation, we indicate to JUnit to execute the method before the execution of any test. Similarly, it is also possible to use the @After annotation to mark a method that needs to run after every single test (for instance to free up some resources). Of course, immutable objects do not need to be reinitialized, so they can be stored as static fields of the class. The code below shows the improvement to our test class TestFoundationPile, which now uses a test fixture.

```
public class TestFoundationPile
{
  private static final Card ACE_CLUBS =
    Card.get(Rank.ACE, Suit.CLUBS);
  private static final Card TWO_CLUBS =
    Card.get(Rank.TWO, Suit.CLUBS);
  private static final Card THREE_CLUBS =
    Card.get(Rank.THREE, Suit.CLUBS);

  private FoundationPile aPile;

  @Before
  public void setUp() { aPile = new FoundationPile(); }
```

```
@Test
public void testCanMoveTo_Empty()
{
  assertTrue(aPile.canMoveTo(ACE_CLUBS));
  assertFalse(aPile.canMoveTo(THREE_CLUBS));
}

@Test
public void testCanMoveTo_NotEmptyAndSameSuit()
{
  aPile.push(ACE_CLUBS);
  assertTrue(aPile.canMoveTo(TWO_CLUBS));
  assertFalse(aPile.canMoveTo(THREE_CLUBS));
}
}
```

This code not only avoids duplication, but also increases the readability of the tests
by decluttering them. The first test in particular is very readable, while the second
only needs to add one line of test-specific initialization. The only regression in test
readability is due to the fact that by using a field to refer to the pile, we lose our flexibility to name the pile with a variable name that describes its state. In this context
this is a small price to pay for the benefit of using the fixture. Although it would always be possible to alias the `aPile` field into an appropriately named variable (e.g.,
`emptyPile`), it is not clear that this would necessarily improve readability, since
aliasing can also hinder code comprehension.

5.6 Tests and Exceptional Conditions

An important point when writing unit tests is that what we are testing is that the
unit under test does what it is expected to. This means that when using design by
contract, it does not make sense to test code with input that does not respect the
method's preconditions, because the resulting behavior is unspecified. For example,
let us consider a version of method `peek` of class `FoundationPile` (introduced in
the previous section) which returns the top of the pile.

```
class FoundationPile
{
  boolean isEmpty() { ... }

  /*
   * @return The card on top of the pile.
   * @pre !isEmpty()
   */
  Card peek() { ... }
}
```

The documented precondition implies that the method cannot be expected to fulfill
its contract (to return the top card) if the precondition is not met. Thus, if we call the

method on an empty pile, there is no expectation to test. The situation is different, however, when raising exceptions is explicitly part of the interface. Let us consider the following slight variant of method `peek()`:

```
class FoundationPile
{
  boolean isEmpty() { ... }

  /*
   * @return The card on top of the pile.
   * @throws EmptyStackException if isEmpty()
   */
  Card peek()
  {
    if( isEmpty() ) { throw new EmptyStackException(); }
    ...
  }}
```

In this case, calling `peek` on an empty pile *should* result in an `EmptyStackException`. This is part of the specified, expected behavior. If no exception is raised when called on an empty pile, then the `peek()` method does not do what is expected, and this means it is faulty. We should have a test to detect this potential fault.

With JUnit 4 there are two main idioms for testing for exceptions. One is to use the `expected` property of the `@Test` annotation:[7]

```
@Test(expected = EmptyStackException.class)
public void testPeek_Empty()
{
    new FoundationPile().peek();
}
```

With this feature, JUnit will automatically fail the test if the execution of the corresponding test method completes without raising an exception of the specified type. This testing idiom is useful, but limited in the sense that the exceptional behavior must be the last thing to happen in the test. In cases where it is desirable to have more flexibility for evaluating exception-related control-flow, the following idiom can be used:

```
@Test
public void testPeek_Empty()
{
  FoundationPile pile = new FoundationPile();
  try
  {
    pile.peek();
    fail();
  }
  catch(EmptyStackException e ) {}
  assertTrue(pile.isEmpty());
}
```

---

[7] This idiom is replaced with the static method `assertThrows` in JUnit 5.

This idiom is a bit more convoluted, but does exactly what we want. If the unit under test (the `peek` method here) is faulty in the sense that it does not raise an exception when it should, the code will keep executing normally and reach the following statement, which will force a test failure using JUnit's `fail()` method. If the unit under test is (at least partially) correct in that it does raise the exception when it should, control flow will immediately jump to the **catch** clause, thereby skipping the `fail();` statement. It is then possible to add additional code below the **catch** clause, as illustrated.

5.7 Encapsulation and Unit Testing

A design issue that often comes up when testing is that to write the test we want, we need some functionality that is not part of the interface of the class being tested. For example, let us consider that the interface to class `FoundationPile` (see Section 5.5) does not include a method to return the number of cards in the pile (e.g., `size()`). Presumably, because `FoundationPile` does not have a `size()` method, and following the principle of information hiding, we can assume that no part of the production code needs this information. However, it would be very convenient for testing to check that, for example, the size of the pile changes as we push cards onto it or pop cards from it. Would it not make sense, then, to add a `size()` method to the interface of our target class? Although experts might disagree, my personal recommendation is to design production code to have the best and tightest encapsulation possible, and let the testing code work around whatever constraints this may impose. A typical solution when an interface does not include a method that would be convenient for testing, is to provide the desired functionality in the form of a *helper method* in the testing class instead. For example:

```java
public class TestFoundationPile
{
  private FoundationPile aPile;

  private int size()
  {
    List<Card> temp = new ArrayList<>();
    int size = 0;

    while( !aPile.isEmpty() ) { size++; temp.add(aPile.pop()); }

    while( !temp.isEmpty() )
    { aPile.push(temp.remove(temp.size() - 1)); }

    return size;
  }

  @Before
  public void setUp() { aPile = new FoundationPile(); }
}
```

There are often many ways to obtain the information we need without polluting the interface of the target class. In cases where the information is difficult to obtain using methods of the class's interface, metaprogramming is a recourse (see Section 5.4).

A related question when writing tests is, how can we test private methods? There are different possible avenues for answering that question, and again experts disagree about which one is best:

- Private methods are internal elements of other, accessible methods, and therefore are not really "units" that should be tested. Following this logic, the code in private methods should be tested indirectly through the execution of the accessible methods that call them;
- The `private` access modifier is a tool to help us structure the project code, and tests can ignore it.

Although I understand the rationale of the first approach, I personally consider that the second option can also be a reasonable strategy. There are many cases where a neat little method can be restricted to a class's scope, but it would still be valuable to test it in isolation. Situations where private methods should probably *not* be tested separately are when their parameters or return type encode detailed information about the internal structure of the class, or make narrow assumptions about the internal implementation of the class.

In cases where it is judged desirable to test a private method, we need to bypass the method's access restriction. This can be done using metaprogramming. For sake of discussion, let us assume that class `FoundationPile` also has a method:

```
private Optional<Card> getPreviousCard(Card pCard) { ... }
```

that we would like to test separately. This is reasonable, because it returns an `Optional<Card>` (see Section 4.5) and takes as input a single `Card`, two basic elements in our design. In our test code, we will thus create a helper method that calls this private method using metaprogramming.

```java
public class TestFoundationPile
{
  private FoundationPile aPile;

  @Before
  public void setUp() { aPile = new FoundationPile(); }

  private Optional<Card> getPreviousCard(Card pCard)
  {
    try
    {
      Method method = FoundationPile.class.
        getDeclaredMethod("getPreviousCard", Card.class);
      method.setAccessible(true);
      return (Optional<Card>) method.invoke(aPile, pCard);
    }
    catch( ReflectiveOperationException exception )
    {
      fail();
      return Optional.empty();
    }
  }

  @Test
  public void testGetPreviousCard_empty()
  {
    assertFalse(getPreviousCard(Card.get(Rank.ACE, Suit.CLUBS)).
      isPresent());
  }
}
```

In the test class, we define a helper method that launches the execution of the unit under test (`getPreviousCard(Card)`) on an instance of `aPile`, which forms part of the test fixture. With this helper method, the code of the test looks pretty normal. However, there is one big difference. Here, the call to `getPreviousCard` is *not* a call to the unit under tests. Instead, the call is to a helper method (of the same name) that uses metaprogramming to call the unit under test while bypassing the access restriction of the **private** keyword.

5.8 Testing with Stubs

The key to unit testing is to test small parts of the code *in isolation*. In some cases, however, factors can make it difficult to test a piece of code in isolation, for example, when the part we want to test:

- triggers the execution of a large chunk of other code;
- includes sections whose behavior depends on the environment (e.g., system fonts);
- involves non-deterministic behavior (e.g., randomness).

Such a case is illustrated in the following design, which is a simplified version of the Solitaire example application. The `GameModel` class has a `tryToAutoPlay()` method that triggers the computation of the next move by dynamically delegating the task to a strategy, which could be any of a number of options (see Figure 5.5). Here we would like to write a unit test for the `GameModel.tryToAutoPlay(...)` method.

Fig. 5.5 Playing strategy in `GameModel`

In this task we face at least four problems:

- Calling the `tryToAutoPlay` method on an instance of `GameModel` will delegate the call to `computeNextMove` on a strategy object, which will involve the execution of presumably complex behavior to realize the strategy. This does not align well with the concept of unit testing, where we want to test small pieces of code in isolation.
- The implementation of the strategy may involve some randomness.
- How can we know which strategy would be used by the game engine? Presumably we need to determine an oracle for the results.
- How is this different from testing the strategies individually?

The way out of this conundrum is the realization that the responsibility of `GameModel.tryToAutoPlay(...)` is not to compute the next move, but rather to delegate this to a strategy. So, to write a unit test that tests that the UUT does what it is expected to do, we only need to verify that it properly relays the request to compute a move to a strategy. This can be achieved with the writing of a *stub*.

A stub is a greatly simplified version of an object that mimics its behavior sufficiently to support the testing of a UUT that uses this object. Using stubs is heavily dependent on types and polymorphism. Continuing with our `tryToAutoPlay` situation, we simply want to test that the method calls a strategy method, so we will define a dummy strategy in the test method:

```
public class TestGameModel
{
  static class StubStrategy implements PlayingStrategy
  {
    private boolean aExecuted = false;

    public boolean hasExecuted()
    { return aExecuted; }

    public Move computeNextMove(GameModelView pModelView)
    {
      aExecuted = true;
      return new NullMove();
    }
  }
}
```

This strategy does nothing except remember that its `computeNextMove` method has been called, and returns a dummy `Move` object called `NullMove` (an application of the NULL OBJECT pattern). We can then use an instance of this stub instead of a "real" strategy in the rest of the test. To inject the stub into the game model, we can rely on metaprogramming:

```
@Test
public void testTryToAutoPlay()
{
  Field strategyField =
    GameModel.class.getDeclaredField("aPlayingStrategy");
  strategyField.setAccessible(true);
  StubStrategy strategy = new StubStrategy();
  GameModel model = GameModel.instance();
  strategyField.set(model, strategy);
  ...
}
```

at which point completing the test is simply a matter of calling the UUT `tryToAuto-Play` and verifying that it did properly call the strategy:

```
@Test
public void testTryToAutoPlay()
{
  ...
  model.tryToAutoPlay();
  assertTrue(strategy.hasExecuted());
}
```

The use of stubs in unit testing can get very sophisticated, and frameworks exist to support this task if necessary.

5.9 Test Coverage

Up to now this chapter covered how to define and structure unit tests from a practical standpoint, but avoided the question of what inputs to provide to the unit under test. Despite the example of exhaustive testing in Section 5.1, it should be clear that for the vast majority of UUTs it is not even physically possible to exhaustively test the input space. For example, as discussed in Section 4.2, the number of different arrangements of cards that an instance of class Deck can take is astronomical (2.2×10^{68}). Even with a cutting-edge CPU, testing any of the methods of class Deck for all possible inputs (i.e., possible states of the implicit parameter) would take an amount of time greater than many times the age of the universe. This is quite incompatible with the requirement that unit tests execute "quickly" (see Section 5.5).

Clearly we need to select some input out of all the possibilities. This is a problem known as *test case selection*, where *test case* can be considered to be a set of input values for an assumed UUT. For example, an instance of Deck with a single ace of clubs in the deck is a test case of the method Deck.draw(). The basic challenge of the test case selection problem is to test *efficiently*, meaning to find a minimal set of test cases that provides us a maximal amount of "testing" for our code. Unfortunately, while it is fairly obvious what a minimal number of test cases is, there is no natural or even agreed-upon definition of what an "amount of testing" is. However, there is a large body of research results and practical experience on the topic of test case selection: enough for many books (see Further Reading for a recommendation). In this section, I only summarize the key theoretical tenets and practical insights necessary to get started with test case selection. There are two basic ways to approach the selection of test cases:

- **Functional (or black-box) testing** tries to cover as much of the *specified* behavior of a UUT as possible, based on some external specification of what the UUT should do. For the Deck.draw() method, this specification is that the method should result in the top card of the deck being removed and returned. There are many advantages to black-box testing, including that it is not necessary to access the code of the UUT, that tests can reveal problems with the specification, and that tests can reveal missing logic.
- **Structural (or white-box) testing** tries to cover as much of the *implemented* behavior of the UUT as possible, based on an analysis of the source code of the UUT. An example is provided below. The main advantage of white-box testing is that it can reveal problems caused by low-level implementation details that are invisible at the level of the specification.

Coverage of functional testing techniques is outside of the scope of this book, so the remainder of this section provides a review of the main concepts of structural testing. Let us consider again the implementation of the canMoveTo method of class FoundationPile (see Section 5.5, the **assert** statement was removed to simplify the discussion).

```
boolean canMoveTo(Card pCard)
{
  if( isEmpty() )
  { return pCard.getRank() == Rank.ACE; }
  else
  {
    return pCard.getSuit() == peek().getSuit() &&
      pCard.getRank().ordinal() ==
        peek().getRank().ordinal()+1;
  }
}
```

Here we can intuitively see that the code structure can be partitioned into different "pieces" that might be good to test. First, there is the case where the pile is empty (the **true** part of the **if** statement), and the case where it is not empty (the **else** block). But then, each of these "pieces" can also be partitioned into different sub-pieces, for example to cover the case where the cards are in the correct sequence, but of different suits. In the general case, things can get hairy, and it is easy to get lost without a systematic way to understand the code.

One classic method for determining what to test is based on the concept of *coverage*. Informally, a *test coverage metric* is a number (typically a percentage) that determines how much of the code executes when we run our tests. Test coverage metrics can then be computed by code coverage tools that keep track of the code that gets executed when we run unit tests. This sounds simple, but the catch is that there are different definitions of what we can mean by "code", in the context of testing. Each definition is a different way to compute "how much testing" is done. Certain software development organizations may have well-defined *test adequacy criteria* whereby test suites must meet certain coverage thresholds, but in many other cases, the insights provided by coverage metrics are used more generally to help determine where to invest future testing efforts. The following are three well-known coverage metrics (there are many others, see Further Reading).

Statement Coverage

Let us start with the simplest coverage metric: *statement coverage*. Statement coverage is simply the number of statements executed by a test or test suite, divided by the number of statements in the code of interest. The following test:

```
@Test
public void testCanMoveTo_Empty()
{
  assertTrue(aPile.canMoveTo(ACE_CLUBS));
  assertFalse(aPile.canMoveTo(THREE_CLUBS));
}
```

achieves $2/3 = 67\%$ coverage, because the conditional statement predicate and the single statement in the **true** branch are executed, and the single statement in the **false** branch is not. The logic behind statement coverage is simply that if a fault is present in a statement that is never executed, the tests are not going to help find it. Although this logic may seem appealing, statement coverage is actually a poor coverage metric. A first reason is that it depends heavily on the detailed structure of the code. We could rewrite the canMoveTo method as follows, and achieve 100% test coverage with exactly the same tests.

```
boolean canMoveTo(Card pCard)
{
  boolean result = pCard.getSuit() == peek().getSuit() &&
      pCard.getRank().ordinal() ==
        peek().getRank().ordinal()+1;
  if( isEmpty() )
  { result = pCard.getRank() == Rank.ACE; }
  return result;
}
```

The second reason is that not all statements are created equally, and there can be quite a bit that goes on in a statement, especially if this statement involves a compound Boolean expression (as is the case of the first statement in the last example).

Branch Coverage

Branch coverage is the number of program "branches" (decision points) executed by the test(s) divided by the total number of branches in the code of interest. In this context, a branch is one outcome of a condition. Branch coverage is a stronger metric than statement coverage in the sense that for the same coverage result, more of the possible program executions will have been tested. Unfortunately, the concept of branch coverage is a bit ambiguous in the literature, due to the different possible interpretations of the term "branch". In the code of canMoveTo, there are only two branches if we only consider the single **if** statement. However, both the **true** and the **false** branches lead to statements that consist of Boolean expressions, which are themselves another type of branch. To be consistent with popular coverage analysis tools, I adopt the definition that Boolean expressions within statements also introduce branches. Although more complex to determine, this definition is also more useful. With this definition, the original code of canMoveTo exhibits eight branches: the **if**, the first **return** statement, the first comparison in the second return statement, and the second comparison in the second return statement. Each of these branches has a **true** and **false** outcome. The only test written so far thus has only $3/8 = 37.5\%$ branch coverage. If we add the other test shown in Section 5.5 to the test suite:

```
@Test
public void testCanMoveTo_NotEmptyAndSameSuit()
{
  aPile.push(ACE_CLUBS);
  assertTrue(aPile.canMoveTo(TWO_CLUBS));
  assertFalse(aPile.canMoveTo(THREE_CLUBS));
}
```

we get $7/8 = 87.5\%$. This is pretty good, but our systematic coverage analysis points out that we are actually missing one branch, which corresponds to the case where the pile is not empty, and the card at the top of the pile and the card passed as argument are of different suits. Generally speaking, branch coverage is one of the most useful test coverage criteria. It is well supported by testing tools and relatively easy to interpret, and also *subsumes* statement coverage, meaning that achieving complete branch coverage always implies complete statement coverage.

Path Coverage

There are other coverage metrics stronger than branch coverage. For example, one could, in principle, compute a *path coverage* metric as the number of execution paths actually executed over all possible execution paths in the code of interest. Path coverage subsumes almost all other coverage metrics, and is a very close approximation of the "entire behavior that is possible to test". Unfortunately, in almost all cases, the number of paths through a piece of code will be unbounded, so it will not be possible to compute this metric. For this reason, path coverage is considered a theoretical metric, useful for reasoning about test coverage in the abstract, but without any serious hope of general practical applicability. Interestingly, the number of paths in the code of `canMoveTo` is actually only five, so, less than the number of branches! The path coverage of the two-test test suite above can thus be computed, at $4/5 = 80\%$. Because the structure of the code is simple, and without loops, this is not overly surprising. However, as soon as loops enter the picture, reasoning about paths becomes problematic.

Insights

This chapter described techniques to structure and implement unit tests for a project, and argued that unit tests can provide valuable feedback on the design of production code. The following insights assume you have decided to adopt unit testing and are using a unit testing framework.

- Every unit test includes the execution of unit under test (UUT), some input data passed to the UUT, an oracle that describes what the result of executing the UUT should be, and one or more assertions that compare the result of the execution with the oracle;
- Design your unit tests so that they are focused, that is, that they isolate and test a small and well-defined amount of behavior;
- Design your unit tests to run fast, be independent from each other, and be repeatable in any computing environment;
- Design your unit tests to be readable: consider using the name of the test and local variables to add clarity about what you are testing and to describe the oracle;

- Organize your test suite cleanly, with a clear mapping between tests and the code units they test. Consider separate source code directories with a parallel package structure for production and test code;
- Metaprogramming is a powerful language feature that allows you to write code to analyze other code. However, it must be used with care in production code, because it is prone to run-time errors;
- Type annotations can provide metadata about certain program elements, which can then be accessed through metaprogramming;
- Use test fixtures to structure your testing code cleanly. Remember that any data used by unit tests must be initialized before every test, since tests are not guaranteed to be executed in any specific order;
- Do not test for unspecified behavior, and in particular for input that does not respect a method's preconditions;
- Exceptions that can be raised are often an explicit part of a method's interface, in which case the raising of exceptions constitutes behavior that can be tested;
- Do not weaken the interface of a class just to provide additional state inspection methods for your tests. Instead, write helper methods in the test class to obtain this information. Consider using metaprogramming for the trickier cases;
- To isolate the behavior of stateful objects that refer to many other objects, consider using stubs to abstract the behavior of the component objects;
- Use test coverage metrics to reason about how much of the program's behavior you are testing. Consider using branch coverage in favor of statement coverage;
- Remember that passing tests does not guarantee that your code is correct.

Code Exploration

An Example of Bug

The details of the bug discussed in Section 5.1 are available on-line at `https://github.com/prmr/JetUML/issues/188`. Clicking on the commit links (e.g., "add failing test") shows the process of first writing tests that exercise the bug, and then fixing it so the tests pass.

Chapter Samples from Solitaire

Most of the examples in this chapter are simplified versions adapted from the actual testing code of the Solitaire project. Here are the actual versions.

Class `TestSuit` provides the complete unit test for `Suit.sameColorAs(Suit)`. This is an exhaustive test with no fixture, pretty much as simple as it gets in terms of unit testing.

In Solitaire, instead of a `FoundationPile` class with four instances, the design involves a single `Foundations` class that stores the four piles in one object and indexes each pile using the enumerated type `FoundationPile`. The rest is very similar to the example in the chapter. Class `TestFoundations` includes four tests for `canMoveTo` that achieve complete branch coverage.

The private method `getPreviousCard(Card)` is actually located in class `Tableau`. This class represents the seven piles of cards that fan downwards in a game of Solitaire. The rest of the code is the same. Class `TestTableau` provides a working implementation of an invocation of `getPreviousCard` using metaprogramming, along with three tests that access the private method in this way.

`TestClipboard` in JetUML

In JetUML, class `Clipboard` supports the usual functionality that allows applications to copy some objects to a temporary storage. Its testing class, `TestClipboard`, provides more realistic examples of some of the features of unit tests.

First, the testing class uses metaprogramming to access two private fields of `Clipboard`: `aNodes` and `aEdges`. The code to access these fields is more efficient than in the simpler examples in the chapter, in that is stores a references to objects of `Field` classes in the instance of the testing class, as opposed to retrieving them anew every time their value is needed.

Second, the testing class uses an additional annotation, `@BeforeClass`, to execute code once before any of the test methods in the class are called. In this case we need to initialize the graphics system before running the tests.

A third note on the design of `TestClipboard` has to do with *what* the unit tests target. Although the majority of tests in the JetUML test suite focus on testing a single method, for `Clipboard` this was not very useful. Instead, each test focuses on testing a specific *usage scenario* for an instance of the class.

Finally, `Clipboard` is a singleton instance in the sense of the SINGLETON design pattern (see Section 4.9). Testing singleton objects is a challenge precisely because it is not possible to create many "fresh" instances of an object. Thus, we need to be especially careful to ensure that the state of our singleton is the same every time a test is executed. For class `Clipboard`, this happens to be easy by design, because any call to `Clipboard.copy(...)` resets the clipboard to the empty state before copying the input objects.

Further Reading

The book *Software Testing and Analysis* by Pezzè and Young [13] provides a comprehensive treatment of testing, including the definition of many test coverage metrics. The Java Tutorial [10] provides a good introduction to annotations and reflection (Java's version of metaprogramming). Documentation on how to use JUnit is available on the JUnit website.

Chapter 6
Composition

This chapter covers:

Concepts and Principles: Divide and conquer, law of Demeter;
Programming Mechanisms: Aggregation, delegation, cloning;
Design Techniques: Sequence diagrams, combining design patterns;
Patterns and Antipatterns: GOD CLASS†, MESSAGE CHAIN† COMPOSITE, DECORATOR, PROTOTYPE, COMMAND

Large software systems are assembled from smaller parts. In object-oriented design, parts are connected through two main mechanisms: composition and inheritance. Composition means that one object holds a reference to another object and delegates some functionality to it. Although this sounds simple, unprincipled composition can lead to a mess of spaghetti code. In this chapter I give a quick refresher on the mechanism of polymorphism and how it can be used to elegantly compose objects together by following some well-known design patterns. The second way of assembling systems is through inheritance, which is more complex and is covered in Chapter 7.

Design Context

This chapter draws its code examples from various problems related to the modeling of card games. The design problems address requirements at different levels of abstraction, from the management of low-level structures to represent a card source, to high-level structures that can represent the entire state of a card game. To support a discussion of a rich variety of potential design alternatives, the examples are not limited to the context of a Solitaire application, but also consider other usage scenarios. For the examples that do target the Solitaire application specifically, knowledge

© Springer Nature Switzerland AG 2019
M. P. Robillard, *Introduction to Software Design with Java*,
https://doi.org/10.1007/978-3-030-24094-3_6

of the game terminology will be useful: see Appendix C for definitions of the main
game concepts and terms and an overview of a game in progress.

6.1 Composition and Aggregation

A general strategy for managing complexity in software design is to define larger
abstractions in terms of smaller ones. This is an example of the general "divide and
conquer" problem-solving strategy. In software design, if we want to organize our
code, data, and run-time computation by separating it in different parts (classes,
methods, objects, etc.), we need a way to specify how the separate pieces interact
together to form a working software application.

In practice one way to assemble different pieces of code, data, or computation,
is through object *composition*. For an object to be composed of other objects means
that one object stores a reference to one or more other objects. Composition is a way
to provide a solution to two common software design situations.

In a first situation, we have one abstraction whose intrinsic *representation* is that
of a collection of other abstractions. For example, in the problem domain a deck
of cards is conceptually a sequence of playing cards, so in a piece of software that
must handle a deck of cards, it would make a lot sense for a `Deck` instance to be
composed of a number of `Card` instances (see Section 2.2). In this situation, object
composition corresponds exactly to our notion of composition from the problem
domain: one object is *essentially* composed of other objects. As another example,
a string (an instance of `String`) is essentially a collection of characters (values of
type **char**). One term often used to refer to the object that is composed of other
objects is the *aggregate*, whereas the objects being aggregated are the *elements*. So,
in our example, class `Deck` is an aggregate of `Card` elements.

A second situation in which composition is helpful is to break down a class that
would otherwise be too big and complex. In object-oriented development it is easy
to follow the path of least resistance and add more of the data and functionality
needed to solve a problem into a single class. This is the path of least resistance
because, as members of the class share private access to each other, no design effort
is required to organize the code. However, this opportunistic approach often leads
to a GOD CLASS†, that is, an unmanageable class that knows everything and does
everything. God classes are a problem because they violate practically every major
principle of good design. To avoid god classes and similar design degradation, we
can use composition to support a mechanism of *delegation*. The idea of delegation
is that the aggregate object delegates some services to the objects that serve a role of
specialized service to the aggregate. This looser form of composition is also known
as *aggregation*.

One important property of composition is that it is *transitive*. An object that
is composed of other objects can, itself, be one component or delegate of another
parent object. Ultimately, many structures in object-oriented programs are *object*

graphs that group simpler component and delegate objects into progressively more and more complex aggregates.

When designing a class, it does not hurt to be conscious of whether we are using composition for the purpose of representation or delegation. However, the purposes are not mutually exclusive, so it is necessary to be comfortable with the gray area where elements can be thought of as either components (i.e., essential parts of the aggregate object) or delegates (i.e., service providers for the aggregate object).

Let us make this whole discussion more concrete by studying the GameModel class of the Solitaire example application. Figure 6.1 shows a simplified class diagram of the GameModel. The diagram shows how class GameModel is an aggregate of one Deck, one CardStack (the discard pile), one Foundations, and one Tableau. A first thing to observe is that in this version of the code, instead of having a Deck class aggregate Card objects using the List library type, I used composition to define a tighter type CardStack that provides a narrow interface dedicated to handling stacks of cards. The following is a partial implementation:

```java
public class CardStack implements Iterable<Card>
{
  private final List<Card> aCards = new ArrayList<>();

  public void push(Card pCard)
  { assert pCard != null && !aCards.contains(pCard);
    aCards.add(pCard);
  }

  public Card pop()
  { assert !isEmpty();
    return aCards.remove(aCards.size()-1);
  }

  public Card peek()
  { assert !isEmpty();
    return aCards.get(aCards.size()-1);
  }

  public void clear() { aCards.clear(); }
  public boolean isEmpty() { return aCards.size() == 0; }
  public Iterator<Card> iterator() { return aCards.iterator(); }
}
```

Technically, a game of Solitaire is just 13 piles of cards. It would definitely have been possible to implement the game by referring to 13 instances of CardStack in GameModel and implementing all the game algorithms in the GameModel class. However, this class would not have been pretty. Instead, the design makes use of classes Foundations and Tableau. As shown in the diagram, these two classes simply reaggregate instances of CardStack. Following the principle of separation of concerns, we can now move a lot of computation to these classes, and delegate to them when necessary.

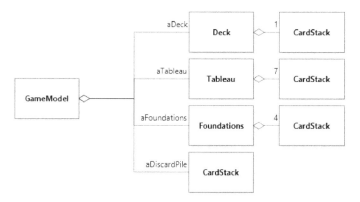

Fig. 6.1 Class diagram of the GameModel. Composition relations are represented using the white diamond decoration. Note that the diamond is on the side of the aggregate. Normally, in a class diagram, model elements that represent a given class are not repeated. In this diagram I took the liberty of repeating CardStack for clarity. All CardStack elements, however, represent the *same* class.

For example, class GameModel needs a method isVisibleInTableau(Card) to determine whether a card is face up or down in the game tableau. In the design of diagram 6.1, this request is delegated to class Tableau:

```
public boolean isVisibleInTableau(Card pCard)
{
    return aTableau.contains(pCard) && aTableau.isVisible(pCard);
}
```

In a class diagram, object composition is represented with an edge decorated with a diamond on the side of the class whose instances hold the reference to the instances of the other class. Note that the UML notation technically allows the distinction between two types of composition: *aggregation* (white diamond) and *composition* (black diamond). As argued above, the difference between these can be murky, and experts disagree on how to choose between aggregation, composition, or just plain association in UML diagrams. I get around the issue by avoiding using the distinction. Because composition is often understood to be a stronger form of aggregation, I exclusively use the white diamond annotation for all types of aggregation/composition (see Section 3.3).

Although it is technically possible to compose objects in arbitrary ways simply by defining fields and passing object references around, unprincipled use of object composition quickly degenerates into overly-complex code. This chapter covers different ways to keep a certain amount of organization in the use of composition through the use of design patterns. The overarching goal of this chapter, however, is to foster a general skill in using composition according to a well-defined design plan with clear underlying rationale.

6.2 The COMPOSITE Design Pattern

As a first principled use of composition, we will consider the situation where we would like to have groups of objects behave like a single object. Let us consider that we are working on a card game that takes as input a source of cards. In Section 3.1, I showed how we can use interfaces to decouple the behavior of a source of cards from its implementation using interface types. The code below repeats the definition of the `CardSource` interface for convenience.

```java
public interface CardSource
{
  /**
   * Removes a card from the source and returns it.
   *
   * @return The card that was removed from the source.
   * @pre !isEmpty()
   */
  Card draw();

  /**
   * @return True if there is no card in the source.
   */
  boolean isEmpty();
}
```

By relying on this interface and the polymorphism it supports, we can write loosely coupled code that can draw cards from any kind of source. The types of card sources we can support with this interface are only limited by our imagination (and actual usage scenarios in card games). For example, we could have a card source that consists of multiple decks of cards, a card source that contains only the four aces, or only face cards, etc. Or any combinations of these schemes (e.g., one deck and four extra aces).

One obvious way to support all these options is to write one class for each option, with each class declaring to implement the `CardSource` interface:

```java
public class Deck implements CardSource { ... }
public class MultiDeck implements CardSource { ... }
public class FourAces implements CardSource { ... }
public class FaceCards implements CardSource { ... }
public class DeckAndFourAces implements CardSource { ... }
```

The main feature of this design decision is that the set of possible implementations of `CardSource` is specified statically (in the source code), as opposed to dynamically (when the code runs). Three major limitations of this static structure are:

- The number of possible structures of interest can be very large. As illustrated by the fifth definition, `DeckAndFourAces`, supporting all possible configurations leads to a *combinatorial explosion* of class definitions.

- Each option requires a class definition, even if it is used very rarely. This clutters the code unnecessarily, because most implementations would probably look very similar.
- In running code, it is very difficult to accommodate the situation where a type of card source configuration is needed that was not anticipated before launching the application.

The above limitations are pretty clearly derived from the static nature of the design. A general solution is to support an open-ended number of configurations by relying on object composition as opposed to class definition. The fundamental idea to support this approach is to define a class that represents multiple CardSources while still behaving like a single one. This core idea is captured as the COMPOSITE design pattern. Figure 6.2 shows a class diagram of the COMPOSITE applied to the CardSource context.

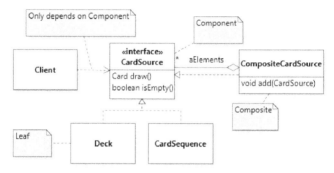

Fig. 6.2 Application of COMPOSITE to CardSource

The diagram shows the application of the pattern, and the roles of each element in the solution template are indicated in notes. In this pattern, the three main roles are *component*, *composite*, and *leaf*. The composite element has two important features:

- It aggregates a number of different objects of the component type (CardSource in our case). Using the component interface type is important, as it allows the composite to compose any other kind of elements, including other composites. In our application, a composite CardSource can aggregate any kind of CardSource: instances of Deck, CardSequence, or anything else that implements CardSource.
- It implements the component interface. This is basically what allows composite objects to be treated by the rest of the code in exactly the same way as leaf elements.

The diagram also captures the important insight that for the COMPOSITE to be effective, client code should depend primarily on the component type, and not manipulate concrete types directly.

An example of object graph created through a COMPOSITE design is illustrated by the object diagram of Figure 6.3.

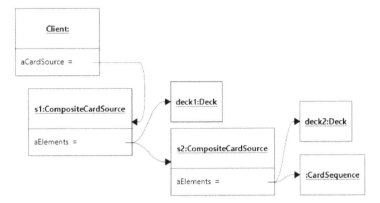

Fig. 6.3 Object diagram representing a sample composite `CardSource`

When applying the COMPOSITE as part of a design, the implementation of the methods of the component interface will generally involve an iteration through all the aggregated elements. As a simple example, in the above design the implementation of method `CompositeCardSource.isEmpty()` would be:

```java
public boolean isEmpty()
{
  for( CardSource source : aElements )
  {
    if( !source.isEmpty() )
    { return false; }
  }
  return true;
}
```

In the case of method `draw`, the behavior is a bit special. Instead of delegating the method call to all elements, we only need to iterate until we can find one card to draw.

```java
public Card draw()
{
  assert !isEmpty();
  for( CardSource source : aElements )
  {
    if( !source.isEmpty() )
    {
      return source.draw();
    }
  }
  assert false;
  return null;
}
```

Because `CompositeCardSource.draw()` is an implementation of the interface `CardSource.draw()`, it has the same preconditions as the interface method. Thus, it does not need to deal with the case where a call is made to `draw` from an empty card source, even if this is a composite. In the first line of the method, we assert that `!isEmpty()`. Here, the call to `isEmpty()` would be to method `isEmpty` of class `CompositeCardSource`, so the following code could be assumed to always find a method to draw.[1] This assumption is further encoded with the **assert false;** statement, which encodes the developer's assumption that if the precondition is respected, the execution should not reach this point. The following **return null;** statement serves no purpose besides making the code compilable.

When applying the COMPOSITE, an important implementation issue to consider is how to add to the composite the instances of the component that it composes. In other words, in our case we need a way to specify which `CardSource` instances form the elements of a `CompositeCardSource`. This can be done in two main ways, each with its strengths and weaknesses.

One way is to provide a method to add elements as part of the composite's interface. This is the method illustrated in Figure 6.2. In turn, this strategy leads to a second design question, which is whether to include the `add` method in the component or not. The more common solution is to not include it in the component, but there may be some situations where it makes more sense to include it on the interface of the component so that the component and all its children have the same interface (see Further Reading).

The second way to initialize composite objects is through their constructor. For example, we could pass a list of card sources as input:

```java
public CompositeCardSource
{
  private final List<CardSource> aElements;

  public CompositeCardSource(List<CardSource> pCardSources)
  {
    aElements = new ArrayList<>(pCardSources);
  }
}
```

Here we use of the copy constructor, to avoid leaking a reference to the private collection structure (see Section 2.5). Another option would be to use Java's varargs mechanism to list each card source individually (see Further Reading):

```java
public CompositeCardSource(CardSource... pCardSources)
```

The main reason for adopting the "add method" strategy is if we need to modify the state of the composite at run time. However, this comes at a cost in terms of design structure and code understandability, because we need to deal with a more complex life-cycle for the composite object and have to manage the difference between the interface of the component (which does not have the `add` method) and

---

[1] This assumes a single-threaded system. Concurrent programming is outside the scope of this book.

the one of the composite (which does). If run-time modification of the composite is not necessary, then it is likely a better option to initialize the composite once and leave it as is. In the context of the CardSource example, it would not result in an immutable composite (we still draw cards), but in other contexts immutability may be an additional advantage.

Some practical aspects related to using the pattern are independent from the structure of the pattern itself. These include:

• The location of the creation of the composite in client code;
• The logic required to preserve the integrity of the object graph induced by this design.

Because these concerns are context-dependent, their solution will depend on the specific design problem at hand. However, it is important to be aware that simply creating a well-designed composite class is not sufficient to have a correct application of the COMPOSITE. For example, with the design of Figure 6.2, it could be possible to write code that results in the object graph of Figure 6.4. However, this outcome is very likely undesirable, because the shared deck instance between source1 and source2 and the self-reference in source2 would lead to unmanageable behavior.

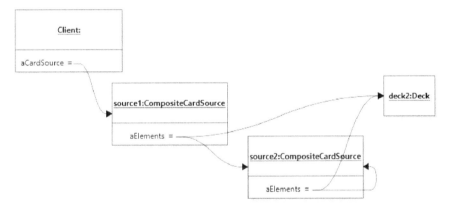

Fig. 6.4 Object diagram showing an abused design for a composite CardSource

6.3 Sequence Diagrams

The use of composition in software design implies design decisions that have to do with how objects collaborate with each other. This means that the impact of composition-related design decisions is reflected on how objects end up calling each other.[2] We can contrast this to more static design decisions, which have to do with how classes depend on each other. For example, an important consequence of the use of the Composite for CardSource is that to determine if a CompositeCardSource is empty, we need to call isEmpty() on some, and possibly all, of its elements.

It can often be helpful to model certain design decisions related to object call sequences. With the UML, this is accomplished through *sequence diagrams*. Just like object diagrams and state diagrams, sequence diagrams model the dynamic perspective on a software system. Like object diagrams and as opposed to state diagrams, sequence diagrams represent a specific execution of the code. They are the closest representation to what one would see when stepping through the execution of the code in a debugger, for example.

To introduce sequence diagrams, and bring home the point that the Composite pattern is really a way to organize how objects interact, Figure 6.5 shows a sequence diagram that models a call to isEmpty() on an instance of CompositeCardSource.

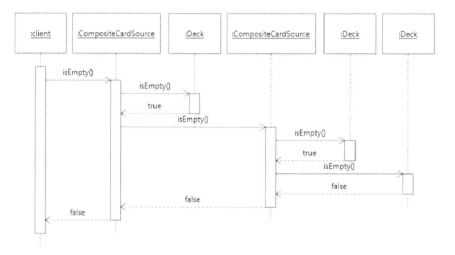

Fig. 6.5 Sequence diagram for a call to isEmpty() on a CompositeCardSource

Each rectangle at the top of the diagram represents an object. An object in a sequence diagram is also referred to as *implicit parameter*, because it is the object upon which a method is called. Consistently with other UML diagrams that represent the system at run time, the object names are underlined and follow the convention name:type as necessary. Here I did not specify a type for the client because it does not matter, and did not specify a name for any of the other objects because it does not matter either.

---

[2] Objects "calling each other" is a linguistic shortcut. The precise, but more cumbersome, phrasing would be "code of a method with a given implicit argument calling methods with other objects as implicit arguments".

In the diagram, we immediately see the recursive descent through an instance of CompositeCardSource. This information cannot be captured in a class diagram, because the notation does not support the specification of the behavior of the different methods, even at an abstract level. This diagram complements the class diagram of Figure 6.2 by showing a dynamic aspect of the design that is invisible on the class diagram.

The dashed vertical line emanating from an object represents the object's *life line*. The life line represents the time (running from top to bottom) when the object exists, that is, between its creation and the time it is ready to be garbage-collected. When objects are placed at the top of the diagram, they are assumed to exist at the beginning of the scenario being modeled. The diagram thus shows an interaction between a client object and an instance of CompositeCardSource and all its component objects, all of which were created before the modeled interaction began. How these objects were created is an example of details left unspecified by a particular diagram.

When representing the type of an object in a sequence diagram, there is some flexibility in terms of what type to represent in the object's type hierarchy. We can use the concrete type of the object or one of its supertypes. As usual when modeling, we use what is the most informative. Here the CompositeCardSource and Deck objects are represented using their concrete type because the only other option is CardSource, which makes the information in the diagram less self-explanatory.

Messages between objects typically correspond to method calls. Messages are represented using a directed arrow from the caller object to the called object. By "called object" I mean "the object that is the implicit parameter of the method call". Messages are typically labeled with the method that is called, optionally with some label representing arguments, when useful. When creating a sequence diagram that represents an execution of Java code, it is likely to be a modeling error if a message incoming on an object does not correspond to a method of the object's interface. Constructor calls are modeled as special messages with the label <<create>>.

Messages between objects induce an activation box, which is the thicker white box overlaid on the life line. The activation box represents the time when a method of the corresponding object is on the execution stack (but not necessarily at the top of the execution stack).

It is also possible to model the return of control out of a method back to the caller. This is represented with a dashed directed arrow. Return edges are optional. I personally only use them to aid understanding when there are complex sequences of messages, or to give a name to the value that is returned to make the rest of the diagram more self-explanatory. Here for example, I included return edges to provide the rationale for subsequent calls in the sequence (given that the execution terminates as soon as isEmpty() returns **false**).

To explore some of the additional modeling features of sequence diagrams and their potential, let us model the use of an iterator in the Iterator pattern (see Section 3.6). Figure 6.6 shows the class diagram of the specific application of Iterator I model with a sequence diagram.

Fig. 6.6 Class diagram of the iterable `Deck`

This diagram shows a version of the `Deck` class that relies on a collection type
`Stack` to store cards. Both the `Deck` and the `Stack` are iterable. The client code,
represented as class `Client`, can refer to instances of class `Deck` as well as the
iterators they return.

Let us look at what happens when the client code makes a call to `Deck.itera-`
`tor()`. Figure 6.7 is the sequence diagram that models a specific execution of
`Deck.iterator()` within client code. The names of model elements are provided
as notes on the diagram.

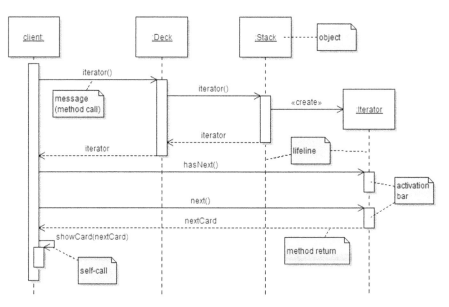

Fig. 6.7 Sequence diagram of an iteration through a `Deck` object

The `iterator()` message to a `Deck` instance leads to the call being *delegated* to
the `Stack` object. The `Stack` object is responsible for creating the iterator. It is also

possible to show the creation of an instance by placing it lower in the diagram, as in the case here for the `Iterator` object. The label "iterator" is used on the return edge from both `iterator()` calls to show (indirectly) that it is the same object being propagated back to the client. In this diagram I also included a return edge from the `next()` method and labeled it "nextCard" to show that the returned object is the one being supplied to the subsequent self-call (a method called on an object from within a method already executing with this object as implicit parameter).

In terms of representing types, here the `Deck` object is represented using its concrete type, but the label `deck:Iterable<Card>` would have been a valid option as well. For the `Iterator` object I used the interface supertype because in practice the concrete type of this object is anonymous and does not really matter.

The distinction between models and complete source code applies to sequence diagrams as well. First, a sequence diagram models a specific execution, not all executions. In the above example, a different execution could have received **false** from `hasNext()` and not called `next()`, or called `next()` twice, etc. These options are not represented, because they are different scenarios. Second, sequence diagrams will naturally omit some details of the execution of the code. We use sequence diagrams to show how objects interact to convey a specific idea. Although the UML supports the specification of looping and conditional statements within a method, these are typically not included in UML sketches and I do not use this notation in the book. Asynchronous calls (which are shown using a half arrow head), are also not covered. Insignificant calls (e.g., to library methods) are typically omitted from sequence diagrams in sketches.

6.4 The DECORATOR Design Pattern

In some cases we would like to optionally have objects of a given type to exhibit special behavior, or have certain extra features. In the example of a `CardSource`, we could imagine that in some cases we might want to print a description of each card drawn on the console or in a file (a process called *logging*). As another example, we might want to keep a reference to every card drawn from a certain source (i.e., *memorizing* the drawn cards). One strategy for meeting this requirement is to enhance the static structure of the design to accommodate the new features. In other words, we can provide additional functionality by writing more classes that have that functionality. Let us consider two possible design solutions for doing this.

Our first solution, which I will call the *specialized class* solution, will be to design one class for each type of feature we want to support. For example, to have a `CardSource` that logs cards drawn, we could define our own special version of `Deck`:

```java
public class LoggingDeck implements CardSource
{
  private final CardStack aCards = ...

  public Card draw()
  {
    Card card = aCards.pop();
    System.out.println(card);
    return card;
  }

  public boolean isEmpty() { return aCards.isEmpty(); }
}
```

Similarly, to have a version of Deck that remembers the cards drawn, we could create a new class MemorizingDeck that stores a reference to every drawn card in a separate structure. Although a strategy that relies on the static structure could work in simple cases, it has several drawbacks.

The main drawback of the specialized class idea is that it offers no flexibility for toggling features on and off at run-time. In other words, it is not easily possible to turn a normal deck into a "memorizing" deck, or to start logging the cards drawn at some arbitrary point in the execution of the code. In Java, it is impossible to change the type of an object at run-time, so the only option would be to initialize a new object and copy the state of the old object into a new object which has the desired features. Such a scheme is not very elegant. However, turning features on or off might be necessary if the user interface allows the player to turn these features on or off during game play.

We can consider a second solution that can accommodate run-time adjustments in the features of an object. I will call this solution the *multi-mode class* solution. With this solution, we provide all possible features within one class, and include a flag value to represent the "mode" the object of the class is in. The resulting code would look like this:

```java
public class MultiModeDeck implements CardSource
{
  enum Mode { SIMPLE, LOGGING, MEMORIZING, LOGGING_MEMORIZING }
  private Mode aMode = Mode.SIMPLE;

  public void setMode(Mode pMode) { ... }

  public Card draw()
  {
    if( aMode == Mode.SIMPLE ) { ... }
    else if( aMode == Mode.LOGGING ) { ... }
    ...
  }
}
```

Although the multi-mode class solution does allow one to toggle features on and off at run-time, it contravenes the important principles presented in Chapter 4 by inducing elaborate state spaces for objects that should otherwise be fairly simple.

It also violates the principle of separation of concerns by tangling the behavior of different features within one class, or even a single method. In the extreme, it can turn a class intended to represent a simple concept into a GOD CLASS†. This thus illustrates that what works is not necessarily what we want. As a consequence of its complexity, the multi-mode class solution also suffers from a lack of extensibility. To add a new feature, we need to add yet more code and branching behavior to account for new modes. With, say, 10 features, it is easy to imagine how the code would become a nightmare of case switches and an instance of SWITCH STATEMENT†. As is often the case in the presence of a potential combinatorial explosion, the key is to move from a solution that relies on defining new classes to a solution that relies on combining objects together.

The DECORATOR design pattern offers just that solution. The context for using the pattern is a design problem where we want to "decorate" some objects with additional features, while being able to treat the decorated objects just like any other object of the undecorated type. Figure 6.8 shows an application of the solution template of DECORATOR to the `CardSource` scenario. The diagram shows the roles played by different elements as notes.

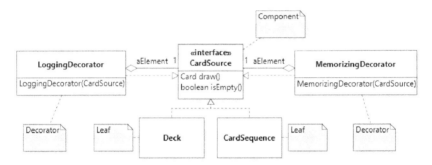

Fig. 6.8 Class diagram of a sample application of DECORATOR

In terms of solution template, the DECORATOR looks very much like the COMPOSITE, except that instead of a composite class we have some decorator classes. Indeed, the design constraints of the decorator class are similar as those of the composite class:

- A decorator aggregates one object of the component interface type (`CardSource` in the example). Using the component interface type is important, as it allows the decorator to "decorate" any other kind of components, including other decorators (and composites).
- It implements the component interface. This is basically what allows decorator objects to be treated by the rest of the code in exactly the same way as leaf elements.

The main question to resolve when applying the DECORATOR is what the methods of the decorator class should do. In a classic use of the DECORATOR, the implementation of the interface's methods that implement the decoration involves two steps, illustrated in the code below:

```java
public class MemorizingDecorator implements CardSource
{
  private final CardSource aElement;
  private final List<Card> aDrawnCards = new ArrayList<>();

  public MemorizingDecorator(CardSource pCardSource)
  { aElement = pCardSource; }

  public boolean isEmpty()
  { return aElement.isEmpty(); }

  public Card draw()
  {
    // 1. Delegate the original request to the decorated object
    Card card = aElement.draw();
    // 2. Implement the decoration
    aDrawnCards.add(card);
    return card;
  }
}
```

One step is to delegate the execution of the original behavior to the element being decorated. In our case, we call `draw()` on the "original" card source (the one being decorated). The other step is to implement the "decoration", which in our case is to add the card to some internal structure. There is no prescribed order for these two steps, although in some case the problem domain may impose an order. In our case, it is clearly necessary to draw a card before we can add it to the internal storage. Finally, although only some methods may involve a behavioral decoration, it is necessary to re-route all methods declared in the component interface to respect the subtyping contract. In our case, this means that we have to implement a method `isEmpty()` that simply returns whether the decorated element is empty.

With the `Decorator` we can easily combine decorations. Because a decorator aggregates a component, combining features becomes as simple as decorating a decorated object. The sequence diagram of Figure 6.9 illustrates the delegation sequence when using a Decorator where we decorated a `Deck` with a `MemorizingDecorator`, and then again with a `LoggingDecorator`, so that the final behavior of `draw()` will be to memorize, log, and return the next card in the card source.

An important constraint when using the Decorator is that for the design to work, decorations must be independent and strictly additive. The main benefit of the Decorator is to support attaching features in a flexible way, sometimes in unanticipated configurations. For this reason, use of the pattern should not require client code to respect elaborate combination rules. As for being additive, this means that the Decorator pattern should not be used to *remove* features from objects. The main reason for this constraint is that it would violate a fundamental principle of object-oriented design introduced in Chapter 7.

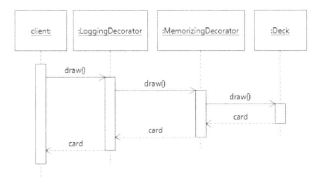

Fig. 6.9 Sequence diagram modeling a call to `draw` on a decorated `Deck`

When implementing the DECORATOR design pattern in Java, it is a good idea to specify as **final** the field that stores a reference to the decorated object, and to initialize it in the constructor. A common expectation when using the DECORATOR is that a decorator object will decorate the same object throughout its lifetime.

Finally, an important consequence of decorating objects using the DECORATOR is that decorated objects *lose their identity*. In other words, because a decorator is itself an object that wraps another object, a decorated object is not the same as the undecorated object. Figure 6.10 illustrates this loss of identity for a simple `CardSource` decoration. In this diagram, we see that the client code holds a reference to a `Deck` instance we call `deck` in a variable `source1`, and a reference to a decorated version of `deck` in `source2`. Although `source1` and `source2` conceptually refer to the *same* card source, the decorated version does not have the same identity as the undecorated version. In other words, `source1 != source2`. This issue of identity loss could be a problem in a code base where, for example, object comparison relies on identity instead of equality. In this case, introducing the DECORATOR pattern would most likely break the design. See Section 4.7 to review the implications of object identity.

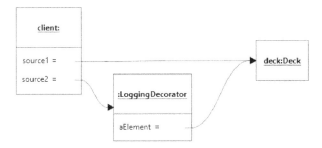

Fig. 6.10 Object diagram of a decorated `Deck`

6.5 Combining COMPOSITE and DECORATOR

Although the DECORATOR and COMPOSITE patterns are distinct and often presented separately, decorator and composite classes can easily co-exist in a type hierarchy. If they implement the same component interface, they can basically work hand-in-hand in supporting composition-based solutions to design problems. The class diagram of Figure 6.11 shows a type hierarchy with one leaf, one composite, and two decorators.

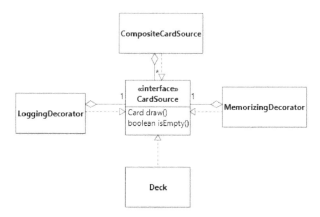

Fig. 6.11 Combining the COMPOSITE and DECORATOR in the same class hierarchy

The object diagram of Figure 6.12 shows a sample object graph that can be induced by this type hierarchy. Note how the graph shows examples of both a decorated composite and a composite of a decorated object.

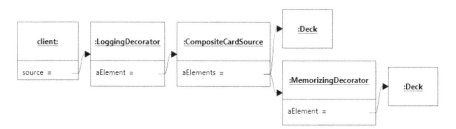

Fig. 6.12 Object graph showing a combination of composite and decorator objects

Although in this chapter I developed the running example of various design options for a card game, it is good to know about the classic scenario supported by the COMPOSITE and DECORATOR patterns. A design context that is a particularly good fit for these patterns is the development of some drawing feature (e.g., for a drawing tool or slideshow presentation application). In this scenario, the component type is a

Figure with a draw() method or something like this. Leaf classes are concrete figures, such as rectangles, ellipses, text boxes, etc. Figure 6.13 shows a class diagram of the domain elements and corresponding design structures.

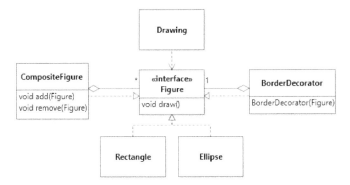

Fig. 6.13 Class diagram of the COMPOSITE and DECORATOR patterns applied to the context of a drawing editor

In this design, the CompositeFigure very naturally supports the end-user feature of "grouping" figures into an aggregate figure. Groups can then be considered single elements, which can then be grouped with other figures and groups, etc. As for the DECORATOR, it allows decorating figures, literally. The example provided on the diagram is that of a decorator that adds a border to the decorated figure, whatever it is. This classic application of the COMPOSITE and DECORATOR patterns is good to know about, because they also provide the conceptually cleanest illustration of the behavior that must be realized by their implementation of the component interface. Specifically, the draw() method of the composite is simply an invocation of the draw() method of all the figures it contains:

```
public void draw()
{
  for( Figure figure : aFigures ) { figure.draw(); }
}
```

For the DECORATOR, the implementation of the draw method would be a clean sequence of one delegation followed by a decoration.

```
public void draw()
{
  aFigure.draw();
  // Additional code to draw the border
}
```

6.6 Polymorphic Object Copying

We are now starting to work with designs that involve combinations of objects and more elaborate object graphs. The use of such dynamic structures has various implications for other aspects of the design. One implication is on object identity (see Section 6.4). Another implication is for designs that rely on object copying.

In Section 2.7, I discussed situations where it is useful to copy some objects, and introduced the idea of copy constructors, which allow a client to make a copy of an object passed as argument:

```
Deck deckCopy = new Deck(pDeck);
```

Copy constructors work fine in many situations, but their main limitation is that a constructor call requires a static reference to a specific class (here, class `Deck`). In designs that make heavy use of polymorphism, this can turn out to be a problem. Consider a design where a `CardSourceManager` holds a collection of `CardSource` objects:

```
public class CardSourceManager
{
  private final List<CardSource> aSources;

  public List<CardSource> getSources()
  {
    // return a copy of aSources;
  }
}
```

In the definition of this class, if we want to return a copy of the list of card sources while protecting the class's encapsulation, we would have to make a copy of every individual card source in `aSources`. However, because `CardSource` is an interface type that must be subtyped, we do not know the precise concrete types of the objects in the list `aSources`, so it is not easy to know what constructor to call. One clumsy solution would be to use a branching statement such as this:

```
if( source.getClass() == Deck.class )
{ return new Deck((Deck) source); }
else if( source.getClass() == CardSequence.class )
{ return new CardSequence((CardSequence) source); })
else if( source.getClass() == CompositeCardSource.class )
{ return new CompositeCardSource((CompositeCardSource) source); }
...
```

Solutions of this nature are not recommended because they essentially void the benefits of polymorphism, namely, to be able to work with instances of `CardSource` no matter what their actual concrete type is. Moreover, this code is also an example of Switch Statement† which completely destroys the extensibility of the design, as it would break as soon as a new subtype of `CardSource` is introduced into the design. Finally, it would be a complete mess to implement because some `CardSource` classes are just wrappers around other card sources. Specifically, because `CompositeCardSource` can aggregate any kind of card source, a copy constructor for this class would also need a branching statement like the above. In brief, in the presence of polymorphism, the use of copy constructors is basically unworkable.

Instead, what we need is a mechanism that provides us with polymorphic object copying. Specifically, we want to be able to make copies of objects without knowing the exact concrete type of the object. In Java, this feature is supported by a mechanism called *cloning*. In general, polymorphic object copying is a complex concept with many potential issues. Java's specific implementation of polymorphic object copying, cloning, is especially tricky to use. The Further Reading section refers to additional resources on cloning. Here I only discuss the main recipe for achieving cloning, and defer additional discussion of the mechanism to Chapter 7, because the explanation requires knowledge of inheritance.

The recipe for making an object cloneable involves four mandatory steps and a fifth, optional step:

1. Declaring to implement the `Cloneable` interface;
2. Overriding the `Object.clone()` method;
3. Calling **super**`.clone()` in the `clone()` method;
4. Catching `CloneNotSupportedException` in the `clone()` method;
5. Optionally, declaring the `clone()` method in the root supertype of a cloneable hierarchy.

Declaring to Implement `Cloneable`

To make it possible to clone a class, the first step is to tag the class as cloneable using the `Cloneable` tagging interface:[3]

```
public class Deck implements Cloneable ...
```

This allows other objects to check whether an object can be cloned, e.g.:

```
if( o instanceof Cloneable ) { clone = o.clone(); }
```

Overriding `Object.clone()`

The second step is to override the `clone()` method. Overriding is covered in detail in Chapter 7. For now, it suffices to say that the root superclass `Object` defines a method `clone()` which, for reasons that will become clear later, *must* be overridden with the **public** access modifier.[4]

```
public Deck clone() ...
```

---

[3] A tagging interface is an interface with no method declaration, intended only to mark objects as having a certain property.

[4] Method `Object.clone()` is declared to be **protected**.

When overriding `clone`, it is also recommend to change its return type from `Object` to the type of the class that contains the new `clone` method.[5]

Calling `super.clone()`

The overridden clone method needs to create a new object of the same class. Although the normal way to create an object is to use a constructor, creating the cloned object should *not* be done through a constructor. The proper way to create the cloned object is by calling the method `clone()` defined in class `Object` by using the call **super**.`clone()`. How a super call works exactly is detailed in Section 7.4. For now, the important thing to know is that the proper way to obtain a clone of the implicit parameter to a call to method `clone()` is as follows:

```
public Deck clone()
{
  // NOT Deck clone = new Deck();
  Deck clone = (Deck) super.clone();
  ...
}
```

The statement **super**.`clone()` calls the `clone()` method in the superclass, which here means method `Object.clone()`. This method is very special. It uses metaprogramming features (see Section 5.4) to return an object of the class from where the call to the method originates. This is special because although the method is implemented in the library class `Object`, it still returns a new instance of class `Deck`.[6]

Method `Object.clone()` is also special because it does not create a new instance of the class by internally calling the default constructor (sometimes there is not even a default constructor). Instead, it reflectively creates a new instance of the class initialized by making a shallow copy of all the instances fields. Whenever a shallow copy is not sufficient, the overridden `clone` method must perform additional steps to more deeply copy some of the fields.

---

[5] This feature, called covariant return types, is available since Java 5. The feature allows overriding methods to have a return type that is more specific than the return type of the method they override.

[6] To understand why the use of a constructor is dangerous, we need to consider the possibility that the method `clone` might be inherited, a topic covered in Chapter 7. If an inherited implementation of `clone()` uses a constructor to create the cloned object, the method will return an object of the wrong type if called on an instance of the subtype. For example, if we have a subclass of `Deck` called `SpecialDeck` and call `clone` on an instance of `SpecialDeck`, the returned object will be of class `Deck`, not `SpecialDeck`. With **super**.`clone()`, the cloned object would be an instance of `SpecialDeck` even if the `clone()` method is inherited from `Deck`.

For example, a reasonable implementation of `clone()` of a class `Deck` could look like this:

```
public Deck clone()
{
  Deck clone = (Deck) super.clone();
  clone.aCards = new CardStack(aCards);
  return clone;
}
```

In this code, the `clone()` method obtains a new instance of `Deck` by using `super.clone()`. However, this would result in a shared (shallow-copied) reference to the value of the field `aCards`, as illustrated in Figure 6.14. Because this outcome would break encapsulation and most likely is incorrect, the clone method makes a new copy of the `CardStack`, this time using a copy constructor given that for `CardStack` there is no requirement to use polymorphic copying.

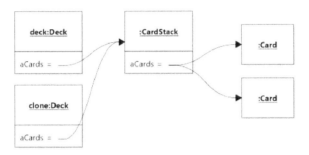

Fig. 6.14 Object diagram of a cloned instance of `Deck`

Catching `CloneNotSupportedException`

Unfortunately, the code in the previous fragment will not compile because **super**.`clone()` declares to throw a checked exception of type `CloneNotSupported-Exception`. This exception is only raised if **super**.`clone` is called from within a class that is not declared to implement `Cloneable` (directly or transitively). If we properly declare our class `Deck` to be `Cloneable`, then we are assured that this exception will never be raised, and we can safely squash it by catching it and doing nothing.

```
public Deck clone()
{
  try
  {
    Deck clone = (Deck) super.clone();
    clone.aCards = new CardStack(clone.aCards);
    return clone;
  }
  catch( CloneNotSupportedException e )
  {
    assert false;
    return null;
  }
}
```

The reason for this awkward exception-handling requirement is that because the default cloning behavior implemented by `Object.clone` (shallow copying) is potentially not appropriate for a class (like `Deck`), a programmer should not be able to call `clone` "accidentally". Having to catch the exception is supposed to force programmers to remember this, although it is not clear to what extent this mechanism is successful.

Adding `clone()` to an Interface

The last, optional, step when using cloning is to add the `clone` method to the super type of a hierarchy of classes whose objects we want to clone. Unfortunately, the `Cloneable` interface does not include the `clone()` method, so that the `clone()` method will not automatically be visible to clients of `Cloneable` types. In other words, this means that if we declare `CardSource` to be cloneable:

```
CardSource extends Cloneable ...
```

it does not mean that we can do:

```
CardSource clone = cardSource.clone();
```

To support this idiom, we need to add `clone()` to the interface (and implement it in all concrete subtypes). A version of `CardSource` meant to be cloneable would thus look like this:

```
public interface CardSource extends Cloneable
{
  Card draw();
  boolean isEmpty();
  CardSource clone();
}
```

As a review example, here is how we would make class `CompositeCardSource` cloneable, assuming that `CardSource` has the above definition

```
public class CompositeCardSource implements CardSource
{
  private final List<CardSource> aSources;

  ...

  public CardSource clone()
  {
    try
    {
      CompositeCardSource clone =
        (CompositeCardSource) super.clone();
      clone.aSources = new ArrayList<>();
      for( CardSource source : aSources )
      {
        clone.aSources.add(source.clone());
      }
      return clone;
    }
    catch(CloneNotSupportedException e ) { return null; }
  }
}
```

With this definition, and assuming all subtypes of `CardSources` properly implement `clone()`, the `clone()` method in `CompositeCardSource` will recursively make a deep copy of all card sources in the composite object.

6.7 The PROTOTYPE Design Pattern

The ability to copy objects polymorphically, as seen in the previous section, is a powerful feature that can be used for a variety of purposes in composition-based designs. One specialized use of polymorphic copying is to support *polymorphic instantiation*. Let us continue with the context of a `CardSourceManager` class, introduced in the previous section. We now wish to add an additional service to the class: a method to return a default card source.

```
public class CardSourceManager
{
  public CardSource createCardSource() { ... }
}
```

The implementation of `createCardSource()` can be trivial if we hard-code the specific type of source to return (e.g., `return new Deck();`). However, what if we want to make it possible to configure `CardSourceManager` so that it is possible to obtain *any* type of `CardSource`, and to change the default card source at run time? In this case, the problems are very similar to the ones discussed in the previous section (i.e., the use of a SWITCH STATEMENT† structure destroys the benefits of polymorphism, etc.).

To create a default card source, one option better than a SWITCH STATEMENT†
would be to use metaprogramming (see Section 5.4), for example by adding a parameter to `createCardSource()` of type `Class<T>`, which specifies the type of the
card source to add. Although workable, solutions of this nature tend to be fragile
and require a lot of error handling.

Another option is to rely on a polymorphic copying mechanism and create new
instances of an object of interest by copying a *prototype object*. This idea is captured
as the PROTOTYPE design pattern. The context for using the PROTOTYPE is the need to
create objects whose type may not be known at compile time. The solution template
involves storing a reference to the prototype object and polymorphically copying
this object whenever new instances are required.

For the `CardSource` scenario, the application of the PROTOYPE would look like
this:

```
public class CardSourceManager
{
  private CardSource aPrototype = new Deck(); // Default

  public void setPrototype( CardSource pPrototype )
  { aPrototype = pPrototype; }

  public CardSource createCardSource()
  { return aPrototype.clone(); }
}
```

Fig. 6.15 Sample application of the PROTOTYPE, with the name of roles indicated in notes

Figure 6.15 shows a class diagram that summarizes the key aspects of the solution template, and indicates the role various elements play in the application of the
pattern. The client is a generic mention to represent any code that needs to perform
instantiation. The prototype is the abstract element (typically an interface) whose
concrete prototype can be switched at run-time. The *products* are the objects that
can be created by copying the prototype.

One nice conceptual benefit of the PROTOTYPE pattern is that normally the option
to create objects of different types does not increase the amount of control flow
(branching statements) in the client class. In a traditional, "mode-based" design,
the `createCardSource()` method would have to check whether the object is in

a specific state to create, say, `Deck` card sources as opposed to other card sources, using a control statement such as an `if` statement. With the PROTOYPE, this branching is done through polymorphism. As the code of the `createCardSource()` method shows, there is no such control statement: the method just makes a copy of whatever object is the current prototype. The Code Exploration section provides additional insights on the use of the PROTOTYPE in practice.

6.8 The COMMAND Design Pattern

Conceptually a *command* is a piece of code that accomplishes something: saving a file, drawing a card from a deck, etc. Intuitively the way to represent a command in code naturally maps to the concept of a function or method, since that is an abstraction that corresponds to a piece of code that will execute. As an example, we can consider the two main state-changing functionalities of a `Deck` class: to draw a card, and to shuffle the cards in deck. To exercise these features, we can just call methods:

```
deck.shuffle();
Card card = deck.draw();
```

However, now that we are studying designs that make principled use of objects, let us consider an alternative idea for representing commands, namely for objects to serve as *manageable units of functionality*. In sophisticated applications, there are many different contexts in which we might want to exercise a functionality such as drawing a card from the deck. For example, we might want to store a history of completed commands, so that we can undo them or replay them later. Or, we might want to accumulate commands and execute them all at once, in batch mode. Or, we might want to parameterize other objects, such as graphical user interface menus, with commands. Requirements such as these point to the additional need to *manage* functionality in a principled way. The COMMAND design pattern provides a recognizable way to manage abstractions that represent commands.

The class diagram of Figure 6.16 shows a sample application of the pattern. The `Command` interface defines an `execute` method and other methods to specify the services required by the clients to manage the commands. In the example, this includes an additional `undo()` method, but other designs may leave it out or have other required services (such as `getDescription()`, to get a description of the command).

The COMMAND pattern has a simple solution template. The template involves defining commands as objects, with an interface for commands that includes a method to execute the command. Another important part of the solution template is for the client to refer to commands through the interface. Despite the simplicity of the solution template, the COMMAND pattern is not necessarily an easy one to apply, because many important design choices induced by the pattern are implementation-dependent. Let us look at some examples from our scenario.

Fig. 6.16 Application of the
COMMAND design pattern
with the name of element
roles in notes

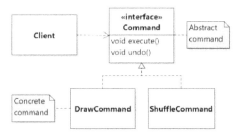

- **Access to command target:** Command execution typically modifies the state of one of more objects, e.g., by drawing a card from a deck. The design must specify how the command gains access to the objects it must act on. Typically this is done by storing a reference to the target within the command object, but other alternatives are possible, including passing arguments to the `execute` method or using closures (see below);
- **Data flow:** In the typical solution template for COMMAND, the interface methods have return type **void**. The design must thus include a provision for returning the result of commands that produce an output, such as drawing a card from a deck;
- **Command execution correctness:** The code responsible for executing commands must ensure that the sequence of execution is correct. For example, the design needs to specify if commands can be executed more than once. The use of design by contract also leads to interesting implications. If commands call code with specified preconditions, the responsibility of respecting the preconditions is transferred to the code executing the command. In our case, a precondition is that we do not call `draw()` on an empty deck. The responsibility for ensuring that this precondition holds normally rests with the client code calling `Deck.draw()`. In the COMMAND pattern, we must ensure that code calling `Command.execute()` can ensure the precondition will be respected in cases where the command happens to be for drawing a card;
- **Encapsulation of target objects:** In some cases, a command object might require operations that are not available in the target object's public interface. For example, to undo the effect of calling `Deck.draw()`, it is necessary to push a card back onto the deck. In our running example class `Deck` does not have a `push` method. The design must include a solution to this issue. One possibility is to have a command factory method located in the class of the object the commands operate on. In our case, this would mean to add a `createDrawCommand()` method in class `Deck` (see below).
- **Storing data:** Some operations supported by commands require storing some data, something that also needs to be designed as part of the pattern's application. For example, in a design context where the undoing of commands is required, the effect of executing a command may have to be cached so that it can be undone. In our case, to undo the drawing of a card from a deck, it is necessary to remember which card was drawn. This information could be stored in the command object directly, or in an external structure accessible by the command object.

To illustrate one point in the design space for each of the concerns above, the code below shows an example of how to support a command to draw cards from a deck. The key idea for this application of the pattern is to use a factory method to create commands that are instances of an anonymous class with access to fields of its outer instance (see Section 4.10). In this design, commands to operate on a Deck instance are obtained directly from the Deck instance of interest. To keep the example simple, I slightly modify the Command interface so that execute() returns an Optional<Card>, which allows some commands to return an instance of Card if applicable. The code also assumes commands are executed only once and undone in the inverse order of that in which they are executed.

```java
public class Deck
{
  private CardStack aCards = new CardStack();

  public createDrawCommand()
  {
    return new Command()
    {
      Card aDrawn = null;
      public Optional<Card> execute()
      {
        aDrawn = draw();
        return Optional.of(aDrawn);
      }

      public void undo()
      {
        aCards.push(aDrawn);
        aDrawn = null;
      }
    }
  }
}
```

With this code, a new "draw" command is created, executed, and undone as follows:

```java
Deck deck = new Deck();
Command command = deck.createDrawCommand();
Card card = command.execute().get();
command.undo();
```

When command.execute() executes, the code in the anonymous class calls draw() on the instance of Deck stored in variable deck, because anonymous classes retain a reference to their outer instance. The resulting card is then stored in a field of the anonymous class, which can then be used by the undo() method. The undo method also accesses the Deck instance through an implicit reference to its outer instance. Because the code is defined within class Deck, a reference to the private member aCards is possible. The Code Exploration section discusses another similar example application of the COMMAND pattern.

Independently of the specific way the pattern is applied, having command objects gives us much flexibility for managing how and when to execute commands on a `Deck` instance.

6.9 The Law of Demeter

When designing a piece of software using aggregation, one can often end up with long delegation chains between objects. For example, Figure 6.17 models the aggregation for card piles in the Solitaire example application.

Fig. 6.17 Aggregation structure for foundation piles in Solitaire

In this design, a `GameModel` object holds a reference to an instance of `Foundations` to manage the four piles of cards of a single suit. In turn, an instance of `Foundations` holds references to four `CardStack` instances, which are specialized wrappers around `List` objects, etc.

There are different ways to use such delegation chains. Figure 6.18 illustrates a hypothetical way to use the aggregation structure for adding a card to a pile.

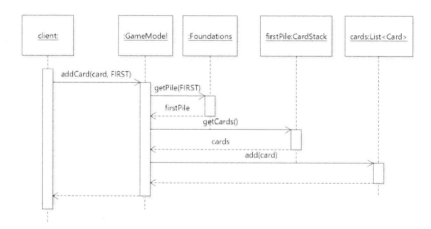

Fig. 6.18 Sample data structure access scenario for the Solitaire game design

In this design the `GameModel` is in charge of all the details of adding a card to a pile, and must handle every intermediate object in the delegation chain. As an example, in this design the implementation of addCard in class GameModel would look like this:

```
aFoundations.getPile(FIRST).getCards().add(pCard);
```

This design violates the principle of information hiding by requiring the code of the GameModel class to know about the precise navigation structure required to add a card to the system. Although this might be obvious in the case of a CardStack returning its List<Card>, exactly the same argument can be made for Foundations returning one of its CardStack. However, the encapsulation quality of intermediate classes in aggregation chains is easier to overlook. The intuition that designs such as this one tend to be suboptimal is captured by the MESSAGE CHAIN† antipattern. The Law of Demeter is a design guideline intended to help avoid the consequences of MESSAGE CHAIN†. This "law" is actually a design guideline that states that the code of a method should only access:

- The instance variables of its implicit parameter;
- The arguments passed to the method;
- Any new object created within the method;
- (If need be) globally available objects.

So, to respect this guideline it becomes necessary to provide additional services in classes that occupy an intermediate position in an aggregation/delegation chain so that the clients do not need to manipulate the internal objects encapsulated by these objects. The solution in our example would be illustrated by Figure 6.19.

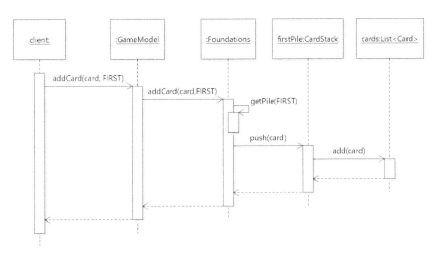

Fig. 6.19 Sample data structure access scenario for the Solitaire game design, which respects the Law of Demeter

In this solution, objects do not return references to their internal structure, but instead provide the complete service required by the client at each step in the delegation chain.

Insights

This chapter presented various techniques for solving design problems by composing objects according to specific patterns.

- Large classes can be simplified by introducing classes whose objects will provide services to the initial class;
- If a design problem requires structures that change at run-time or can be combined, consider building the structures by combining objects, as opposed to defining new classes for each possible structure;
- Use the COMPOSITE when you need to manipulate collections of objects the same way as single ("leaf") objects;
- Use the DECORATOR when you need to add functionality to certain objects, while being able to use them in place of "regular" objects;
- The COMPOSITE and DECORATOR can be combined easily, especially if they share the same component type;
- Applying well-known object composition patterns is not sufficient to ensure the code is correct: typically, client code remains responsible for ensuring that the use of the pattern does not result in defective object graphs;
- Sequence diagrams can help communicate important arrangements of method calls between objects in a design;
- Use polymorphic copying (cloning) to make copies of objects whose concrete type is not known at compile time. If the type is known at compile time, favor the simpler technique of copy constructors;
- Be careful when using Java's cloning mechanism, as it involves many error-prone steps;
- Polymorphic copying can also be used as a way to create fresh instances of objects whose type is not known at compile time, a technique called the PROTOTYPE pattern;
- For designs where function objects need to be explicitly managed by client code, for example to store them or share them between code locations, the COMMAND design pattern provides a recognizable solution template;
- When applying the COMMAND pattern, be careful not to break the encapsulation of classes simply to allow command objects to operate on target objects;
- Unless there is an explicit reason not to, respect the Law of Demeter.

Code Exploration

Commands in Solitaire

The Solitaire example application relies on the COMMAND pattern. The command role is taken up by the Move interface. The implementations of Move illustrate a diversity of ways that commands can be realized. Classes CardMove and RevealTop-

Move are private inner classes of GameModel so that they can refer to the private fields and methods of their outer instance, as discussed in Section 4.10. The command to represent discarding a card from the deck is very simple and thus implemented as an anonymous class instantiated as part of the initialization of a field aDiscardMove. An alternative option would have been to create new instances of discard move in a factory method. To me both options are almost equivalent in terms of design quality. Because it does not refer to the state of a GameModel, field NULL_MOVE is a constant and declared as static. The null move represents the situation where it is not possible to make a move in the game. This is an application of NULL OBJECT (see Section 4.5). Class CompositeMove realizes the role of the composite in the COMPOSITE pattern. In the game it is used to combine atomic moves, such as taking a card from a tableau pile and flipping the card underneath it to reveal it. Finally, one implementation of Move is a stub, used for testing (see Section 5.8).

Delegation in GameModel

The design of the Solitaire project is consistent with the diagram of Figure 6.1. Note how some methods of class GameModel simply delegate the call to their aggregated objects. Examples include getScore(), getSubStack(...), getTableauPile, and isVisibleInTableau(...).

Cloning in JetUML

In JetUML, classes Line and Point show simple examples of cloning. The application also uses cloning for the Edge and Node class hierarchies. However, understanding cloning in these more complex cases requires a good grasp of inheritance, which is covered in Chapter 7.

Commands in JetUML

JetUML provides a different example of the use of the COMMAND pattern. In Jet-UML, DiagramOperation fulfills the role of command. However, in this design, there are only two concrete command types: SimpleOperation and Compound-Operation. SimpleOperation is a wrapper for a function object that can be used to encapsulate any non-compound command using a functional-programming flavored design. I revisit this style in Chapter 9. In contrast, CompoundOperation is a typical implementation of a composite in the COMPOSITE pattern.

Prototype Object in JetUML

The design of the JetUML tool bar relies on the PROTOTYPE pattern to create
new nodes in a diagram. The `DiagramTabToolBar` class aggregates a number of
`SelectableToolButton` which, in turn, aggregate an instance of the `Node` to create when the button is clicked. When the user presses a mouse button on the canvas,
the code asks the toolbar to return the prototype associated with the button, and
clones it to create the new node. Figure 6.20 shows the main participants in this
interaction.

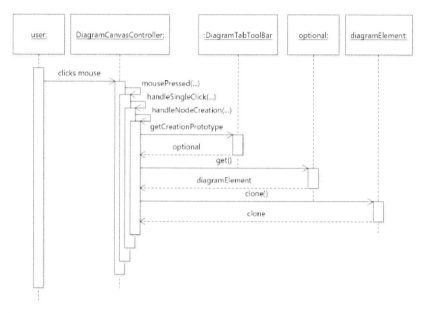

Fig. 6.20 Use of the PROTOTYPE in JetUML

Further Reading

The Gang of Four book [6] has the original, detailed treatment of the COMPOSITE,
DECORATOR, PROTOTYPE, and COMMAND patterns. Their description of the patterns
include useful complementary discussions of the implications of using the pattern.
For example, the presentation of the COMPOSITE pattern includes an extended discussion of the trade-off between *transparency* and *safety* (in the type-checking sense)
involved around the decision of whether to declare the child management operations
in the component interface or not.

In terms of mechanisms of the Java language, the API documentation for `Object.clone()` provides additional details of the cloning protocol in Java. Item 13 in *Effective Java* [1], titled "Override `clone` judiciously", provides eight pages of advice on using this mechanism. Information on variable arguments ("varargs") can be found on the Oracle website in the list of enhancements for Java SE 5.0.

The "home page" for information on the Law of Demeter can be found at
`http://www.ccs.neu.edu/home/lieber/LoD.html`.

Chapter 7
Inheritance

This chapter covers:

> **Concepts and Principles:** Code reuse, extensibility, Liskov Substitution Principle;
>
> **Programming Mechanisms:** Inheritance, subtyping, downcasting, object initialization, super calls, overriding, overloading, abstract classes, abstract methods, final classes, final methods;
>
> **Design Techniques:** Inheritance-base reuse, class hierarchy design;
>
> **Patterns and Antipatterns:** TEMPLATE METHOD.

Inheritance is a programming language mechanism that allows us to create objects from definitions provided in multiple, inter-related classes. It is a powerful feature that offers a natural solution to many design problems related to code reuse and extensibility. At the same time, it is a complex mechanism that can all too easily be misused. This chapter provides a review of inheritance and presents the major design rules and patterns involving it.

Design Context

The examples in this chapter discuss the design of two type hierarchies: card sources and moves. The card source hierarchy follows the examples of the previous chapters where instances of objects that are subtypes of a `CardSource` interface are used to provide card instances to be used in card games. The second context is the design of a hierarchy of subtypes of an interface `Move` which, together, realize an application of the COMMAND design pattern as seen in Section 6.8.

© Springer Nature Switzerland AG 2019
M. P. Robillard, *Introduction to Software Design with Java*,
https://doi.org/10.1007/978-3-030-24094-3_7

7.1 The Case for Inheritance

So far we have seen many situations where we can leverage polymorphism to realize various design features. Polymorphism helps make a design extensible by decoupling client code from the concrete implementation of a required functionality. The class diagram of Figure 7.1 exemplifies this benefit by showing a `GameModel` that depends only on a general `CardSource` service whose concrete realization can be one of at least three options: a typical `Deck` of cards, a `MemorizingDeck` that remembers each card drawn, and a `CircularDeck` that replaces drawn cards at the bottom of the deck.

Fig. 7.1 Polymorphic reference to a `CardSource` service

This design is extensible because in principle the `GameModel` can work with any card source. As discussed in Chapter 3, in Java polymorphism relies intrinsically on the language's subtyping mechanism. The key to supporting various options for a `CardSource` is the fact that the different concrete implementations of the service are subtypes of the `CardSouce` interface type.

Although the design illustrated is clean from the point of view of polymorphism, it has one major weakness from the point of view of the implementation of the various card source alternatives. This weakness would become apparent as soon as we would start to implement the class hierarchy of Figure 7.1. The issue is that the services defined by the `CardSource` interface are similar, and likely to be implemented in similar ways.[1] Figure 7.2 shows a slightly different variant of the class diagram that emphasizes the implementation of the concrete `CardSources` instead of the polymorphism. As is now more evident from the diagram, all three implementations of `CardSource` hold a reference to a `CardStack` delegate. Moreover:

- In all cases the implementation of method `isEmpty()` is simply a delegation to `aCards.isEmpty()`
- In all cases the implementation of method `draw()` pops a card from `aCards`: the only difference between the three options is small variants for the remain-

---

[1] This assumes a standard implementation, and not an application of the DECORATOR, which would be challenging in the case of `CircularDeck` because of the requirement to use a service (adding cards to the source) that is not defined on the component interface.

Fig. 7.2 Implementations of the `CardSource` service

der of the implementation of `draw` (e.g., to re-insert the card in the deck in the `CardStack` of `CircularDeck`).

So here we can say that the design induces DUPLICATED CODE†, also known as *code clones*. There is an extensive literature on the topic of duplicated code, but the bottom line is that it is a good idea to avoid it.

Problems of redundancies such as the one illustrated here can be improved by reorganizing the design. One mechanism of object-oriented programming languages that is especially effective for supporting code reuse (and thus avoiding DUPLICATED CODE†) is *inheritance*. Inheritance directly supports code reuse and extensibility because it allows us to define some classes in terms of other classes. The key idea of inheritance is to define a new class (the *subclass*) in terms of how it adds to (or extends) an existing *base class* (also called the *superclass*). Inheritance avoids repeating declarations of class members because the declarations of the base class will automatically be taken into account when creating instances of the subclass.

In class diagrams, inheritance is denoted by a solid line with a white triangle pointing from the subclass to the superclass. Figure 7.3 illustrates a variant of our design where `MemorizingDeck` and `CircularDeck` are defined as subclasses of the `Deck` base class.

Fig. 7.3 Inheritance-based
design for `CardSource`

7.2 Inheritance and Typing

In Java the subclass-superclass relation is declared using the **extends** keyword:

```
public class MemorizingDeck extends Deck
{
  private CardStack aDrawnCards;
}
```

To understand the effect of inheritance in code, it is important to remember that a class is essentially a template for creating objects. Defining a subclass MemorizingDeck as an extension of a superclass Deck means that when objects of the subclass are instantiated, the objects will be created by using the declaration of the subclass *and* of the declaration of the superclass. The result will be a single object. The run-time type of this object will be the type specified in the **new** statement. However, just as for interface implementation, inheritance introduces a suptyping relation. For this reason, an object can always be assigned to a variable of its superclass (in addition to its implementing interfaces).

```
Deck deck = new MemorizingDeck();
CardSource source = deck;
```

In the code above, a new object of run-time type MemorizingDeck is created and assigned to a variable named deck of compile-time type Deck. This is legal because MemorizingDeck is a subtype of Deck. The second line of the code example shows another relation between variables and values of different, yet related, types. The code declares a variable of type CardSource and assigns the value deck to it. The compile-time type of deck is Deck, which is a subtype of CardSource. For this reason, the compiler allows the assignment. At run time, it will turn out that the concrete type of deck is MemorizingDeck. However, because MemorizingDeck is a subtype of both Deck and CardSource, there is no problem.

In this chapter, the distinction between compile-time type and run-time type will become increasingly important. In our case, when an instance of MemorizingDeck is assigned to a variable of type Deck, it does not "become" a simple deck or "lose" any of its subclass-specific fields. In Java, once an object is created, its run-time type remains unchanged. All the variable reassignments accomplish in the code above is to change the type of the variable that holds a reference to the object. The run-time type of an object is the most specific type of an object when it is instantiated. It is the type mentioned in the **new** statement, and the one that is represented by the object returned by method getClass() (see Section 5.4). The run-time type of an object never changes for the duration of the object's lifetime. In contrast, the compile-time (or static) type of an object is the type of the *variable* in which a reference to the object is stored at a particular point in the code. In a correct program the static type of an object can correspond to its run-time type, or to any supertype of its run-time type. The static type of an object can be different at different points in the code, depending on the variables in which an object is stored. Let us consider the following example:

```
public static boolean isMemorizing(Deck pDeck)
{ return pDeck instanceof MemorizingDeck; }

public static void main(String[] args)
{
  Deck deck = new MemorizingDeck();
  MemorizingDeck memorizingDeck = (MemorizingDeck) deck;
  boolean isMemorizing1 = isMemorizing(deck); // true
  boolean isMemorizing2 = isMemorizing(memorizingDeck); // true
}
```

At the first line of the `main` method an object is created that is of run-time type `MemorizingDeck` and assigned to a variable of type `Deck`. As stated above, the run-time type of this object remains `MemorizingDeck` throughout the execution of the code. However, at the following line the static type of the variable that stores the original object is `MemorizingDeck`, and within the body of method `isMemorizingDeck` it is `Deck` (a formal parameter is a kind of variable, so the type of a parameter acts like a type of variable). Because the run-time type of the object never changes, the value stored in both `isMemorizing1` and `isMemorizing2` is **true**.

Downcasting

To make the code above compile, it is necessary to use as *cast* operator `(MemorizingDeck)`. In brief, a cast operator is necessary to enable unsafe type conversion operations. An example of an unsafe conversion between primitive types is to convert a **long** value into an **int** value (which may cause an overflow). Similarly, because a reference to a `Deck` is not guaranteed to refer to an instance of `MemorizingDeck` at run time, it is necessary to flag the risky conversion using a cast operator, a process known as *downcasting*.[2] When using inheritance, subclasses typically provide services in addition to what is available in the base class. For example, a class `MemorizingDeck` would probably include the definition of a service to obtain the list of cards drawn from the deck:

```
public class MemorizingDeck extends Deck
{
  public Iterator<Card> getDrawnCards() { ... }
}
```

Because of the typing rules discussed in Chapter 3, it is only possible to call methods that are applicable for a given static type. So if we assign a reference to an object of run-time type `MemorizingDeck` to a variable of type `Deck`, then we will get a compilation error if we try to access a method of the subclass:

```
Deck deck = new MemorizingDeck();
deck.getDrawnCards();
```

---

[2] The direction implied in the term is a consequence of the convention that in type hierarchies, the "top" of the hierarchy is usually considered to be the root of the hierarchy

This makes a lot of sense. The code above would be type unsafe. Because references to an instance of any subtype of Deck can be stored in variable Deck, there is no guarantee that, at run-time, the object in the variable will actually define a getDrawnCards() method. If, based on our knowledge of the code, we are "sure" that the object will always be of type MemorizingDeck, we can downcast the variable from a supertype down to a subtype:

```
MemorizingDeck memorizingDeck = (MemorizingDeck) deck;
Iterator<Card> drawnCards = memorizingDeck.getDrawnCards();
```

Downcasting involves some risks because a downcast encodes an assumption that the run-time type of the object referred to in the variable is of the same type as (or a subtype of) the type of the variable. In a way the code above would be a little bit like writing:

```
assert deck instanceof MemorizingDeck;
```

If the assumption is wrong, most likely due to a programmer error, then the execution of the code cannot proceed, and the downcast will raise a ClassCast-Exception. For this reason, downcasting code will often be protected by control structures to assert the run-time type of an object, such as:

```
if( deck instanceof MemorizingDeck )
{
  return ((MemorizingDeck)deck).getDrawnCards();
}
```

Singly-Rooted Class Hierarchy

Java supports *single inheritance*, which means that a given class can only declare to inherit from (i.e., extend) a single class. This is in contrast to languages such as C++, which support *multiple inheritance*. However, because the superclass of a class can also be defined to inherit from a superclass, classes can have, in effect, more than one superclass. In fact, classes in Java are organized into a *single-rooted class hierarchy*. If a class does not declare to extend any class, by default it extends the library class Object. Class Object thus constitutes the root of any class hierarchy in Java code. The complete class hierarchy for variants of Deck thus includes class Object, as illustrated in Figure 7.4. Because the subtyping relation is transitive,[3] objects of class MemorizingDeck can thus be stored in variables of type Object, etc.

---

[3] In a transitive relation, if *A* is related to *B* and *B* is related to *C*, then *A* is related to *C* within the same relation.

Fig. 7.4 Complete class hierarchy for `Deck`

7.3 Inheriting Fields

With inheritance, the subclass inherits the declarations of the superclass. The consequences of inheriting field declarations are quite different from those of method
declarations, so I discuss these separately.

Field declarations define the structure of information stored by the instantiated
object. When creating a new object, this object will have a field for each field declaration in the class named in the **new** statement, and each of its superclasses, transitively. Given the following class hierarchy:

```
pulic class Deck implements CardSource
{
    private final CardStack aCards = new CardStack();
    ...
}

public class MemorizingDeck extends Deck
{
    private final CardStack aDrawnCards = new CardStack();
    ...
}
```

objects created with the statement **new** `MemorizingDeck();` will have two fields:
`aCards` and `aDrawnCards`. It does not matter that the fields are private. Accessibility
is a static concept, meaning that it is only relevant for the source code. The fact that
the code in class `MemorizingDeck` cannot access (or *see*) the field declared in its
superclass does not change anything about the fact that this field is inherited. For
the fields to be accessible to subclasses, it is possible to set their access modifier
to **protected** instead of **private**, or to access their value through a getter. Type
members declared to be **protected** are only accessible within methods of the same
class, classes in the same package, and subclasses in any package.

The inheritance of fields creates an interesting problem of data initialization.
When an object can be initialized with default values, the process is simple. In
our case, if we assign the default values using the field initialization statement as
in the above statements (i.e., = **new** `CardStack();`), and rely on the default (i.e.,

parameterless) constructors,[4] we can expect that creating a new instance of class `MemorizingDeck` will result in an instance with two fields of type `CardStack`, each referring to an empty instance of `CardStack`.

However, it is often the case that object initialization requires input data. For example, what happens if we want to make it possible to initialize a deck with a set of cards supplied by the client code? For example:

```
Card[] cards = {Cards.get(Rank.ACE, Suit.CLUBS),
                Card.get(Rank.ACE, Suit.SPACES)};
MemorizingDeck deck = new MemorizingDeck(cards);
```

In such situations it becomes important to pay attention to the order in which the fields of an object are initialized. The general principle in Java is that the fields of an object are initialized "top down", from the field declarations of the most general superclass down to the most specific class (the one named in the **new** statement). In our example, `aCards` would be initialized, then `aDrawnCards`. This order is achieved simply by the fact that the first instruction of any constructor is to call a constructor of its superclass, and so on.[5] For this reason, the order of constructor calls is "bottom up".

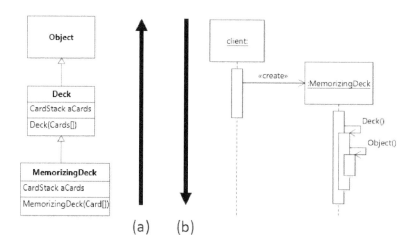

(a)   (b)

Fig. 7.5 Order of constructor call (a) and object construction (b). The calls to the constructors of a superclass are self-calls.

---

[4] In Java, if no constructor is declared for a class, a default constructor with no parameter is invisibly made available to client code. Declaring any non-default constructor in a class disables the automatic generation of a default constructor.

[5] If the superclass declares a constructor with no parameter, this call does not need to be explicit.

In our running example, declaring:

```
public class MemorizingDeck extends Deck
{
  private final CardStack aDrawnCards = new CardStack();

  public MemorizingDeck(Card[] pCards)
  {
    /* Automatically calls super() */
    ...
  }
}
```

means that the default constructor of `Deck` is called and terminates before the code of the `MemorizingDeck` constructor executes. It is also possible to invoke the constructor of the superclass explicitly, using the **super**(...) call. However, if used, this call must be the first statement of a constructor. Although it illustrates how constructor calls are chained, the example above does not quite do what we want, because it ignores the input cards. However, with the initialization mechanism we have seen so far, it becomes relatively easy to pass input values "up" to initialize fields declared in a superclass. In our case we want to store the input cards into the `aCards` field defined by the `Deck` superclass. We would accomplish this as follows:

```
public class Deck
{
  private final CardStack aCards = new CardStack();

  public Deck(){} // Relies on the field initialization

  public Deck(Card[] pCards)
  {
    for( Card card : pCards )
    { aCards.push(card); }
  }
}

public class MemorizingDeck extends Deck
{
  private final CardStack aDrawnCards = new CardStack();

  public MemorizingDeck(Card[] pCards)
  { super(pCards); }
}
```

Here the only statement of the `MemorizingDeck` constructor is an *explicit* call to the constructor of the superclass, which passes in the initialization data. Once the **super** call terminates, the execution of the constructor of the same class continues with the initialization of the `aDrawnCards` field.

Calling the constructor of the superclass with **super**(...) is very different from calling the constructor of the superclass with a **new** statement. In the latter case, two different objects are created. The code:

```
public MemorizingDeck(Card[] pCards)
{
  new Deck(pCards);
}
```

calls the default constructor of Deck, then *also* creates a new Deck instance, different from the instance under construction, immediately discards the reference to this instance, and then completes the initialization of the object. This code would not serve many useful purposes.

7.4 Inheriting Methods

Inheriting methods is different from inheriting fields because method declarations do not store information that represents the state of an object, and so do not require any initialization. Instead, the implications of method inheritance center around the question of *applicability*. By default, methods of a superclass are applicable to instances of a subclass. For example, if we define a method shuffle() in class Deck, it will be possible to call this method on an instance of its subclass MemorizingDeck:

```
MemorizingDeck memorizingDeck = new MemorizingDeck();
memorizingDeck.shuffle();
```

This "feature" is nothing special, and really is only a consequence of what a method represents and the rules of the type system. Here it is worth remembering that an instance (i.e., non-static) method is just a different way to express a function that takes an object of its declaring class as its first argument. For example, the method shuffle() in Deck:

```
public class Deck implements CardSource
{
  private CardStack aCards = new CardStack();

  public void shuffle()
  {
    // The 'this' keyword is optional in this case. It is used
    // here to contrast with the alternative below.
    this.aCards.clear();
    this.initialize();
  }

  private void initialize()
  { /* Adds all 52 cards to aCard in random order */ }
}
```

is more or less equivalent to the static method:

```
public class Deck implements CardSource
{
  private CardStack aCards = new CardStack();

  public static void shuffle(Deck pThis)
  {
    pThis.aCards.clear();
    pThis.initialize();
  }

  private void initialize()
  { /* Adds all 52 cards to aCard in random order */ }
}
```

In the first case the function is invoked by specifying the target object *before* the call: `memorizingDeck.shuffle()`. In this case we refer to the `memorizingDeck` parameter as the *implicit parameter*. A reference to this parameter is accessible through the **this** keyword within the method.[6] In the second case the function is invoked by specifying the target object as an *explicit* parameter, so after the call: `shuffle(memorizingDeck)`. In this case to clear any ambiguity it is usually necessary to specify the type of the class where the method is located, so `Deck.shuffle(memorizingDeck)`. What this example illustrates is that methods of a superclass are automatically applicable to instances of a subclass because instances of a subclass can be assigned to a variable of any supertype. In our example, because it is legal to assign a reference to a `MemorizingDeck` to a parameter of type `Deck`, the `shuffle()` method is applicable to instances of any subclass of `Deck`.

In some cases, a method inherited from a superclass does not do quite what we want. In our running example, this would be the case for method `draw()`, which in the `Deck` base class simply draws a card from the deck:

```
public class Deck implements CardSource
{
  private CardStack aCards = new CardStack();

  public Card draw()
  { return aCards.pop(); }
}
```

Here using `Deck`'s version of method `draw()` on instances of `MemorizingDeck` through inheritance does not do what we need, because that method does not memorize anything. In such cases, we need to *redefine*, or *override*, the behavior of the inherited method by supplying an implementation in the subclass that only applies to instances of the subclasses. For method `draw()` we would want:

---

[6] The **this** keyword is optional to refer to the members of a class from within the class declaration, as it can be inferred by the compiler if left out.

```
public class MemorizingDeck extends Deck
{
  private CardStack aDrawnCards = new CardStack();

  public Card draw()
  {
    Card card = aCards.pop();
    aDrawCards.push(card);
    return card;
  }
}
```

Unfortunately, this code will not compile because the code of method `draw()` in `MemorizingDeck` refers to private field `aCards` of class `Deck`. Because private fields are only accessible within the class where they are declared, this field is not visible in other classes, including subclasses. One possible workaround is to define `Deck.aCards` as **protected** instead. This is the typical use case for **protected** fields: to allow subclasses to manipulate some structure of the superclass when overriding methods. Unfortunately, increasing the visibility of `aCards` from **private** to **protected** has a corresponding negative impact on encapsulation, because now it is possible to refer to the field, and thus mutate the object it refers to, from many different classes instead of just one. To circumvent this issue, we can resort to other alternatives, including the use of *super calls*, introduced a bit further below.

Overriding inherited methods has a major consequence on the design of an object-oriented application, because it introduces the possibility that multiple method implementations apply to an object that is the target of a method invocation. For example, in the code:

```
Card card = new MemorizingDeck().draw();
```

both `Deck.draw()` and `MemorizingDeck.draw()` are applicable and can thus legally be used. Which one is used? For the program to work, the programming environment (the Java Virtual Machine,) must follow a consistent *method selection algorithm*.

For overridden methods, the selection algorithm is relatively intuitive: when multiple implementations are applicable, the run-time environment selects the *most specific one* based on the *run-time type of the implicit parameter*. Again, the run-time type of an object is the "actual" class that was instantiated: the class name that follows the **new** keyword, or the class type represented by the object returned by a call to `Object.getClass()`. Because the selection of an overridden method relies on run-time information, the selection procedure is often referred to as *dynamic dispatch*, or *dynamic binding*. It is important to remember that type information for variables is ignored for dynamic dispatch. So, in this example:

```
Deck deck = new MemorizingDeck();
Card card = deck.draw();
```

the method `MemorizingDeck.draw()` would be selected, even though the static (compile-time) type of the target object is `Deck`.

In some cases it is necessary to bypass the dynamic binding mechanism and link
to a specific, statically-predictable method implementation. In Java, however, for
instance methods it is only possible to do so by referring to the implementation of
the method that is being directly overridden. This exception to the usual dynamic
binding mechanism is intended to support the common case where a method is
overridden to provide behavior *in addition* to what the inherited method does. To
illustrate this case, let us return to the issue of overriding method `draw()` in class
`MemorizingDeck`. This time, we will do it without declaring `Deck.aCards` to be
protected.

The key insight we use to accomplish this is to observe that to draw a card from
`aCards`, we can also use `Deck`'s own `draw()` method. So what we want would be a
little bit like this:

```java
public class MemorizingDeck extends Deck
{
  private CardStack aDrawnCards = new CardStack();

  public Card draw()
  {
    Card card = draw(); // Problematic
    aDrawCards.push(card);
    return card;
  }
}
```

Here, the naive intention is that by calling `draw()` inside `MemorizingDeck.-`
`draw()`, we can execute the code of `Deck.draw()` and thus draw a card from
`aCards`. Unfortunately this does not work precisely because of the dynamic binding
mechanism described above. Because the call to `draw()` within `MemorizingDeck.-`
`draw()` will be dispatched on the same object, the same method implementation will
be selected, endlessly. The result will be a *stack overflow* error, because the method
will recursively call itself without a termination condition.

What we really want, here, is to refer *specifically* to `Deck.draw()` within
`MemorizingDeck.draw()`. In other words, we want to *statically* bind the method
call `draw()` to the implementation located in `Deck.draw()`. In Java, to refer to the
specific implementation of a method located in the superclass *from within a subclass*, we use the keyword **super** followed by the method call.

```java
public class MemorizingDeck extends Deck
{
  public Card draw()
  {
    Card card = super.draw();
    aDrawCards.push(card);
    return card;
  }
}
```

This mechanism is informally referred to as a super call. Its effect is to statically
bind the method call to the first implementation of the method found by going up

the class hierarchy. The implementation does not need to be in the immediate super-class, but there needs to be at least one inherited method that can be selected in this way.

Annotating Overridden Methods

For a method to effectively override another one, it needs to have the same signature as the one it overrides.[7] This requirement for matching method signatures opens the door to errors with mystifying consequences.

For example, let us say we want to override the `equals` and `hashCode` methods for class `Deck`, as discussed in Section 4.7, and we proceed as follows:

```java
public class Deck implements CardSource
{
  public boolean equals(Object) { ... }
  public int hashcode() { ... }
}
```

With these definitions we would expect that instances of `Deck` could be stored in collections such as a `HashSet` without problems, given that we are properly overriding `hashCode()` to ensure equal instances of `Deck` have the same hash code. Except that we are not! Actually the name of the method declared in `Deck` is `hashcode()` and not `hashCode()`. Although we expect `Object.hashCode()` to be overridden, the hard-to-see, one-character difference in the name means that the method is, in fact, not overridden. Unless we notice the name difference, the bugs this problem would cause could be very hard to explain.

To avoid situations like these, where we expect a method to be overridden when it is not, we can use Java's `@Override` annotation (see Section 5.4 for a review of annotation types). The goal of this annotation is to allow programmers to formally state their intent to override a method. The compiler can then check this intent against reality and warn of any mismatches. In practice, this means that if a method annotated with `@Override` does not actually override anything, a compilation error is raised. The case for using `@Override` annotations is very compelling, and personally I use them systematically.[8]

7.5 Overloading Methods

As we saw above, overriding methods allows programmers to declare different versions of the same method, so that the most appropriate method will be selected based

---

[7] Technically, it could have a *subsignature* as defined in Section 8.4.2 of the Java Language Specification. However, this subtlety is outside the scope of this book, so for simplicity we can consider that the match in terms of method names, parameter types, and declared exceptions, must be exact.

[8] For conciseness, overriding annotations are, however, not included in the code examples in the chapters.

on the run-time type of the implicit parameter. Java and many other programming languages support another mechanism for specifying different implementations of the "same" method, this time by selecting the method based on the types of the *explicit* parameters. This mechanism is known as *overloading*. A typical example of overloading can be found in math libraries such as `java.lang.Math`, which provide basic functions such as `abs` (absolute value) for arguments of different primitive types, such as `int` and **`double`**. Another typical application of overloading is for constructors. For example, Section 7.3 discusses a scenario where two constructors for `MemorizingDeck` are provided, one that takes no argument, and one that takes an array of `Card` instances.

The main thing to know about overloading is that the selection of a specific overloaded method or constructor is based on the number and *static* types of the *explicit* arguments. The selection procedure is to find all *applicable* methods and to select the *most specific* one. Let us consider the following version of `MemorizingDeck`, which overloads the constructor with three different versions:

```java
public class MemorizingDeck extends Deck
{
    private CardStack aDrawnCards = new CardStack();

    public MemorizingDeck()
    { /* Version 1: Does nothing besides the initialization */ }

    public MemorizingDeck(CardSource pSource)
    { /* Version 2: Copies all cards of pSource into
       * this object */ }

    public MemorizingDeck(MemorizingDeck pSource)
    { /* Version 3: Copies all cards and drawn cards of pSource
       * into this object */ }
}
```

If we call a constructor for `MemorizingDeck`, three versions of the constructor are available to fulfill the task. In some cases, which version is selected can be trivially deduced. For instance, if we call the constructor and supply no argument, clearly, version 1 will be selected. However, things can be tricky when the types of overloaded versions are related to each other within a type hierarchy. The following code illustrates the situation:

```java
MemorizingDeck memorizingDeck = new MemorizingDeck();
Deck deck = memorizingDeck;

Deck newDeck1 = new MemorizingDeck(memorizingDeck);
Deck newDeck2 = new MemorizingDeck(deck);
```

Here the constructor of `MemorizingDeck` is invoked three times. In the first call, it is obvious that the default constructor (with no parameter) is selected. In the second call, the constructor used is version 3, which might be intuitive in this example because `MemorizingDeck` is both the run-time type of the argument object and the static type of the variable holding a reference to it. However, it can appear surprising that for `newDeck2`, it is version 2 of the constructor that is used. That is because in this case the static type of the argument passed to the constructor is `Deck`. Because `Deck` is a subtype of `CardSource` but *not* a subtype of `MemorizingDeck`, the only applicable overload is version 2. If we change the type of `deck` from `Deck` to `MemorizingDeck`, then version 3 is the one that will be selected. Note that the types of variables `newDeck1` and `newDeck2` play no role whatsoever in the selection algorithm for overloaded methods and constructors.

Although overloading provides a convenient way to organize small variants of a general computation, the use of this mechanism can easily lead to hard-to-understand code. This is especially the case when the types of the parameters to overloaded versions of a method or constructor are related within a type hierarchy, as illustrated above. For this reason I recommend avoiding overloading methods except for widely used idioms (such as constructor overloading or library methods that support different primitive types). In many designs, the same properties can be obtained without overloading (i.e., by giving different names to the methods that take different types of arguments).

7.6 Inheritance Versus Composition

Inheritance provides an alternative to composition as a design approach to deal with situations where some objects are "extended" versions of another. To explore some of the differences between the two, let us consider the composition vs. inheritance alternatives for meeting the requirements for a `MemorizingDeck`.

With composition, we can define a class `MemorizingDeck` that implements `CardSource` but *aggregates* a simple deck. The methods of `MemorizingDeck` will then *delegate* their call to methods on the `Deck` object.

```java
public class MemorizingDeck implements CardSource
{
  private final CardStack aDrawCards = new CardStack();
  private final Deck aDeck = new Deck();

  public boolean isEmpty()
  { return aDeck.isEmpty(); }

  public void shuffle()
  {
    aDeck.shuffle();
    aDrawnCards.clear();
  }

  public Card draw()
  {
    Card card = aDeck.draw();
    aDrawnCard.push(card);
    return card;
  }
}
```

In contrast, with inheritance, the cards in the deck are not stored in a separate deck, but rather referred to from a field *inherited* from the superclass. In terms of methods, `shuffle()`, `isEmpty()`, and `draw()` are also inherited from the superclass, so they do not need to be redefined to delegate the call, as in composition. In our example we only need to override `shuffle()` and `draw()` to account for the memorization. Method `isEmpty()` can be directly inherited and still do what we want. In the code of the overridden methods, the delegation to another object is replaced by a super call, which executes on the *same* object.

```java
public class MemorizingDeck extends Deck
{
  private final CardStack aDrawCards = new CardStack();

  public void shuffle()
  {
    super.shuffle();
    aDrawnCards.clear();
  }

  public Card draw()
  {
    Card card = super.draw();
    aDrawnCard.push(card);
    return card;
  }
}
```

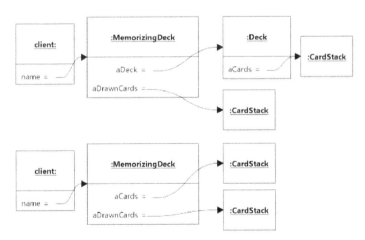

Fig. 7.6 Two implementations for `MemorizingDeck`: Composition-based (top), and inheritance-based (bottom)

The main difference between the two approaches is the number of `Deck` objects involved (see Figure 7.6). The composition-based approach provides a solution that requires combining the work of two objects: a basic `Deck` object and a "wrapper" (or "decorator") object `MemorizingDeck`. Thus, as discussed in Section 6.4, the identity of the object that provides the full `MemorizingDeck` set of features is different from that of the other object that provides the basic card handling services of the deck. In contrast, the use of a `MemorizingDeck` subclass creates a *single* `MemorizingDeck` object that contains all the required fields.

In most situations, it may be possible to realize a design solution using either inheritance or composition. Which option to choose will ultimately depend on the context. Composition-based reuse generally provides more run-time flexibility. This option should therefore be favored in design contexts that require many possible configurations, or the opportunity to change configurations at run-time. At the same time, composition-based solutions provide fewer options for detailed access to the internal state of a well-encapsulated object. In contrast, inheritance-based reuse solutions tend to be better in design contexts that require a lot of compile-time configuration, because a class hierarchy can easily be designed to provide privileged access to the internal structure of a class to subclasses (as opposed to aggregate and other client classes).

7.7 Abstract Classes

There are often situations where locating common class members into a single superclass leads to a class declaration that it would not make sense to instantiate. As a running example for this section and the next, I continue to develop the concept of command objects as introduced in Section 6.8. Let us assume that for a card game application we decide to apply the COMMAND pattern and use the following definition of the command interface.

```
public interface Move
{
  void perform();
  void undo();
}
```

This interface is pretty self-explanatory. A "move" represents a possible action in the game. Calling `perform()` on any subtype of `Move` performs the move, and calling `undo()` undoes the move. The class diagram of Figure 7.7 shows a hypothetical application of the COMMAND pattern. Following a common naming convention, classes that implement the interface include the name of the interface as a suffix (e.g., `DiscardMove` represents the move that discards a card from the deck). At a glance the diagram reveals a redundancy: each concrete command class stores an aggregation to an instance of `GameModel`, which the implementation of `perform()` and `undo()` will rely on when executing the respective commands. In terms of source code, this would look very similar: a field of type `GameModel` (called `aModel` in the diagram). As pointed out in Section 7.1, avoiding CODE DUPLICATION† is the very motivation for inheritance, so we should "pull up" the field `aModel` into a common superclass. However, there is a big difference between the `Deck` class

Fig. 7.7 Abstract and concrete commands

example of Section 7.1 and the command example discussed here. With a `Deck` base class and various subclasses that specialize it, *it makes sense to instantiate the base class*. If we want an instance of a `Deck` with no frills, we do **new** `Deck()` and we have what we want. In the case of commands, what would be the base class? One option is to arbitrarily select one concrete command and use it as the base class, as illustrated by the diagram of Figure 7.8.

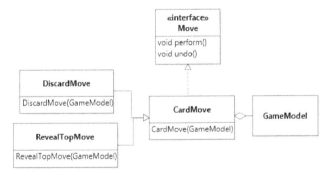

Fig. 7.8 Abuse of inheritance: the members of the base class end up being completely redefined instead of specialized

Although this could work, it is not good design. An important principle of inheritance is that a subclass should be a "natural" subtype of the base class that extends the behavior of the base class. In our case, a `DiscardMove` is not really a specialized version of a `CardMove`, they are just two different moves. First, `CardMove` may define non-interface methods that make no sense for users of its subclass (e.g., `getDestination()` to get the destination when moving a card). Second, this idea is risky, because `DiscardMove` and `RevealTopMove` automatically inherit the `perform()` and `undo()` methods of class `CardMove`, which need to be completely overridden to implement the actual move we want. If we forget to implement one (`undo()` for example), then calling `perform()` will do one thing, and calling `undo()` will undo something else! These types of bugs can be very hard to catch. I will return to the issue of design ideas that abuse inheritance in Section 7.10. To use inheritance properly here, we need to create an entirely new base class, and have all "actual" commands inherit it, as shows in Figure 7.9.

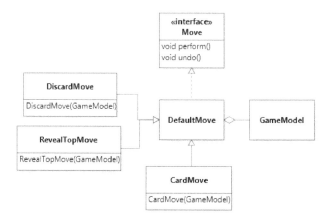

Fig. 7.9 Inheritance with additional base class

Now we avoid the hack of having subclasses that morph their superclass into something entirely different. However, at the same time we have a problematic situation: what is a `DefaultMove`, really? What would the implementation of `perform()` and `undo()` actually do? Here, even using some sort of default behavior seems questionable, because that would bring us back to the idea of using a base class that is not conceptually a base for anything. A key observation to move forward is that our new base class represents a purely abstract concept that needs to be refined to gain concreteness. This design situation is directly supported by the *abstract class* feature of a programming language. Technically, an abstract class represents a correct but *incomplete* set of class member declarations.

In Java a class can be declared abstract by including the keyword **abstract** in its declaration. It is also a common practice to prefix the identifier for an abstract class with the word `Abstract`. Hence, in our design the `DefaultMove` should be called `AbstractMove`, and its definition would look like this:

```
public abstract AbstractMove implements Move
{
  private final GameModel aModel;

  protected AbstractMove(GameModel pModel)
  { aModel = pModel; }

  ...
}
```

Declaring a class to be abstract has three main consequences:

- The class cannot be instantiated, which is checked by the compiler. This is a good thing because abstract classes should represent abstract concepts that it makes no sense to instantiate. Another typical example, besides abstract commands, would be something like an `AbstractFigure` in a drawing editor. Unlike concrete figures (rectangles, ellipses), an abstract figure has no geometric representation, so in most designs something like that would be likely to end up as an abstract class.
- The class no longer needs to supply an implementation for all the methods in the interface(s) it declares to implement. This relaxing of the interface contract is type-safe because the class cannot be instantiated. However, any concrete (i.e., non-abstract) class will need to have implementations for all required methods. What this means in our case is that, even though `AbstractMove` declares to implement `Move`, we do not have to supply an implementation for `perform()` and `undo()` in the abstract class. However, this assumes that non-abstract subclasses of `AbstractMove` will supply this missing implementation.
- The class can declare new abstract methods using the same **abstract** keyword, this time placed in front of a method signature. In practice this means adding methods to the interface of the abstract class, and thereby forcing the subclasses to implement these methods. The usage scenario for this is a bit specialized, and I will cover it in detail in Section 7.9. However, for now, we can just say that in most designs abstract methods are typically called from within the class hierarchy: by methods of the base class, by methods of the subclasses, or both.

Note that because abstract classes cannot be instantiated, their constructor can only be called from within the constructors of subclasses. For this reason it makes sense to declare the constructors of abstract classes **protected**. In our running example, the constructor of `AbstractMove` would be called by the constructor of subclasses to pass the required reference to the `GameModel` "up" into the base class:

```
public class CardMove extends AbstractMove
{
  public CardMove(GameModel pModel)
  {
    super(pModel);
  }
}
```

7.8 Revisiting the DECORATOR Design Pattern

In Section 6.4, we saw how we can use the DECORATOR pattern to add feature elements, or "decorations", to an object at run-time. The key idea of the DECORATOR is to define these decorations using wrapper classes and composition as opposed to subclasses. Figure 7.10 reproduces Figure 6.8, which shows a class diagram of the sample application of DECORATOR to the `CardSource` design context.

Fig. 7.10 Class diagram of a sample application of DECORATOR

When a design involves multiple decorator types, as in this example, each decorator class will need to aggregate an object to be decorated. This introduces the kind of redundancy that inheritance was designed to avoid. Thus, we can use inheritance to "pull up" the aElement field into an abstract decorator base class, and define concrete decorator subclasses that then only need to deal with the specific decoration. This solution, shown in Figure 7.11, is a good illustration of a design that combines ideas of composition (as seen in Chapter 6) and inheritance. Specifically, a decorator object is of a subtype that *inherits* the aElement field, which is then used to *aggregate* the instance of CardSource that is being decorated.

Fig. 7.11 Class diagram of a sample application of DECORATOR that uses inheritance

With this design, the AbstractDecorator includes default delegation to the decorated element.

```java
public class AbstractDecorator implements CardSource
{
  private final CardSource aElement;

  protected AbstractDecorator(CardSource pElement)
  { aElement = pElement; }

  public Card draw() { return aElement.draw(); }

  public boolean isEmpty() { return aElement.isEmpty(); }
}
```

It is worth noting that the `aElement` field is private. This means concrete decorator classes will not have access to it. This level of encapsulation is workable because normally in the DECORATOR, decorated elements are only accessed through the methods of the component interface. In this case, subclasses can simply use the implementation of the interface methods they inherit from `AbstractDecorator` to interact with the decorated object. As an example, the following is a basic implementation of a `LoggingDecorator` that outputs a description of the cards drawn to the console.

```java
public class LoggingDecorator extends AbstractDecorator
{
  public LoggingDecorator(CardSource pElement)
  { super(pElement); }

  public Card draw()
  {
    Card card = super.draw();
    System.out.println(card);
    return card;
  }
}
```

Class `LoggingDecorator` does not supply an implementation of `isEmpty()` because the one it inherits, which delegates the call to `aElement`, does what we want. As for `draw`, the method is redefined to do a basic draw operation using the inherited method, print the card, then return it to complete the require behavior.

7.9 The TEMPLATE METHOD Design Pattern

One potential situation with inheritance is when some common algorithm applies to objects of a certain base type, but a part of the algorithm varies from subclass to subclass. To illustrate this situation, let us go back to the design context of creating and managing moves in the Solitaire application, as discussed above in Section 7.7 and illustrated in Figure 7.9 (with `DefaultMove` renamed to `AbstractMove`). In this context we also assume that `aModel`'s access modifier is **protected**.

Let us assume that calling method `perform()` on moves *of any type* should accomplish three actions: *1)* Add the move to an undo stack, possibly located in the `GameModel`;[9] *2)* Perform the actual move; *3)* Log the move by writing out a description of what happened. This algorithm can be described with the following code, which could be in any concrete subclass of `AbstractMove`:

---

[9] This is not necessarily the best idea from a separation of concerns standpoint, but I use this example for simplicity. The Code Exploration section points to what might be a better alternative for accumulating commands.

```
public void perform()
{
  aModel.pushMove(this);
  /* Actually perform the move */
  log();
}
```

In this code, the first statement of method `perform()` pushes the current move object onto a command stack located in the game model. The block comment corresponds to the actual implementation of the move, which would vary from move to move. The final statement implements some logging of the move, for example by printing the name of the command class to the console. Let us assume the same approach is used for `undo()`, with moves being popped instead of pushed. Because parts of the code are common, it will benefit from being "pulled up" to the `AbstractMove` superclass for two main reasons:

- So that it can be reused by all concrete `Move` subclasses, thereby avoiding DUPLICATED CODE†;
- So that the design is robust to errors caused by inconsistently re-implementing common behavior. Specifically, we want to prevent the possibility that a developer could later declare a new concrete subclass of `Move` and supply it with an implementation of method `perform()` that does not do steps 1 and 3, for example.

Because the implementation of `perform()` needs information from subclasses to actually perform the move, it cannot be completely implemented in the superclass.[10] The solution to this problem is to put all the common code in the superclass, and to define some "hooks" to allow subclasses to provide specialized functionality where needed. This idea is called the TEMPLATE METHOD design pattern. The name relates to the fact that the common method in the superclass is a "template", that gets "instantiated" differently for each subclass. The "steps" are defined as non-private[11] methods in the superclass. The code below further illustrates the solution template for the TEMPLATE METHOD:

---

[10] Although, technically, it would be possible to have a SWITCH STATEMENT† in `perform()` that checks the concrete type of the object using **instanceof** or `getClass()` and executes the appropriate code for all commands, this would introduce a dependency cycle between the base class and its subclasses, and completely destroy the benefits of polymorphism. A bad idea of epic proportions.

[11] The "step methods" can have default, public, or protected visibility depending on the design context. However, they cannot be private because private methods cannot be overridden. This constraint makes sense because private methods are technically not visible outside of their class, and overriding requires method signature matching across classes.

```
public abstract class AbstractMove implements Move
{
  protected final GameModel aModel;

  protected AbstractMove(GameModel pModel)
  { aModel = pModel; }

  public final void perform()
  {
    aModel.pushMove(this);
    execute();
    log();
  }

  protected abstract void execute();

  private void log()
  { System.out.println(getClass().getName()); }
}
```

In this code example, the implementation of method `perform()` introduces two new concepts related to inheritance: *final* methods (and classes) and *abstract method declarations* in classes.

Final Methods and Classes

In Java, declaring a method to be `final` means that the method cannot be overridden by subclasses. The main purpose for declaring a method to be `final` is to clarify our intent, as designers, that a method is not meant to be overridden. One important reason for preventing overriding is to ensure that a given constraint is respected. Final methods are exactly what is needed for the TEMPLATE METHOD, because we want to ensure that the template is respected for all subclasses. By declaring the `perform()` method to be `final`, subclasses cannot override it with an implementation that would omit the call to `pushMove` or `log()`.

The use of the `final` keyword with methods has an effect that is different from the use of the same keyword with fields and local variables (see Section 4.6). The use of `final` with fields limits how we can assign values to variables, and does not involve inheritance, dynamic dispatch, or overriding.

The `final` keyword can also be used with classes. In this case, the behavior is consistent with the meaning it has for methods: classes declared to be `final` cannot be inherited. Inheritance in effect broadens the interface of a class by allowing extensions by other classes. As demonstrated in Figure 7.8 and as will be further discussed in the next section, inheritance is a powerful mechanism that can easily be misused. A good principle to follow with inheritance is "design for inheritance or else prohibit it" [1, Item 19]. In other words, inheritance should be used to support specific extension scenarios (as the one illustrated in this section), or not used at all. Because by default, it is possible to inherit from a class, the mechanism needs to be explicitly disabled to prohibit its use. Generally, stating that a class cannot be inherited tends to make a design more robust because it prevents unanticipated effects caused by inheritance. In our current example, we could decide to make immediate subclasses of `AbstractMove` **final** to make it clear to other readers of the code that the class hierarchy should not be extended through inheritance beyond a single level of concrete move subclasses.

Although performance is not a major aspect of this book, it is also worth noting that declaring classes and methods to be final can also have some positive implications for the execution speed of a program, because the absence of dynamic dispatch for final classes means that code can be optimized to run more quickly.

Abstract Methods

In the implementation of the `perform()` template method in `AbstractMove`, the second step is to perform the actual move. Within class `AbstractMove`, this step is meaningless given that an abstract move does not represent any concrete move we could perform. For this reason, we need to leave out the actual execution of the move. However, we cannot leave this step out *entirely*, because as part of our template we do need to specify that executing the move needs to happen, and needs to happen specifically after the move is pushed to the move stack and before the move execution is logged. In our design we thus specify that this computation needs to happen by calling a method. However, because in Java all methods that are called need to be declared, we must add a new method declaration. In this example I called it `execute()`, because we cannot give it the same name as the template method (this would result in a recursive call). Because we do not have any implementation for `execute()`, we can defer the implementation to the subclasses. This is allowed because `AbstractMove` is declared to be **abstract**, so there is no issue if the class's interface is not fully implemented. Although it sometimes makes sense to declare abstract methods to be public, here I declare `execute()` to be protected because the only classes that really need to see this method are the subclasses of `AbstractMove` that must supply an implementation for it.

Summary of the Pattern

The declaration of class `AbstractMove`, above, illustrates the key ideas of the solution for TEMPLATE METHOD. The following points are also important to remember about the use of the pattern:

- The method with the common algorithm in the abstract superclass is the *template method*; it calls the concrete and abstract *step methods*;
- If, in a given context, it is important that the algorithm embodied by the template method be fixed, it could be a good idea to declare the template method **final**, so it cannot be overridden (and thus changed) in subclasses;
- It is important that the abstract step method has a different signature from the template method for this design to work. Otherwise, the template method would

recursively call itself, quite possibly leading to a stack overflow; following the advice of Section 7.5 about avoiding unnecessary overloading, I would recommend actually using a different name in all cases.

- The most likely access modifier for the abstract step methods is **protected**, because in general there will likely not be any reason for client code to call individual steps that are intended to be internal parts of a complete algorithm. Client code would normally be calling the template method;
- The steps that need to be customized by subclasses do not necessarily need to be abstract. In some cases, it will make sense to have a reasonable default behavior that could be implemented in the superclass. In this case it might not be necessary to make the superclass abstract. In our example, there is a default implementation of `log()` that can be overridden by subclasses. In a different context, it might make more sense to declare this method abstract as well.

When first learning to use inheritance, the calling protocol between code in the super- and subclasses can be a bit confusing because, although it is distributed over multiple classes, the method calls are actually dispatched to the *same target object*. The sequence diagram in Figure 7.12 illustrates a call to `perform()` on a `DiscardMove` instance. As can be seen, although it is implemented in subclasses, the call to the abstract step method is a self-call.

Fig. 7.12 Call sequence in the TEMPLATE METHOD

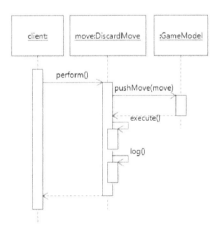

7.10 Proper Use of Inheritance

Inheritance is both a code reuse and an extensibility mechanism. This means that a subclass inherits the declarations of its superclass, but also becomes a subtype of its superclass (and its superclass's superclass, and so on). To avoid major design flaws, inheritance should only be used for *extending* the behavior of a superclass. As such, it is bad design to use inheritance to restrict the behavior of the superclass, or to use inheritance when the subclass is not a proper subtype of the superclass.

Restricting What Clients of Base Classes Can Do

As an example of a design idea to limit what a superclass can do using our running example of a deck of cards, let us say that in some design context we need to have decks of cards that should never be shuffled. Given that we already have a class (Deck) that defines everything we need to instantiate a deck, would it not be easy to simply subclass Deck to somehow "deactivate" the shuffling:

```java
public class UnshufflableDeck extends Deck
{
  public void shuffle() {/* Do nothing */}
}
```

or,

```java
public class UnshufflableDeck extends Deck
{
  public void shuffle()
  { throw new OperationNotSupportedException(); }
}
```

Actually, both versions are a bad design decision because they conflict directly with the use of polymorphism, which supports calling operations on an object independently of the concrete type of the object. Let us consider the following hypothetical calling context:

```java
private Optional<Card> shuffleAndDraw(Deck pDeck)
{
  pDeck.shuffle();
  if( !pDeck.isEmpty() )
  { return Optional.of(pDeck.draw()); }
  else
  { return Optional.empty(); }
}
```

This code will compile and, given the interface documentation of Deck, should do exactly what we want. However if, when the code executes, the run-time type of the instance passed into shuffleAndDraw happens to be an UnshufflableDeck, the code will either not work as expected (first variant, the deck silently does not get shuffled), or raise an exception (second variant). There is clearly something amiss here.

The intuition that inheritance should only be used for extension is captured by the *Liskov substitution principle* (LSP). The LSP basically states that subclasses should not restrict what clients of the superclass can do with an instance. Specifically, this means that methods of the subclass:

• Cannot have stricter preconditions;
• Cannot have less strict postconditions;

- Cannot take more specific types as parameters;
- Cannot make the method less accessible (e.g., from **public** to **protected**);
- Cannot throw more checked exceptions;
- Cannot have a less specific return type.

This list seems like a lot of things to remember when designing object-oriented software, but the whole point of the principle is that once we have assimilated its logic, we no longer need to remember specific elements in the list. In addition, all situations except for the first two points are prevented by the compiler. Nevertheless, at first some of these points can seem a bit counter-intuitive, so let us consider concrete scenarios.

Remembering our interface CardSource, which has method isEmpty() and a method draw() with the precondition !isEmpty(), we can design a new subclass of Deck that draws the highest of the two top cards on the deck, and replaces the lowest one back on top of the deck.

```
public class Deck implements CardSource
{
  protected final CardStack aCards = new CardStack();

  public Card draw() { return aCards.pop(); }
  public boolean isEmpty() { return aCards.isEmpty(); }
}

public class DrawBestDeck extends Deck
{
  public Card draw()
  {
    Card card1 = aCards.pop();
    Card card2 = aCards.pop();
    Card high = // identify highest card between card1 and card2
    Card low = // identify lowest card  between card1 and card2
    aCards.push(low);
    return high;
  }
}
```

This code is simple and easy to understand, which can be a symptom of good design. There is a catch, however: for this solution to work, the deck needs to have at least two cards in it. How can we deal with this? One solution is to rework the code of the draw override to handle both cases:

```
public Card draw()
{
  Card card1 = aCards.pop();
  if( isEmpty() ) { return card1; }
  Card card2 = aCards.pop();
  ...
}
```

However, this code is not as elegant as the first version, it is more costly to test, etc. Given that we know about design by contract (see Section 2.8), why not simply declare the precondition that, to call `draw()` on an instance of `DrawBestDeck`, there needs to be at least two cards in the deck?

```
public class DrawBestDeck extends Deck
{
  public int size() { return aCards.size(); }

  public Card draw()
  {
    assert size() >=2;
    ...
  }
}
```

This makes the precondition stricter (i.e., less tolerant), and thus violates the LSP. This is because the mere presence of the subclass makes code like this unsafe for cases where a deck has only one card.

```
if( deck.size() >=1 ) { return deck.draw(); }
```

Actually, in our specific example, the idea is bad for an additional, if less fundamental, reason. Because the inteface `CardSource` does not have a `size()` method, it is not possible to check the precondition polymorphically. To check that a call to `draw()` respects all preconditions, it would thus be necessary to do:

```
Deck deck = ...
Optional<Card> result = Optional.empty();
if( deck instanceof DrawBestDeck &&
    ((DrawBestDeck)deck).size() >= 2 ||
      !deck.isEmpty() )
{ result = Optional.of(deck.draw()); }
```

Ultimately, we solved nothing by trying to make the overridden version of `draw()` simpler, because the size check simply migrated to the client, acquiring some additional complexity in the process.

Similarly, the LSP is the reason why Java does not allow overriding methods to take more specific types as parameters or have less specific types as return types. Let us say we add a method `init(Deck)` to the interface of `Deck` that re-initializes the target instance to contain exactly the cards in the argument. If we have a `MemorizingDeck` in our class hierarchy, we might be tempted to override `init` in `MemorizingDeck` to initialize both the cards and the drawn cards, as illustrated in Figure 7.13.

Fig. 7.13 Invalid attempt at method overriding that does not respect the LSP

Although this code will compile, it will actually create an *overloaded* version of init as opposed to an *overridden* version, as perhaps expected. This is extremely confusing. The systematic use of the @Override annotation (see Section 7.4) would help flag this as a problem, but otherwise, the code would lead to very mysterious executions, given that the result of both calls to init would be different in the code below:

```
Deck deck = new Deck();
MemorizingDeck memorizingDeck = new MemorizingDeck();
Deck mDeck = memorizingDeck;
deck.init(memorizingDeck); // Calls MemorizingDeck.init
deck.init(mDeck); // Calls Deck.init
```

The reason for this seemingly strange behavior is again to ensure the design respects the LSP. If clients of the base class Deck can call init and pass in instances of *any* subtype of Deck, then it would be limiting what they can do to require the clients to only pass certain subtypes to init (like MemorizingDeck).

The case of return types simply inverses the logic: if a method returns an object of a certain type, it should be possible to assign it to a variable of that type. If subclasses can redefine methods to return more general types, then it would no longer be possible to complete the assignment. For example, let us say that in a (bad) design, a developer adds a version of Deck that contains a joker card, and that objects that represent jokers are not subtypes of Card, but merely subtypes of the Object root type. Then calls like this:

```
Card card = deck.draw();
```

would become problematic if some versions of method draw() can return objects that are not subtypes of Card.

The classic example of a violation of the LSP is the so-called Circle–Ellipse problem, wherein a class to represent a circle is defined by inheriting from an Ellipse class and preventing clients from creating any ellipse instance that does not have equal proportions. This violates the LSP because clients that use an Ellipse base class can set the height to be different from the width, and introducing a Circle subclass would eliminate this possibility:

```
Ellipse ellipse = getEllipse();
// Not possible if ellipse is an instance of Circle
ellipse.setWidthAndHeight(100, 200);
```

How to avoid the Circle–Ellipse problem in practice will, as usual, depend on the context. In some cases, it may not be necessary to have a type Circle in the first place. For example, in a drawing editor, user interface features could be responsible for assisting users in creating ellipses that happen to be circles, while still storing these as instances of Ellipse internally. In cases where a type Circle can be useful, it might make sense to have different Circle and Ellipse classes that are siblings in the type hierarchy, etc.

Subclasses That Are Not Proper Subtypes

Inheritance accomplishes two things (see Section 7.2):

- It reuses the class member declarations of the base class as part of the definition of the subclass;
- In introduces a subtype–supertype relation between the subclass and the superclass.

To use inheritance properly, it has to make sense for the subclass to need *both* of these features. A common abuse of inheritance is to employ it only for reuse, and overlook the fact that subtyping does not make sense:

> Inheritance is appropriate only in circumstances where the subclass really is a *subtype* of the superclass. In other words, a class *B* should extend a class *A* only if an "is-a" relationship exists between the two classes. [1, p. 92]

Some well-known acknowledged violations of this principle include the library type `Stack` (which inappropriately inherits from `Vector`), and `Properties` (which inappropriately inherits from `Hashtable`). When subtyping is not appropriate, composition should be used.

Insights

This chapter introduced inheritance as a mechanism to support code reuse and extensibility.

- Use inheritance to factor out implementation that is common among subtypes of a given root type and avoid DUPLICATED CODE†;
- UML class diagrams can describe inheritance-related design decisions effectively;
- To the extent possible, use the services provided by a subclass through polymorphism, to avoid the error-prone practice of downcasting;
- Even in the presence of inheritance, consider keeping your field declarations private to the extent possible, as this ensures tighter encapsulation;
- Subclasses should be designed to complement, or specialize, the functionality provided by a base class, as opposed to redefining completely different behavior;
- Use the `@Override` annotation to avoid hard-to-find errors when defining overriding relations between methods;
- Because it can easily lead to code that is difficult to understand, keep overloading to a minimum. Overloading is best avoided altogether when the parameter types of the different versions of a method are in a subtyping relation with each other;
- Inheritance- and composition-based approaches are often viable alternative when looking for a design solution. When exploring inheritance-based solutions, consider whether composition might not be better;

- Ensure that subclasses that extend a base class can also be considered meaningful subtypes of the base class, namely that instances of the subclass are in a "is-a" relation with the base class;
- Ensure that any inheritance-based design respects the Liskov substitution principle. In particular, do not use inheritance to restrict the features of the base class;
- If some of the fields and methods that can be isolated through inheritance do not add up to a data structure that it makes sense to instantiate, encapsulate them in an abstract class;
- Remember that abstract classes can define abstract methods, and that methods of the abstract class can call its own abstract methods. This way you can use abstract classes to define abstract implementations of algorithms;
- Consider using the TEMPLATE METHOD pattern in cases where an algorithm applies to all subclasses of a certain base class, except for some steps of the algorithm that must vary from subclass to subclass;
- If there is no obvious scenario for overriding a method, consider declaring it `final`. Similarly, if there is no specific reason for a class to be extensible using inheritance, consider declaring it `final`.

Code Exploration

Inheritance is a specialized mechanism that it only makes sense to use to provide design solutions for the specific kinds of contexts discussed in this chapter. The main implication for this specialization is that inheritance is used less often than composition. For example, the two more basic example applications discussed in this book, the Minesweeper and Solitaire projects, are completely realized without the help of inheritance.[12] The JetUML project, however, provides numerous examples of class hierarchies that illustrate many of the aspects discussed in this chapter.

Edge Class Hierarchy

JetUML defines a class hierarchy rooted at interface `Edge` (itself a subinterface of the more general `DiagramElement`). There is a lot going on in the `Edge` hierarchy. This discussion will focus on how I used subclasses to progressively extend the data stored by edge objects.

The immediate implementation type for interface `Edge` is `AbstractEdge`. As it turns out, this class already inherits another abstract class `AbstractDiagramElement`. Class `AbstractDiagramElement` groups declarations that apply to both nodes and edges, whereas its subclass `AbstractEdge` adds fields that are only relevant to edges. These fields include a reference to the start and end node for the edge,

---

[12] With the exception of the subclassing necessary to use the graphical user interface framework, introduced in Chapter 8.

the diagram in which the edge is located, and an additional `View` object discussed below. The separation between `AbstractDiagramElement` and `AbstractEdge` illustrates how in practice it might be necessary to have multiple abstract classes inheriting from each other.

Among the different subclasses of `AbstractEdge`, let us focus on `SingleLabelEdge`. This class is also abstract! It simply adds one field that corresponds to a label on the edge. Thus, `SingleLabelEdge` can be subclassed by any class intended to represent a UML edge that has at least one label. For example, `ReturnEdge` (which represents a return edge in a sequence diagram) is a concrete subclass because return edges only need one label. However, some edges require three labels. `ThreeLabelEdge` is a fourth abstract class down the `Edge` class hierarchy that adds two more label fields, for a total of three. The following class down the inheritance hierarchy is `ClassRelationshipEdge`. This class serves no real purpose, and is an artifact of a previous design that will be refactored eventually. The classes that represent actual edges are the leaves of the class hierarchy, and their names map to the names of UML edges (aggregation, generalization, etc.). Note how these classes are declared to be final.

NodeView Class Hierarchy

The `Edge` class hierarchy discussed above provides a rich illustration of field inheritance. In contrast, the `NodeView` hierarchy provides many interesting examples of method inheritance. In JetUML, *views* are objects that specialize in handling the position and look of diagram objects. If we include the methods inherited from its super-interface `DiagramElementView`, the methods of the `NodeView` interface include things like `draw`, `getBounds`, `getConnectionPoints`, etc. All things that have to do with the geometry of the nodes.

Let us start our study of the `NodeView` hierarchy at the top, with a look at `AbstractNodeView`. One thing to note already is that the class does not provide an implementation for the interface methods `draw` or `getBounds()`. This is consistent with the concept of abstract classes. Here it would be meaningless to draw something that is not concrete, so we leave it out.

The implementation of method `contains()`, however, involves an interesting quirk: it calls the object's own `getBounds()` method, for which no implementation is provided in the `AbstractNodeView` class. This is an example where we can provide a complete implementation for one service (to see if a point is contained in a node) by relying on the existence of another service (getting the bounds for a node) whose implementation is delegated to the subclasses.

Another example of interesting collaboration between classes within a type hierarchy is the relation between `InterfaceNodeView` and its subclass `ClassNodeView`. These represent the views for the corresponding nodes in a class diagram. The nodes are very similar, except for the fact that class nodes have a box for attributes, which interface nodes do not have. The two views thus require very similar algorithms for computing the size of the node, with only small variants to account for the middle box for attributes for class nodes. The commonality is achieved by defining methods `computeTop()` and `computeBottom()` in `InterfaceNodeView`, which are then used to compute `getBounds()`. All three methods can then be inherited by `ClassNodeView`. However, for `computeTop()` to work for *both* class and interface nodes, it needs to know whether there is a middle compartment below the top or not. This information is obtained through a protected method `needsMiddleCompartment` defined in class `InterfaceNodeView`. Thus, when method `draw` gets called on `ClassNodeView`, it calls "up" its inherited method `getBounds()`, which calls `computeTop()`, which calls `needsMiddleCompartment`, which gets dynamically dispatched "down" to the implementation defined in `ClassNodeView`. As this example illustrates, sharing code between superclasses and subclasses can get a bit tricky.

Further Reading

The Java Tutorial [10] has a section on interfaces and inheritance that provides complementary material on inheritance, with a focus on the programming language aspects.

In terms of design guidelines, Chapter 4 of *Effective Java* [1], titled "Classes and Interfaces" provides many items of guidance that have influenced the content of this chapter. Examples include Item 18, "Favor composition over inheritance" and Item 19 "Design and document for inheritance or else prohibit it", both of which are referenced in the chapter.

Chapter 8
Inversion of Control

This chapter covers:

> **Concepts and Principles:** Inversion of control, Model–View–Controller (MVC) decomposition, callback method;
> **Programming Mechanisms:** Application framework, event loop, Graphical User Interface (GUI) component graph;
> **Design Techniques:** Adapter inheritance, event handling, GUI design;
> **Patterns and Antipatterns:** Pairwise Dependencies†, Observer, Visitor.

Inversion of control is a powerful idea in software design. Simply stated, it involves reversing the usual flow of control from caller code to called code to achieve a better separation of concerns and looser coupling. It allows us to build sophisticated applications while keeping the overall design complexity down to a manageable level. One of the main realizations of the principle takes the form of the Observer pattern. This pattern is pervasive in software development, and it is realized by most graphical user interface toolkits on most software development platforms, from desktop to web to mobile applications.

Design Context

Inversion of control brings the level of discussion to a higher level of abstraction that needs to consider the design of an entire application. To be able to focus on the issue of inversion of control, this chapter introduces new design contexts. The context used as a running example for the chapter is that of a small application to allow the user to select and view a number in different formats (e.g., Arabic vs. Roman numerals). A different context, of an inventory management system, is introduced in Section 8.4 to provide an additional example. I return to the design of recursive

© Springer Nature Switzerland AG 2019
M. P. Robillard, *Introduction to Software Design with Java*,
https://doi.org/10.1007/978-3-030-24094-3_8

card source structures seen in previous chapters to introduce the VISITOR pattern in
Section 8.8. In the Code Exploration section, I then discuss how the concepts introduced in this chapter apply in the context of the card game applications discussed in
previous chapters.

8.1 Motivating Inversion of Control

One concrete situation that motivates inversion of control in software design is when
a number of stateful objects need to be kept consistent. An example from the programming domain itself is an integrated development environment like Eclipse or
IntelliJ IDEA, which presents different views of the source code. In Eclipse, for example, the Package Explorer and Outline views shows the structure of a class that
can also be viewed in the source code editor (see Figure 8.1). If a user changes the
class declaration, for example by adding a field in the source code editor, this change
is immediately reflected in all the different views. Likewise, if the user reorders the
method declarations in the Outline view, the new order of method declarations is
reflected in the source code editor. Hence, we could say that the problem we are trying to solve is one of *synchronization*,[1] where we are trying to keep different objects
consistent with each other.

Fig. 8.1 Three different views of the source code in Eclipse

To isolate the issue of view synchronization, I distilled the design problem into
a toy application called LuckyNumber. The application allows a user to select a
number (presumed to be lucky) between 1 and 10 inclusively. The interesting part
of the application, however, is that users can select their lucky number in different
ways, for example by entering the digit(s) that represent the number, typing out the
name of the number in English, or selecting it from a slider (see Figure 8.2).

---

[1] The term *synchronization* is often used in the context of concurrent programming, a topic that is
outside the scope of this book.

Fig. 8.2 Screenshot of the
LuckyNumber application

In the application, each horizontal panel allows the user to view the number in a specific way, but also to change the number. If the number is changed in one panel, the change is immediately reflected in all other panels. In addition to its current features, one requirement for this application is that it can be extended to accommodate any additional type of view. For example, old-fashioned users may request the option to select their number using Roman numerals, geeky users may want to use binary notation, etc.

A consequence of implementing this functionality naively is to be left with complete PAIRWISE DEPENDENCIES†. With PAIRWISE DEPENDENCIES†, whenever the user changes the number in a panel, this panel directly contacts all other panels and updates their view of the number. Figure 8.3 illustrates these dependencies in a class diagram.

Fig. 8.3 Example of PAIR-
WISE DEPENDENCIES†

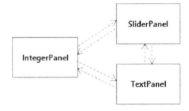

This design suffers from at least the following two related limitations:

- **High coupling**: Each panel explicitly depends on many other panels. Panels could be of different types and require different types of interactions. For example, to update the number it may be necessary to call `setDigit` on one panel and `setSliderValue` on a different panel.
- **Low Extensibility**: To add or remove a panel, it is necessary to modify all other panels. For example, to remove the slider panel, it would be necessary to modify all other panels to remove the statements that update the slider panel. Similarly, to add a Roman numeral panel, it would be necessary to change every panel to add some statements to manage the new panel, etc.

What is even worse, is that the impact of these issues increases quadratically with the number of panels, given that there are $n \cdot (n-1)$ directed edges in a complete graph with n vertices. In the initial application with three panels, we need six call dependencies to keep all panels synchronized. This may not seem like much, but if we throw in a Roman numeral panel and a binary notation panel, for a total of five, then we need 20 dependencies scattered over five components, just to keep a single number consistent. This is poor separation of concerns, because a significant amount of code will be required to manage the dependencies that is likely to end up tangled with code that more directly supports the required logic (e.g., adjusting a slider). The code will also be less understandable, harder to test, etc.

8.2 The Model–View–Controller Decomposition

One way out of using complete pairwise dependencies to synchronize multiple representations of the same data is to separate abstractions responsible for *storing data* from abstractions responsible for *viewing data*, from abstractions responsible for *changing data*. This key insight is generally known as *Model–View–Controller* (MVC) from the name of the three abstractions. The *Model* is the abstraction that keeps the unique copy of the data of interest. In our simple context, that would be the lucky number. The *View* is, not surprisingly, the abstraction that represents one view of the data. Generally in a MVC decomposition there can be more than one view of the same model. This is illustrated in the LuckyNumber application by the presence of different views for something as simple as a single integer. Finally, the *Controller* is the abstraction of the functionality necessary to change the data stored in the model.

The origin of the MVC is somewhat obscure. The idea can be traced back to the late 1970s and Xerox PARC researchers working on SmallTalk software, but there is little besides a few memos in terms of written reports on the original development of the concept. Currently, the term MVC is used fairly loosely. Some software developers refer to it as a design pattern. Others refer to it as something slightly different called an "architectural pattern" or "architectural style" (a bit like a design pattern, but at a higher level of design abstraction). Some refer to it simply as a general concept. Finally, some web technology platforms use the terms model, view, and controller to refer to specific software components. Because I see the main benefit of the Model–View–Controller as a guideline to separate concerns, I like to think of it simply as a *decomposition* (of concerns). In this sense, it is more general than a design pattern, because it does not include a solution template that is specific enough to apply directly.

The lack of a well-defined solution template for the MVC means that there is little guidance on how to realize the idea in practice. This also means that there are innumerable ways to go about separating the model, view, and controller in a design context. For example, the model could be a single object, or a collection of objects. The view and controller could be different objects, or fused together. In the latter case, the separation of concerns would be organized along the interfaces of objects rather than the objects themselves (see Section 3.8 on the idea of interface segregation).

Such a vague concept as the MVC is not easy to grasp in itself when learning software design. Fortunately, there exists a related idea that is much more concrete, namely the OBSERVER pattern.

8.3 The OBSERVER Design Pattern

The central idea of the OBSERVER pattern is to store data of interest in a specialized object, and to allow other objects to *observe* this data. The object that stores the data of interest is called alternatively the *subject*, *model*, or *observable*,[2] and it corresponds to the Model abstraction in the Model–View–Controller decomposition. For this reason, the *context* for the OBSERVER corresponds to the motivation discussed in Section 8.1: we want a simple way to manage multiple objects interested in the same data. The class diagram of Figure 8.4 illustrates how this is realized for the LuckyNumber application.

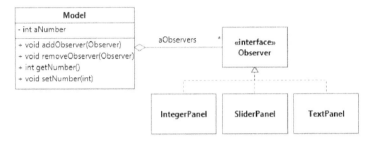

Fig. 8.4 Application of the OBSERVER to the LuckyNumber application

In this situation, the object in charge of keeping the data is an instance of `Model`. Here an instance of `Model` keeps track of a single integer and allows clients to query and change this integer.

Linking Model and Observers

Where things become interesting is that the `Model` class also includes an aggregation to an `Observer` interface, with methods to add and remove `Observer` instances from its collection. This is also called *registering* (or *deregistering*) observers. The mechanism for managing observers can be trivially implemented, for example:

---

[2] See Section 3.2 on the use of the "–able" suffix to name interfaces.

```
public class Model
{
  private int aNumber = 5;
  private ArrayList<Observer> aObservers = new ArrayList<>();

  public void addObserver(Observer pObserver)
  { aObservers.add(pObserver); }

  public void removeObserver(Observer pObserver)
  { aObservers.remove(pObserver); }
}
```

Classes that define objects that would be interested in observing the model must then declare to implement the `Observer` interface:

```
class IntegerPanel implements Observer { ... }
```

Through polymorphism, we thus achieve loose coupling between the model and its observers. Specifically:

- The model can be used without any observer;
- The model is aware that it can be observed, but its implementation does not depend on any concrete observer class;
- It is possible to register and deregister observers at run time.

Control Flow Between Model and Observers

A first key question about the relation between a model an its observers is, how do the observers learn that there is a change in the state of the model that they need to know about? The answer is that whenever there is a change in the model's state worth reporting to observers, the model should let the observers know by cycling through the list of observers and calling a certain method on them. This method has to be defined on the `Observer` interface and is usually called a "callback" method because of the inversion of control that it implies. We talk of inversion of control because to find out information from the model the observers do not call a method on the model, they instead "wait" for the model to call them (back). This idea is often referred to as the "Hollywood Principle" ("don't call us, we'll call you"). That is also why the method that is called by the model on the observer is called a "callback". Continuing with the movie industry metaphor, the name of the method to call back is a bit like the phone number of the prospective actor. If the casting agent determines that the actor should be auditioned, they will call the number. Likewise, if the model determines that the observers should be notified, it will call their callback method.

In the case of the LuckyNumber application, an appropriate name for the callback method would be `newNumber`, given that this is the method that will be called whenever the model needs to inform its observers that it has changed the number it is storing. We can thus define this method in the `Observer` interface:

```java
public interface Observer
{
  void newNumber(int pNumber);
}
```

When first learning about callbacks, their logic can be a bit puzzling, especially if the name of the callback is ambiguous. In the case above, it may look like the method is intended to *set* a new number on an observer, because it would be called like this:

```java
someObserver.newNumber(5);
```

However, the method name should not be mentally read as "set number to this new value", but rather as "the model has a new number, here it is". In other words, the idea of a callback is not to *tell observers what to do*, but rather to *inform* observers about some change in the model, and let them deal with it as they see fit (through the logic provided in the callback). The analogy with the movie studio still works. If an actor (the observer) gets an audition, the studio might call them and say "you have an audition", but not specify the details of how to react to this information (e.g., by preparing, arranging transportation, etc.). The lesson here is that to help others easily understand a design, it is a good practice to name callback methods with a name that describes a state-change situation, as opposed to a command. In our case, other explicit names for the callback method would include `numberChanged` and `hasNewNumber`.

Once we have a callback defined, within class `Model`, we can create a helper method, called a *notification method*[3] that will notify all observers and provide them with the number they should know about:

```java
public class Model
{
  private void notifyObservers()
  {
    for(Observer observer : aObservers)
    { observer.newNumber(aNumber); }
  }
}
```

To ensure that the model dutifully notifies observers whenever a state change occurs, two strategies are possible:

- A call to the notification method must be inserted in every state-changing method; in this case the method can be declared **private**;
- Clear documentation has to be provided to direct users of the model class to call the notification method whenever the model should inform observers. In this case the notification methods needs to be non-private.

As usual, which strategy is better depends on the context. In cases where notifications can simply be issued for every model change, the first method provides a

---

[3] In Java the notification method cannot be called simply `notify()`, because a legacy method with this name is already defined in class `Object`.

simpler life cycle for the state of the model. However, in certain cases, notifying observers with every state change may lead to some performance problems. For example, if we had a model that could be initialized with a large collection of data items by adding each item one at a time, notifying observers after each individual addition may dramatically degrade the performance while providing no benefit. In situations such as this one, it may be better to change the model *silently* (without notifying the observers), and then trigger a notification once the batch operation is done. In cases where such flexibility is needed, the second strategy can provide it.

The sequence diagram of Figure 8.5 illustrates what happens when we change the model on the "LuckyNumber" application, using the first strategy.

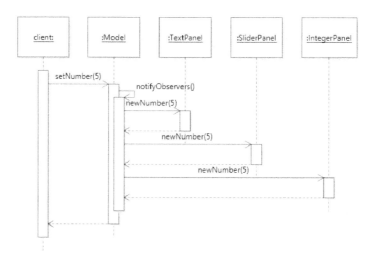

Fig. 8.5 Call sequence for the OBSERVER

Inside the state-changing method `setNumber(int)`, we added a call to `notifyObservers` to loop through each observer and call the method `newNumber` on each. The implementation of the `newNumber` callback dictates how each observer reacts to the change in state. In the case of the LuckyNumber application, each observer deals with the callback in a different way. For example, the `IntegerPanel` simply sets the number of the integer in a text field; the `TextPanel` looks up the name of the integer in an array (for example), and sets the value of the text field to that string; the `SliderPanel` positions the slider to correspond to the value, etc.

Data Flow between Model and Observers

The second key question about the relation between a model and its observers is, how do the observers access the information that they need to know about from the model? Two main strategies are available. The first strategy is to make the information of interest available through one or more parameters of the callback. This strategy is also known as the *push* data-flow strategy because the model is explicitly "pushing" data of a pre-determined structure to the observers.

Applying this strategy to our context, we could define the callback method to include a parameter that represents the number most recently stored in the model. This is the strategy that was illustrated above with the `newNumber(int)` callback.

```
public interface Observer
{ void newNumber(int pNumber); }
```

This way, whenever a callback method is called on an observer, the implementation of the callback can obtain the value of interest from the argument bound to the parameter. For example, relevant parts of the implementation of the `IntegerPanel` would look like this:

```
class IntegerPanel implements Observer
{
  // User interface element that represents a text field
  private TextField aText = new TextField();

  ...

  public void newNumber(int pNumber)
  { aText.setText(Integer.toString(pNumber)); }
}
```

This strategy makes one big assumption: that we know in advance what type of data from the model the observers will be interested in. In our case this strategy looks like a good fit because there is nothing but a single integer that observers could be interested in. However, this is not the general case. For example, we could enhance the model to remember each lucky number ever selected, and the timestamp of its selection. Observers now have more data to choose from. Given the context, we could still assume that the most common case for an observer will be to show the most recent number, but more sophisticated observers might want to show the last three numbers, for example, or the amount of time a certain number remained selected.

As another example, let us consider that we want to turn the `Deck` class discussed in previous chapters into a model. What would observers be interested in? Again, one usage scenario stands out: to show the card drawn. So we could fix this expectation with the callback:

```
public interface DeckObserver
{ void cardDrawn(Card pCard); }
```

However, in some cases this might be too strict. Some observers might be interested in the number of cards left in the deck, or they may want to know about the top card, etc.

A more flexible strategy is instead to let observers "pull" the data they want from the model using query methods defined on the model. Appropriately, this approach is known as the *pull* data-flow strategy. To convert the design of the LuckyNumber application to use the pull strategy, we could exchange the `pNumber` parameter with one that would refer to the entire model:

```
public interface Observer
{ void newNumber(Model pModel); }
```

That way, the data to put in the text field must be obtained from the model:

```
class IntegerView implements Observer
{
  // User interface element that represents a text field
  private TextField aText = new TextField();

  ...

  public void newNumber(Model pModel)
  { aText.setText(Integer.toString(pModel.getNumber())); }
}
```

Now, any data available through the methods of class `Model` also becomes available to the observers. To implement the pull data flow strategy, observers must have a reference to the model, but this reference must not necessarily be provided as an argument to the callback method. Another option is to initialize observer objects with a reference to the model (stored as a field), and simply refer to that field as necessary. This design is illustrated in the class diagram of Figure 8.6. Here the design makes it clear that the reference to the model is obtained through the constructor.

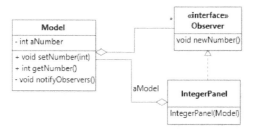

Fig. 8.6 Class diagram of LuckyNumber as a model using the pull data-flow strategy for observers

At first glance, it may look like the pull data-flow strategy introduces a circular dependency between a model and its observers, given that both depend on each other. However, the crucial difference is that in this design, the model does not know the concrete type of its observers. Through interface segregation, the only slice of behavior that the model needs from observers is their callback methods. This being said, one of the main drawbacks of the pull data-flow strategy is that it does, indeed, increase the coupling between model and its observers. In the design of Figure 8.6, observers can not only call `getNumber()`, they can also call `setNumber(int)`! In other words, by holding a reference to the model, observers have access to much more of the interface of the model than they need. Fortunately, we saw how to deal with this situation with the Interface Segregation Principle (ISP, see Section 3.2). To apply ISP to our design, we could create a new interface `ModelData` that only includes the getter methods for the model, and only refer to this type in the observers. Figure 8.7 illustrates this solution.

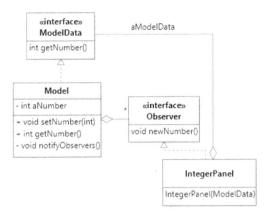

Fig. 8.7 Class diagram of the pull method with ISP

Although I presented them here separately, the push and pull strategies can be trivially combined, for example by specifying a callback that includes a parameter for both data from the model and a reference back to the model. This design would not be very useful in our scenario, but I include its implementation for sake of illustration:

```
public interface Observer
{ void newNumber(int pNumber, Model pModel); }
```

In general, supporting both strategies can help increase the reusability of the `Observer` interface at the cost of a more complex design that may include situations where one parameter is not used.[4] At the other extreme, for simple design contexts it may be the case that the only information that needs to flow between the model and the observers is the fact that a given callback method was invoked. In such cases, neither the push nor the pull strategy is required: receiving the callback invocation is enough information for the observers to do their job. An observer that serves as a counter of a type of event would be one example.

As a final remark regarding the flow of data between the model and its observers, it is worth noting that in the examples above, none of the callbacks return any value (i.e., they have return type **void**). This is not a design decision, but rather a constraint of the pattern. Because the model is supposed to ignore how many observers it has, it can be tricky for observers to attempt to manage the model by returning some value. Technically, it is possible to declare the return type of callbacks to be non-void, and to aggregate the results across many invocations. For example, one could design the callback to return **true** if it somehow succeeded in responding to the callback (and **false** otherwise), and have the model apply a logical operator on the results. Such schemes represent uncommon and possibly abusive use of the pattern. When

---

[4] The Java library includes a pair of types, `Observable` and `Observer`, where `Observer` defines the single callback **void** `update(Observable, Object)`, which supports both data-flow strategies.

starting out with the OBSERVER, my recommendation is to always declare callbacks to return **void**.

Event-Based Programming

One way to think about callback methods is as *events*, with the model being the *event source* and the observers being the *event handlers*. Within this paradigm, the model generates a series of events that correspond to different state changes of interest, and other objects are in charge of reacting to these events. What events correspond to in practice are simply method calls. Thinking about observers as event handlers helps realize that we actually have a lot of flexibility when designing callbacks. In the LuckyNumber application, the design to date has involved a single callback, newNumber. However, for sake of discussion, we can imagine a situation where a Model might be used by observers that are sometimes interested only if the lucky number increased (or, conversely, decreased), or whether the number is set to its maximum or minimum value. Implementing this feature in the current design would be a bit clumsy: every observer would have to store a copy of the number, and check it against the new number just to determine if it has increased or decreased, in addition to checking for maximum or minimum value. We can do things differently by adjusting the design of the callbacks to explicitly capture the events of interest:

```
public interface Observer
{
  void increased(int pNumber);
  void decreased(int pNumber);
  void changedToMax(int pNumber);
  void changedToMin(int pNumber);
}
```

With this design, observers do not need to store a copy of the old number, and they can be notified of precisely the event they are interested in.[5] In cases where an observer does not need to react to an event, the unused callbacks can be implemented as "do-nothing" methods. In the class below, it is assumed that the events are mutually exclusive, namely that the event increased means "increased but not to the maximum value", and similarly for decreased.

```
class IncreaseDetector implements Observer
{
  public void increased(int pNumber)
  { System.out.println("Increased to " + pNumber); }

  public void decreased(int pNumber) {}
  public void changedToMax(int pNumber) {}
  public void changedToMin(int pNumber) {}
}
```

---

[5] Whether we need the parameter for the changeToMax and changeToMin methods depends on the context, i.e., whether the minimum and maximum values are known globally.

If this "do nothing" situation occurs too often, it is possible to implement a "do nothing" class and inherit from it instead. Such "do nothing" classes are sometimes called *adapters*:

```
public class ObserverAdapter implements Observer
{
  public void increased(int pNumber) {}
  public void decreased(int pNumber) {}
  public void changedToMax(int pNumber) {}
  public void changedToMin(int pNumber) {}
}
```

With an adapter, the "do nothing" behavior becomes inherited, and observers can override only the subset of callbacks that correspond to the events they need to respond to:

```
class IncreaseDetector extends ObserverAdapter
{
  public void increased(int pNumber)
  { System.out.println("Increased to " + pNumber); }
}
```

In some cases, extensive use of "do nothing" code might point to a mismatch between the varied needs of observers and the design of the callbacks. Again, it is possible to rely on the interface segregation principle to clean things up. In our situation, we could define *two* observer interfaces that correspond to more specialized event handlers. For example:

```
public interface ChangeObserver
{
  void increased(int pNumber) {}
  void decreased(int pNumber) {}
}

public interface BoundsReachedObserver
{
  void changedToMax(int pNumber) {}
  void changedToMin(int pNumber) {}
}
```

With two abstract observers, concrete observers can be more targeted and only register for the sets of events they need to respond to. The trade-off for more flexibility is a slightly heavier interface for the `Model` class, because it now has to support two lists of observers with their corresponding registration methods.

Summary

The context for using the OBSERVER is fairly rich: it involves situations where many objects should be able to observe some data, and become aware of changes to the state of this data, while minimizing the coupling between the data and the observers of that data. Given a class that represents the data (the *model*), the solution template for the pattern involves making objects of this class observable by aggregating a number of *abstract observers* (usually defined with an interface). The following are the usual variation points when applying the OBSERVER:

- What callbacks methods to define on an abstract observer. An abstract observer can have any number of callbacks that can correspond to different types of events;
- What data flow strategy to use to move data between the model and observers (push, pull, none, or both);
- Whether to use a single abstract observer or multiple ones. Multiple abstract observers with different combinations of callbacks give observers more flexibility to respond to certain events or not;
- How to connect observers with the model if observers need to query or control the model. Here the use of the interface segregation principle is recommended;
- Whether to include a notification helper method and, if so, whether to make this method public or private. If public, clients with references to the model get to control when notifications are issued. If private, it is assumed that the method is called at appropriate places in the state-changing methods of the model.

The listing below shows the complete code of the `Model` and `Observer` type declarations for the variant that uses the push data-flow strategy.

```java
public interface Observer { void newNumber(int pNumber); }

public class Model
{
  private List<Observer> aObservers = new ArrayList<>();
  private int aNumber = 5;

  public void addObserver(Observer pObserver)
  { aObservers.add(pObserver); }

  public void removeObserver(Observer pObserver)
  { aObservers.remove(pObserver); }

  private void notifyObservers()
  {
    for(Observer observer : aObservers)
    { observer.newNumber(aNumber); }
  }

  public void setNumber(int pNumber)
  {
    if( pNumber <= 0 ) { aNumber = 1; }
    else if( pNumber > 10 ) { aNumber = 10; }
    else { aNumber = pNumber; }
    notifyObservers();
  }
}
```

8.4 Applying the OBSERVER Design Pattern

Although the basic idea of the OBSERVER is not overly complex, applying it involves making numerous design decisions. To provide some insights on the process of applying the OBSERVER pattern and further illustrate the rationale behind some of the trade-offs involved, the following discusses a sample application of the pattern for a different scenario:

> We need an inventory system capable of keeping track of electronic equipment. An Item of equipment records a serial number and production year (both of type **int**). An Inventory object aggregates zero or more objects of type Item. Clients can add or remove Items from the Inventory at any time. Various entities are interested in changes to the state of the Inventory. For example, it should be possible to show the items in the Inventory in a ListView. It should also be possible to view a PieChart representing the proportion of Items in the Inventory for each production year (e.g., 2017 = 25%; 2018 = 30%, etc.). Views should be updated whenever items are added or removed from the Inventory.

Fig. 8.8 Class diagram of the domain elements for the inventory context

As a first approach to this design problem we can model the basic elements of the domain with a class diagram, shown in Figure 8.8. This diagram captures all the relevant domain elements, but little else. The following step is to set up a basic OBSERVER solution. At this stage this requires realizing which domain object plays which role in the pattern. In our case the object containing the observable data would be an instance of Inventory, and the objects observing this data would be PieChart and ListView. The refined design is shown in Figure 8.9. To relate the observers to the model, the solution now includes an abstract observer in the form of the Observer interface.

The basic mechanism for linking observers with the Inventory is now in place. At this point we need to define one or more callback methods. Because there are only two possible events in this simple context (adding and removing items), there are two choices for callback methods:

- A single callback method that indicates that the state of the inventory has changed (i.e., an item was added or removed);
- One callback to indicate an item was added, and a different callback to indicate than an item was removed.

The first option would end up being called something like inventoryChanged. Concrete observers who care about whether an item was either added or removed

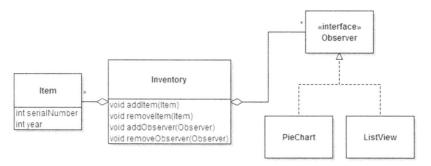

Fig. 8.9 Basic application of the OBSERVER to the inventory context

would need a way to determine this information. The information could be passed as an argument to the callback (e.g., through a value of an enumerated type ADDED or REMOVED), or by some other means (e.g., storing whether the last item was added or removed in the model and accessing this information through a getter). In our context, such schemes are starting to look unnecessary convoluted. To carry the information of what type of event happened in the model, we will choose the option of using two different callback methods to represent the two different types of events.

The next question is how to tell observers *which* item has been added or removed. Our options are to use the push or pull data flow strategies. Let us try both, starting with the pull strategy. With this approach, we could include a reference to the Inventory that changed as part of the callback, and add a method getLastItemAddedOrRemoved() that returns the last item that was either added to or removed from the inventory. Figure 8.10 shows a class diagram that illustrates the design decisions so far. If to have a single method to return the last item added or removed seems awkward, we can also use two methods, getLastItemAdded() and getLastItemRemoved(). However, in this case we have to store two additional pieces of information instead of one and, depending on the design of the Inventory class, this may make the life cycle of the object more complex (see Section 4.4).

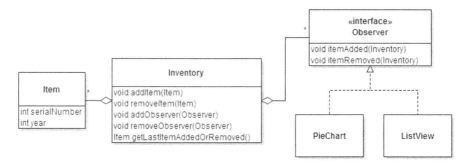

Fig. 8.10 Application of the OBSERVER to the inventory context with two callback methods using the pull data-flow strategy

Another option, somewhat more radical, would be *not* to provide a way to get the last item added or removed, and force observers to update themselves by going through the entire inventory on each event notification. One way to do this would be to make the `Inventory` class implement `Iterable<Item>` so that the concrete observers can iterate through the entire list of items. In this case, the code implementing a callback would look like this:

```
public class PieChart implements Observer
{
  public void itemAdded(Inventory pInventory)
  {
    for( Item item : pInventory ) {...}
  }
  ...
}
```

Although it may sound inefficient, this decision makes sense in some contexts where the data set is small and where observers are likely to be more interested in the complete data set rather than individual changes.

Returning to our context, let us now explore the push data-flow strategy instead. Passing the added or removed item to the observers as an argument to the callback seems like a more effective choice in our case, because it eliminates the need to capture whether an item of interest was added or removed. With this strategy we would end up with callback methods `itemAdded(Item)` and `itemRemoved(Item)`.

Another question to consider at this point is how to trigger notifications. Here, having a single `notifyObservers(Item)` does not work well, because this method would need to determine which callback method to call on the observers (`itemAdded` or `itemRemoved`). Given the simplicity of the context, I would choose to simply invoke the callback methods directly in `addItem` and `removeItem`. The code below shows the implementation of `addItem`, and Figure 8.11 shows the current design.

```
public class Inventory
{
  public void addItem(Item pItem)
  {
    aItems.add(pItem);
    for( Observer observer : aObservers )
    { observer.itemAdded(pItem); }
  }
  ...
}
```

Assuming two observers are registered with the inventory (one instance of `PieChart` and one instance of `ListView`), a sequence that illustrates an item being added is shown in Figure 8.12. The figure helps illustrate the distinction between a *command* and a *callback*. The method invoked on the model is a command, and its name uses the imperative mood ("add [an] item"). In contrast, methods invoked on the observers are callbacks, and their name uses the past participle, to indicate a past event ("[an] item [was] added"). The use of effective names greatly contributes to the understandability of applications of the OBSERVER pattern.

Fig. 8.11 Application of the OBSERVER to the inventory context with two callback methods using the push data-flow strategy

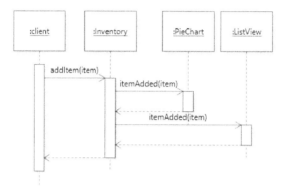

Fig. 8.12 Sequence diagram modeling an invocation of `addItem` on an inventory

Finally, let us assume that, after using this design in a version of the system, a new type of observer is added, called the `TransactionLogger`. This type of observer is only interested in items being added to the inventory. In the current design, the class would have to implement the `itemRemoved` callback to do nothing. In this case, we can improve the design to allow different types of observers to register for only the events they care about. However, this doubles the number of observer management methods on the model. Figure 8.13 shows a class diagram that captures this new design decision.

8.5 Introduction to Graphical User Interface Development

In many technologies, the code that implements the Graphical User Interface (GUI) portion of an application makes heavy use of the OBSERVER. This section and the next two are an introduction to GUI development that serves the dual purpose of introducing the concept of an *application framework* and reinforcing knowledge of the OBSERVER pattern through its application in a new context. This part of the chapter

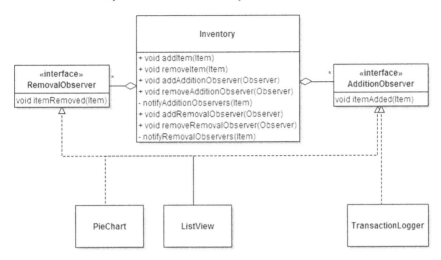

Fig. 8.13 Example of a model with two abstract observers

is based on JavaFX, an extensive GUI framework for the Java language. However, the general concepts presented here apply to other GUI development frameworks. Conceptually, the code that makes up a GUI application is split into two parts:

- **The framework code** consists of a *component library* and an *application skeleton*. The component library is a collection of reusable types and interfaces that implement typical GUI functionality: buttons, windows, etc. The application skeleton is a GUI application that takes care of all the inevitable low-level aspects of GUI applications, and in particular monitoring events triggered by input devices and displaying objects on the screen. By itself, the application skeleton does not do anything visible: it must be extended and customized with *application code*.
- **Application code** consists of the code written by GUI developers to extend and customize the application skeleton so that it provides the required user interface functionality.

A GUI application does not execute the same way as the script-like applications we write when learning to program. In such programs, the code executes sequentially from the first statement of the application entry point (the `main` method in Java) and the flow of control is entirely dictated by the application code. With GUI frameworks, the application must be started by *launching* the framework using a special library method. The framework's skeleton application then starts an *event loop* that continually monitors the system for input from user interface devices. Throughout the execution of the GUI application, the framework remains in control of calling the application code. The application code, written by the GUI developers, only get executed at specific points, in response to calls by the framework. This process is thus a clear example of inversion of control. Application code does not tell the framework what to do: it waits for the framework to call it.

Figure 8.14 illustrates the essence of the relation between the LuckyNumber application and the JavaFX framework. The class diagram shows how the application code defines a `LuckyNumber` class that inherits from the framework's `Application` class. To launch the framework, the following code is used:

Fig. 8.14 Relation between application and framework code for the LuckyNumber application

```
public class LuckyNumber extends Application
{
  public static void main(String[] pArgs)
  { launch(pArgs); }

  @Override
  public void start(Stage pPrimaryStage)
  { ... }
}
```

This code calls the static method `Application.launch`, which launches the GUI framework, instantiates class `LuckyNumber` and then executes method `start()` on this instance.[6] With this setup, class `LuckyNumber` is effectively used as the connection point between the application code used to extend the GUI and the framework code in charge of running the show.

Conceptually, the application code for a GUI application can be split into two categories: the *component graph*,[7] and the *event handling code*.

The component graph is the "actual" interface and is comprised of a number of objects that represent both visible (e.g., buttons) and invisible (e.g., regions) elements of the application. These objects are organized as a tree, with the root of the tree being the main window or area of the GUI. In modern GUI frameworks, constructing a component graph can be done by writing code, but also through configuration files that can be generated by GUI building tools. Ultimately, the two approaches are equivalent, because once the code runs the outcome is the same:

---

[6] Method `launch` uses metaprogramming to discover which application class to instantiate, a bit like `Object.clone()` detects which class to clone.

[7] In the documentation for JavaFX, the component graph is called the *scene graph*.

a tree of plain Java objects that form the user interface. The design of the library classes that support the construction of a component graph makes heavy use of polymorphism and the COMPOSITE and DECORATOR patterns. In JavaFX, the component graph for a user interface is typically instantiated in the application's `start(Stage)` method.

Once the framework is launched and displaying the desired component graph, its event loop will automatically map low-level system events to specific interactions with components in the graph (e.g., placing the mouse over a text box, clicking a button). In common GUI programming terminology, such interactions are called *events*. Unless specific application code is provided to react to events, nothing will happen as a result of the framework detecting an event. For example, clicking on a button will graphically show the button to be clicked using some user interface cue, but then the code will simply continue executing without having any impact on the application logic. To build interactive GUI applications, it is necessary to *handle* events like button clicks and other user interactions. Event handling in GUI frameworks is an application of the OBSERVER pattern, where the model is a GUI component (e.g., a button). Handling a button click, or any similar event, then just becomes a question of defining an observer and registering it with the button. The next two sections detail how to design component graphs and handle events on GUI components.

8.6 Graphical User Interface Component Graphs

The component graph is the collection of objects that forms what we usually think of as the interface: windows, textboxes, buttons, etc. At different stages in the development of a graphical user interface, it can be useful to think about this user interface from four different point of views, or perspectives: user experience, logical, source code, run-time.

The User Experience Perspective

The user experience perspective corresponds to what the user experiences when interacting with the component graph. Figure 8.2, shown earlier in this chapter, shows the user experience perspective on the component graph for the LuckyNumber application. Because not every object in the component graph is necessarily visible, it is important to remember that the user experience perspective does not show the complete picture of the application. This picture is complemented by the other three perspectives.

The Logical Perspective

The logical perspective on the graphical user interface is a way to think about it from the point of view of the hierarchical organization of UI components, independently of their definition in code. Figure 8.15 shows the logical perspective on the LuckyNumber application. This model of the component graph shows that the user interface consists of one `Slider` instance and two `TextField` instances, each wrapped in a `Parent` region component, which are themselves children of an outer region of type `GridPane`, which is the child of the top-level element of the component graph, the `Scene`.[8]

Fig. 8.15 Logical perspective on the LuckyNumber application

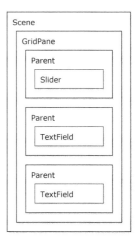

The logical perspective is often a useful complement to the other perspectives, because it shows how components relate to each other hierarchically without getting cluttered by the visual rendering of the components or details of the source code. In simpler applications, where there is a minimum of visual overlap between components, the logical view can also serve as a sketch of the physical arrangement of objects in a layout.

The Source Code Perspective

The source code perspective shows the kind of information about the component graph that is readily available from the declarations of the classes of the objects that form the component graph. This information is best summarized by a class diagram. Figure 8.16 models the source code perspective on the component graph of the LuckyNumber application. Despite the application being tiny, the diagram

---

[8] Technically in JavaFX the `Scene` needs to be set as the child of a further parent called a `Stage`, but one could argue that the `Stage` is not really part of the component graph.

shows that a lot of code is required to instantiate its component graph. Let us walk through this diagram.

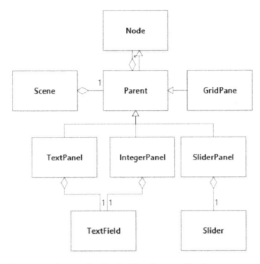

Fig. 8.16 Source code perspective on the LuckyNumber application

The Scene holds a reference to the root node of the component graph, something we can deduce from the fact that it is not a subtype of Node, and no class in the diagram aggregates it. The Scene class aggregates class Parent. This may be puzzling at first, because in my logical model of the component graph, I indicated that the Scene contains a GridPane. This is an example of polymorphism in use. To allow users to build any kind of application, the Scene library class accepts any subtype of type Parent as its child object. In turn, Parent is a subtype of the general Node type that adds functionality to handle children nodes. In JavaFX, all objects that can be part of a component graph need to be a subtype of Node, either directly or, more generally, indirectly by inheriting from other subtypes of Node. The fact that Parent nodes, which can contain children nodes, are themselves of type Node shows that the design of the GUI component hierarchy is an application of the COMPOSITE pattern.

By continuing our investigation of the diagram, we find class GridPane as a subtype of Parent. This is the reason it is possible to add a GridPane to a scene. A GridPane is a type of user interface Node that specializes in organizing its children into a grid. I used it for LuckyNumber to easily lay out the number views vertically on top of each other.

In the LuckyNumber application, a GridPane contains a set of Parent components. In the general case, a GridPane can contain any subtype of Node. However, in my design of the application, I created three classes that inherit from Parent: TextPanel, IntegerPanel, and SliderPanel. These classes represent the three views of the number in the Model–View–Controller decomposition. By defining these classes as subclasses of Parent, I achieve two useful properties:

- I *reuse* the "parenting" functionality of `Parent` to easily add a widget (e.g., a slider) to a `Node`;
- By defining my view classes as subtypes of `Node`, I make it possible to add them as children of a `GridPane` through polymorphism.

The remainder of the diagram shows how the tree would generate its leaves: the `SliderPanel` aggregates a `Slider` instance, and both the `TextPanel` and the `IntegerPanel` aggregate a `TextField` instance. Note that because this is a class diagram and not an object diagram, the fact that both `TextPanel` and `IntegerPanel` have an association to the `TextField` model element does *not* mean that their instance would refer to the same `TextField` instance!

The diagram of Figure 8.16, already somewhat involved, actually omits, for clarity, many intermediate types in the inheritance hierarchy for nodes. For example, the diagram shows `GridPane` to be a direct subclass of `Parent`. In reality, `GridPane` is a subclass of `Pane`, which itself is a subclass of `Region`, which is a subclass of `Parent`. Figure 8.17, while still an incomplete model, shows a bigger picture of the class hierarchy that can be leveraged to define component graphs in JavaFX.

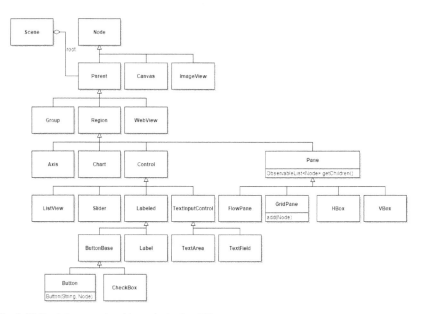

Fig. 8.17 Partial `Node` class hierarchy in JavaFX

The Run-time Perspective

The run-time perspective is the instantiated component graph for a graphical interface. This perspective can best be represented as an object diagram. Figure 8.18 shows the instantiated component graph for LuckyNumber. Conceptually close to the logical view, it differs by making object identities explicit while losing, in this case, the relative positioning of graphical components.

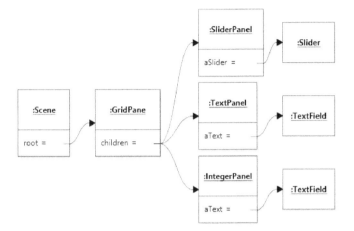

Fig. 8.18 Run-time perspective of the LuckyNumber user interface

Defining the Object Graph

In Section 8.5 I mentioned how after the framework starts it calls the `start` method of the main application class (`LuckyNumber` in our case). This `start` method is the natural integration point for extending the framework, and this is where we put the code that builds the component graph. The code below is the minimum required to get the application to create the LuckyNumber component graph. In practice, this kind of code would typically be extended with additional configuration code and organized using helper methods. The additional configuration code can be used to beautify the application, for example by adding margins around components, a title to the window, etc. The JavaFX functionality to generate component graphs from configuration files is outside the scope of this book.

```
public class LuckyNumber extends Application
{
  public void start(Stage pStage)
  {
    Model model = new Model();

    GridPane root = new GridPane();
    root.add(new SliderPanel(model), 0, 0, 1, 1);
    root.add(new IntegerPanel(model), 0, 1, 1, 1);
    root.add(new TextPanel(model), 0, 2, 1, 1);

    pStage.setScene(new Scene(root));
    pStage.show();
  }
}
```

The first statement of method `start` is to create an instance of `Model`. This instance will play the role of the model in the OBSERVER pattern. It is related to the construction of the component graph because, as detailed later, some of the components in the graph need access to the model. The second statement creates a `GridPane`, which is an invisible component used for assisting with the layout of children components. The local variable that holds a reference to this component is helpfully named `root` to indicate that it is the root of the component graph. Then, three application-defined components are added to the grid. The parameters to the `add` method indicate the column and row index and span. For example, the statement:

```
root.add(new SliderPanel(model), 0, 0, 1, 1);
```

specifies to add an instance of the `SliderPanel` in the top-left cell in the grid, and span only one column and one row. Because `SliderPanel` is a subtype of `Parent`, and thus a subtype of `Node`, it can be added to the grid. Another important thing to note about the instantiation of the panel components is that their constructor takes as argument a reference to the model.

The last two statements of the method are not really related to the construction of the component graph, but are nevertheless crucial steps in the creation of the GUI. The statement with the call to `setScene` creates a `Scene` from the component graph and assigns it to the framework's `Stage`. Finally, the last statement requests that the framework display the `Stage` onto the user's display.

For additional insights on the creation of the component graph, the code below shows the relevant part of the constructor of the `IntegerPanel` (the other panels are very similar).

```
public class IntegerPanel extends Parent implements Observer
{
  private TextField aText = new TextField();
  private Model aModel;

  public IntegerPanel(Model pModel)
  {
    aModel = pModel;
    aModel.addObserver(this);
    aText.setText(new Integer(aModel.getNumber()).toString());
    getChildren().add(aText);
    ...
  }

  public void newNumber(int pNumber)
  { aText.setText(new Integer(pNumber).toString()); }
}
```

This code illustrates a number of insights about the design of the component graph. First, as already mentioned, the application-defined `IntegerPanel` class extends the framework-defined `Parent` class so that it can become part of the component graph. Second, an instance of `IntegerPanel` aggregates a framework-defined `TextField` component. However, the mere fact of defining an instance variable of type `TextField` inside the class does not add the `TextField` to the component graph. To do this, it is necessary for the `IntegerPanel` to add the instance of `TextField` to itself, something that is done with the call `getChildren()` `.add(aText)`. Method `getChildren()` is inherited from class `Parent`, and used to obtain the list of children of the parent user interface `Node`, to which the `TextField` instance can then be added.

The `IntegerPanel` instance also maintains a reference to the `Model`. The reason for this is that the `IntegerPanel` needs to act as a controller for the `Model`, something that will be explained in more detail in the next section. Also, it is worth noticing how the `IntegerPanel` is an observer of the `Model` instance: it declares to implement `Observer`, it registers itself as an observer upon construction (second statement of the constructor), and it supplies an implementation for the `newNumber` callback. As expected, the behavior of the callback is to set the value of the `TextField` user interface component with the most recent value in the model, obtained from the callback parameter.

As a final insight on the design of the component graph, we can note how the instance of `Model` created in method `start` (see preceding code fragment) is stored in a *local variable*. In other words, the application class `LuckyNumber` does *not* manage an instance of the model: this is only done within each panel. This design decision is to respect the guideline provided in Chapter 4, to keep the number of fields to a minimum. Without care, application-defined user interface components can easily become a GOD CLASS† bloated with numerous references to stateful objects, which makes a design much harder to understand.

8.7 Event Handling

In GUI frameworks, objects in the component graph act as models in the OBSERVER. Once the framework is launched, it continually goes through a loop that monitors input events and checks whether they map to events that can be observed by the application code. This process is illustrated in Figure 8.19.

Fig. 8.19 The event loop in a GUI framework

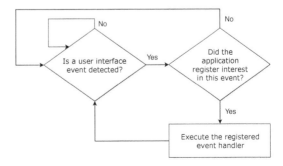

Typically, events are defined by the component library supplied by the framework. For example, the `TextField` user interface component defines an "action" event. According to its class documentation "The action handler is normally called when the user types the ENTER key". This means that an instance of `TextField` can play the role of the model in the OBSERVER. Figure 8.20 shows the correspondence between the code elements and the roles in the OBSERVER pattern.

Fig. 8.20 Correspondence between `TextField` and the roles in the OBSERVER

Handling the action event on a text field is thus pretty straightforward. All we need to do is to:

- **Define a handler for the event.** This means defining a class that is a subtype of `EventHandler<ActionEvent>`. The class will be our event handler class.
- **Instantiate a handler.** This means creating an instance of the class we defined in the previous step. The instance will be our event handler instance, or more simply event handler, or even just "handler".
- **Register the handler.** This means calling the registration method on the model and passing the handler as an argument. In the case of `TextField`, we need to call `setOnAction(handler)`. It is worth noticing an interesting design choice for this application of OBSERVER: it is only possible to have a single observer for a `TextField`.

Although the basic mechanism for specifying and registering event handlers is always the same, one design choice that must be resolved is where to place the definition of the handling code. For this, two main strategies are possible:

- **To define the handler as a function object** using an anonymous class or a lambda expression (see Section 3.4). This is a good choice if the code of the handler is simple and does not require storing data that is specific to the handler;
- **To delegate the handling to an element of the component graph** by declaring to implement the observer interface. This is a good choice if the code of the handler is more complex or requires knowing about many different aspects of the internal structure of the target component.

Let us see how these two options can be realized in the context of the LuckyNumber application. Using the function object strategy, we could complete the code of the constructor of `IntegerPanel` as follows:

```
public class IntegerPanel extends Parent implements Observer
{
  private TextField aText = new TextField();
  private Model aModel;

  public IntegerPanel(Model pModel)
  {
    aModel = pModel;
    aModel.addObserver(this);
    aText.setText(new Integer(aModel.getNumber()).toString());
    getChildren().add(aText);
    aText.setOnAction(new EventHandler<ActionEvent>()
      {
        public void handle(ActionEvent pEvent)
        {
          int number = 1;
          try{ number = Integer.parseInt(aText.getText()); }
          catch(NumberFormatException pException )
          { /* Just ignore. We use 1 instead. */ }
          aModel.setNumber(number);
        }
      });
  }
}
```

With this strategy, the constructor of IntegerPanel creates a function object using an anonymous class and, at the same time, registers this object to become the handler of the action event on the text field. The behavior of the handler is to serve as the controller for the model.

At this point in the design of the application, we now have *two* applications of the OBSERVER at play. One subject is the Model being observed by all three panels, and another subject is the IntegerPanel's TextField that is observed by the anonymous function object. Figure 8.21 captures the design. Naturally, in the finished application, we would also need an event handler for the text panel and the slider panel, which would bring the total number of applications of the OBSERVER to four.

In the case of the LuckyNumber application, one alternative to using function objects for defining handlers is to delegate the handling of GUI events to the panels themselves. In our case, this would mean declaring IntegerPanel to implement both Observer and EventHandler<ActionEvent>. The Observer interface is the same one as before, used to receive callbacks when the model (the number) is changed. The difference in this case is the addition of the EventHandler interface, which allows the IntegerPanel to respond to the event that corresponds to the "Enter" key being pressed in the panel's text field.

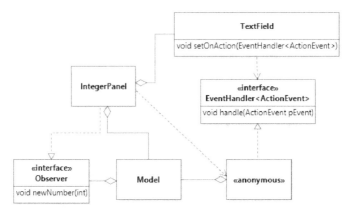

Fig. 8.21 Two applications of the OBSERVER pattern

```
public class IntegerPanel extends Parent implements Observer,
  EventHandler<ActionEvent>
{
  private TextField aText = new TextField();
  private Model aModel;

  public IntegerPanel(Model pModel)
  {
    aModel = pModel;
    aModel.addObserver(this);
    aText.setText(new Integer(aModel.getNumber()).toString());
    getChildren().add(aText);
    aText.setOnAction(this);
  }

  public void handle(ActionEvent pEvent)
  {
    int number = 1;
    try { number = Integer.parseInt(aText.getText()); }
    catch(NumberFormatException pException )
    { /* Just ignore. We'll use 1 instead. */ }
    aModel.setNumber(number);
  }

  public void newNumber(int pNumber)
  { aText.setText(new Integer(pNumber).toString()); }
}
```

There are two main implications of this choice on the code. First, the `handle`
method needs to be declared directly in class `IntegerPanel`. Second, the argument
passed to `aText.setOnAction` is now **this**, because it is the `IntegerPanel` instance itself that is now responsible for handling the event.

Although both design options for locating the handler code are workable, for the
LuckyNumber application I prefer the function object alternative. The handler code

is just a few lines long, and with the function object the behavior of the handler is located with other code that initializes the text field, so everything is in one place. Although there is an element of subjectivity to this argument, the use of function objects to specify GUI handlers is a common practice. In the absence of a good reason to do things otherwise, my recommendation would be to use it by default.

8.8 The VISITOR Design Pattern

Inversion of control can be useful to create loosely coupled design solutions in contexts other than applications of the OBSERVER pattern and event handling mechanisms. An additional recognized use for inversion of control is the VISITOR design pattern. The *context* for applying the VISITOR pattern is when we want to make it possible to support an open-ended number of operations that can be applied to an object graph, but without impacting the interface of the objects in the graph. To illustrate such a context, we will use yet another variant of the CardSource type hierarchy. Figure 8.22 shows a design where different types of concrete card sources have the CardSource interface in common, but then different individual interfaces for services other than draw() and isEmpty();

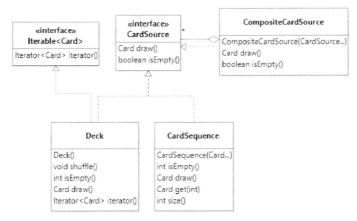

Fig. 8.22 Design context for a sample application of the VISITOR. The constructor uses the vararg construct to accept an unspecified number of cards as argument. The mechanism is also employed by the constructor of CompositeCardSource.

In this design, there are three different types of card sources. Although they all implement the CardSource interface, their commonality ends there. Class Deck can be shuffled and is iterable. A CardSequence can be initialized with a predetermined list of cards, but cannot be shuffled and is not iterable. Instead, elements in a CardSequence can be accessed through an integer index. For this reason, the class also includes a size() method. Finally, CompositeCardSource is a fairly standard application of the Composite with a very narrow interface (i.e., it offers no services besides those of `CardSource`). In this example as well as in general, the reason classes that implement an interface have methods other than the ones in the interface is simply that each class is intended to work in a specific context where its additional methods are necessary and, to respect the interface segregation principle, the only methods in the common type are those used by all contexts (see Section 3.8).

The above design will fulfill its mandate as long as the client code only requires the limited functionality it currently provides. Problems will start arising, however, when we start needing additional functionality from the card sources. Examples of operations that may be necessary at some point include:

- Printing to the console a description of each of the cards in the source;
- Obtaining the number of cards in the card source;
- Removing a certain card from a card source;
- Determining if a card source contains a certain card;
- Obtaining an iterator over all the cards in the source;

Because all the concrete card source classes share a common supertype, there is a straightforward solution to the problem of adding these operations: we can simply define new methods on the `CardSource` interface, one per operation, and implement them in each subclass. For example, we could make `CardSource` extend `Iterable<Card>`, and add the methods `print()`, `size()`, `remove(Card)`, and `contains(Card)` to its declaration. If such a solution is a good fit in a design context, then we can adopt it and we do not need the Visitor pattern. However, adding methods to an interface has drawbacks and limitations:

- The interface of `CardSource` will get much bigger. Not all methods might be used in all usage contexts. As mentioned above, there is a risk of violating the interface segregation principle;
- For a versatile data structure that can be used as a library, it may be hard to anticipate which operations are going to be necessary in the future. Adding operations that end up unused is a clear case of Speculative Generality†. In fact, if the code is indeed distributed as a library, future users may not be able to, or want to, change the code to add additional operations.

The Visitor provides a solution in such a context by supporting a mechanism whereby it is possible to define an operation of interest in a separate class and "inject" it into the class hierarchy that needs to support it. In our case, this means we could write a separate class to implement the `contains(Card)` operation, and use this class to determine if any concrete `CardSource` contains the card of interest.

Abstract and Concrete Visitors

The cornerstone of the Visitor pattern is an interface that describes objects that can "visit" objects of all classes of interest in an object graph. This interface is appropriately called the *abstract visitor*. An abstract visitor follows a prescribed structure: it contains one method with signature `visitElementX(ElementX pElementX)` for each different type of concrete class `ElementX` in the object structure.[9] In our case, the abstract visitor would be defined as follows:

```
public interface CardSourceVisitor
{
  void visitCompositeCardSource( CompositeCardSource pSource );
  void visitDeck( Deck pDeck );
  void visitCardSequence( CardSequence pCardSequence );
}
```

As usual, a *concrete visitor* is an implementation of this interface. In the VISITOR pattern, we implement one concrete visitor for each operation of interest. In a concrete visitor, each `visitElementX` method provides the behavior of the operation as applied to a given class. For example, a simple visitor that prints all the cards in a card source to the console would be defined as such:

```
public class PrintingVisitor implements CardSourceVisitor
{
 public void visitCompositeCardSource(CompositeCardSource pSource)
 {}

 public void visitDeck(Deck pDeck)
 {
   for( Card card : pDeck)
   { System.out.println(card); }
 }

 public void visitCardSequence(CardSequence pCardSequence)
 {
   for( int i = 0; i < pCardSequence.size(); i++ )
   { System.out.println(pCardSequence.get(i)); }
 }
}
```

The first thing to notice in this code is that method `visitCompositeCardSource` does not do anything. Because composite card sources do not store cards directly (they store other card sources), we can defer the printing behavior to the actual card sources they aggregate. How this works exactly is described below. The second thing to notice is that methods `visitDeck` and `visitCardSequence` do not require `Deck` and `CardSequence` to have the same interface: they can use whatever methods are available on the concrete type to implement the required behavior.

Another interesting observation about the implementation of the concrete visitor is that it provides a way to organize code in terms of *functionality* as opposed to *data*. In a classic design, the code to implement the printing operation would be scattered throughout the three card source classes. In this design, all this code in located in a single class. One of the benefits of the VISITOR is thus to allow a different style of

---

[9] Technically, the methods can be overloaded, which would lead to the more compact form `visit(ElementX pElementX)`. For the reasons discussed in Section 7.5, I recommend avoiding overloading by using the longer form.

assignment of responsibilities to classes, and thus a separation of concerns along a different criterion (functionality-centric vs. data-centric).

Integrating Operations into a Class Hierarchy

Although a concrete visitor separates a well-defined operation into its own class, it still needs to be integrated with the class hierarchy that defines the object graph on which the operation will be applied (henceforth simply referred to as the "class hierarchy"). This integration is accomplished by way of a method, usually called `accept`, that acts as a gateway into the object graph for visitor objects. An `accept` method takes as single argument an object of the abstract visitor type (`CardSourceVisitor` in our case). Unless there is good reason not to, we normally define the `accept` method on the common supertype of the class hierarchy:

```
public interface CardSource
{
  Card draw();
  boolean isEmpty();
  void accept(CardSourceVisitor pVisitor);
}
```

The implementation of `accept` by concrete types is where the integration really happens. This implementation follows a prescribed formula: to call the `visit` method for the type of the class that defines the `accept` method. For example, the implementation of `accept` for class `Deck` is:

```
public void accept(CardSourceVisitor pVisitor)
{ pVisitor.visitDeck(this); }
```

and the one for class `CardSequence` is:

```
public void accept(CardSourceVisitor pVisitor)
{ pVisitor.visitCardSequence(this); }
```

The only difference between the two implementations of `accept` is the specific `visitElementX` method that is being called. The version of `accept` for the `CompositeCardSource` class is a bit more involved, and is discussed further below, in the section "Traversing the Object Graph".

Figure 8.23 shows the result of applying the VISITOR to our context. The figure includes two concrete visitors to emphasize that the goal of the pattern is to support adding multiple operations to a class hierarchy.

With the `accept` method in place, executing an operation on the object graph is now a matter of creating the concrete visitor object that represents the operation, and passing this object as argument to method `accept` on the target element:

```
PrintingVisitor visitor = new PrintingVisitor();
Deck deck = new Deck();
deck.accept(visitor);
```

Figure 8.24 shows the result of calling accept on an instance of `Deck`. The client code, which holds the reference to the concrete visitor, calls `accept` on an instance

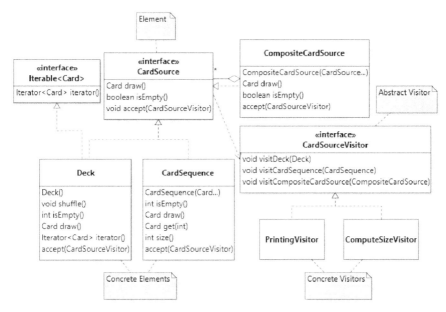

Fig. 8.23 Sample application of the VISITOR pattern with the name of the roles in notes

of `Deck` with the visitor as argument. The `accept` method then calls back the appropriate method on the visitor. In this sequence, the `visitDeck` method qualifies as a callback method. With complex object structures, it may not always be easy or even possible to determine when a `visit` method will be called. Just like in the OBSERVER pattern, the model calls its observers back at the appropriate time, in the VISITOR, concrete elements call the visitors at the appropriate time.

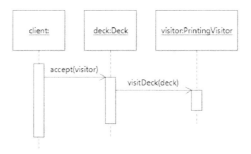

Fig. 8.24 Sequence diagram of a call to an `accept` method in an application of VISITOR

Traversing the Object Graph

So far in our application of the VISITOR we have left out a critical aspect of the pattern: the traversal of the object graph. Any object graph with more than one element
will have an aggregate node as its root. In our case this is CompositeCardSource,
so let us look at what happens when we apply an operation to such a node. Let us
say we implement accept for this class similarly as for Deck and CardSequence:

```
public class CompositeCardSource implements CardSource
{
  public void accept(CardSourceVisitor pVisitor)
  {
    pVisitor.visitCompositeCardSource(this);
  }
}
```

Then, if we call accept on an instance of CompositeCardSource, the method simply invokes its callback visitCompositeCardSource, which does nothing.

The two core ideas of the VISITOR pattern are to (1) enable the integration of an
open-ended set of operations that (2) can be applied by traversing an object graph,
often a recursive one. For the traversal aspect of the pattern to be applicable, at least
one element type in the target hierarchy needs to serve as an aggregate for other
types. In our case this role is played by CompositeCardSource. Let us consider
the object graph illustrated in Figure 8.25. If we want to print the cards reachable
through the root card source, we would need to traverse the entire graph to find all
the cards. We would also need to do such a traversal to count the total number of
cards in a source, remove all instances of a specific card, etc.

Fig. 8.25 Sample object graph generated by the CardSource types

There are two main ways to implement the traversal of the object graph in the
VISITOR. One option is to place the traversal code in the accept method of aggregate
types. The other option is to place this code in the visit methods that serve as
callbacks for aggregate types.

In our case, placing the traversal code in the accept method is relatively straightforward:

```
public class CompositeCardSource implements CardSource
{
  private final List<CardSource> aElements;

  public void accept(CardSourceVisitor pVisitor)
  {
    pVisitor.visitCompositeCardSource(this);
    for( CardSource source : aElements )
    { source.accept(pVisitor); }
  }
}
```

Because the traversal code is implemented within the class of the aggregate, it can refer to the private field that stores the aggregation (aElements). This access to private structures is one major motivation for implementing the traversal code within the accept method. I discuss additional advantages and disadvantages of this choice below. Figure 8.26 shows the beginning of the call sequence that results from calling accept on the root target node of Figure 8.25. From this figure it becomes easier to visualize the concrete visitor as an implementation of callback methods: some independent code traverses an object structure and calls the visitElementX callbacks as appropriate, and methods of the visitor object simply respond to these visitation notifications. The fact that the traversal code is implemented in accept is visible by the fact that some calls to accept originate from the activation bar of a different accept invocation.

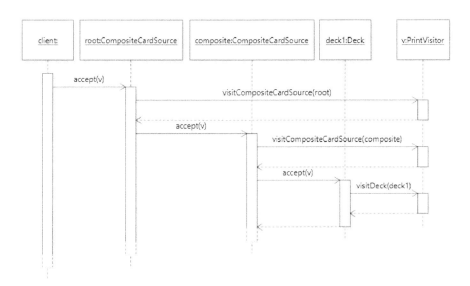

Fig. 8.26 Partial call sequence resulting from a call to root.accept on the object graph of Figure 8.25 when the traversal code is implemented in the accept method

The second option for implementing the traversal code is to put it in the visit method that corresponds to the element types that are aggregates. In our case this means, as before, `CompositeCardSource`. Unfortunately, in our context it is not possible to implement this option directly, because the aggregate class offers no public access to the `CardSource` objects it aggregates. Because the code of the `visit` methods is in a separate class, we need a way to access the objects stored by the private field `aElements`. To make this work we make `CompositeCardSource` iterable over the `CardSource` instances it aggregates. However, this requirement to decrease the level of encapsulation of the class is a disadvantage of this design decision.

```java
public class CompositeCardSource implements CardSource,
  Iterable<CardSource>
{
  private final List<CardSource> aElements;

  public Iterator<CardSource> iterator()
  { return aElements.iterator(); }
  ...
}
```

With this additional service available on `CompositeCardSource`, we can now remove the traversal code from the `accept` method and update the code of `visit-CompositeCardSource` in our concrete visitor:

```java
public class PrintVisitor implements CardSourceVisitor
{
  public void visitCompositeCardSource(
    CompositeCardSource pCompositeCardSource)
  {
    for( CardSource source : pCompositeCardSource )
    { source.accept(this); }
  }
  ...
}
```

Figure 8.27 shows the corresponding call sequence on the root of the object graph illustrated in Figure 8.25.

As we have seen above, the main advantage of placing the traversal code in the `accept` method is that it can help achieve stronger encapsulation because the internal structures can be accessed without being part of the class's interface. The main disadvantage of placing the traversal code in the `accept` method, however, is that the traversal order is fixed in the sense that it cannot be adapted by different visitors. In our very simple example, the traversal order did not really matter. But let us say that in our print visitor we care about the order in which the cards are printed. The code for the `accept` method, above, implements a pre-order traversal (visit the node, then the children). Some operations, however, might require a post-order traversal (visit the children, then the node). If the traversal code is implemented in `accept`, concrete visitors cannot change it. In a nutshell, if encapsulation of target elements is more important, it is better to place the traversal code in the `accept` method. If the ability to change the traversal order is more important, then it is better to place the traversal code in the `visit` method.

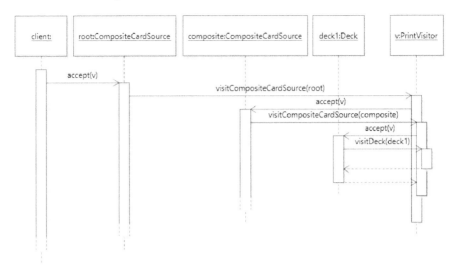

Fig. 8.27 Partial call sequence resulting from a call to `root.accept` on the object graph of Figure 8.25 when the traversal code is implemented in the `visit` method

Using Inheritance in the Pattern

The question of where to place the traversal code brings up the issue of code DUPLI-CATED CODE† again. If we place the traversal code in the `visit` methods, and have more than one concrete visitor class, every class is bound to repeat the traversal code in its `visit` method. A common solution to alleviate this issue is to define an **abstract** visitor class to hold default traversal code.[10] In our case, the following would be a good implementation of an **abstract** visitor class:

```
public abstract class AbstractCardSourceVisitor
  implements CardSourceVisitor
{
  public void visitCompositeCardSource(
    CompositeCardSource pCompositeCardSource)
  {
    for( CardSource source : pCompositeCardSource )
    { source.accept(this); }
  }

  public void visitDeck(Deck pDeck) {}

  public void visitCardSequence(CardSequence pCardSequence) {}
}
```

There are two important things to observe about this implementation. First, I retained the interface. Because most concrete visitors would be implemented as sub-

---

[10] Here it is important to distinguish between an **abstract** visitor *class* and an abstract *visitor*, which is usually an interface.

classes of AbstractCardSourceVisitor, one can wonder, why not simply use this abstract class to serve in the role of abstract visitor, and get rid of the interface? The general reason is that interfaces promote more flexibility in a design. For example, one concrete drawback of using an abstract class is that, because Java only supports single inheritance, defining the abstract visitor as an abstract class prevents classes that already inherit from another class to serve as concrete visitors.

The second notable detail in the above code is that the visit methods for classes Deck and CardSequence are implemented as empty placeholders. Given that AbstractCardSourceVisitor is declared **abstract**, we do not need these declarations. However, providing empty implementations for visit methods allows the abstract visitor class to serve as an adapter (Section 8.3 introduced the idea of adapter classes). In more realistic applications of the pattern, the element type hierarchy can have dozens of different types, with a corresponding high number of visit methods. With empty implementations, concrete observers only need to override the methods that correspond to types they are interested in visiting.

As an example, the following declaration creates an anonymous visitor class that prints the number of cards in every CardSequence in a card source structure, and ignores the rest. Because the class inherits the traversal code, card sequences aggregated within composite card sources will also be reached.

```java
CardSourceVisitor visitor = new AbstractCardSourceVisitor()
   {
     public void visitCardSequence(CardSequence pSequence)
     { System.out.println(pSequence.size() + " cards"); }
   };
```

As a more elaborate example, the following implements a visitor that prints a representation of the object graph that includes the nesting depth of a card source type:

```java
public class StructurePrinterVisitor
  extends AbstractCardSourceVisitor
{
  private int aTab = 0;

  private String tab()
  {
    StringBuilder result = new StringBuilder();
    for( int i = 0; i < aTab; i++ )
    { result.append(" "); }
    return result.toString();
  }

  public void visitCompositeCardSource(
    CompositeCardSource pCompositeCardSource)
  {
    System.out.println(tab() + "Composite");
    aTab++;
    super.visitCompositeCardSource(pCompositeCardSource);
    aTab--;
  }
```

```
public void visitDeck(Deck pDeck)
{ System.out.println(tab() + "Deck"); }

public void visitCardSequence(CardSequence pCardSequence)
{ System.out.println(tab() + "CardSequence"); }
}
```

The result of using this visitor on the object graph of Figure 8.25 would be:

```
Composite
  Deck
  Composite
  Deck
  CardSequence
```

This example introduces two new aspects to our discussion so far. First, the visitor is *stateful*, i.e., it stores data. Specifically, the class defines a field aTab that stores the depth of the element currently being visited. Depth increases when visiting the elements aggregated by a composite card source. Correspondingly, the second notable aspect in the code above is the *reuse of the traversal code through a super call*. Here, the pre-order traversal implemented in the abstract visitor class is what we need. However, additional code is required when visiting a composite card source. To make this possible, visitCompositeCardSource is overridden to manage the indentation level, and a super call is made to trigger the traversal code at the appropriate point.

Supporting Data Flow in Visitor Structures

So far our examples of concrete visitors have carefully avoided the issue of data flow, because the PrintVisitor neither requires input nor produces output. Most realistic operations, however, do involve some data flow. For example, a visitor to compute the total number of cards in a card source must be able to return this number. As another example, an operation to determine if a certain card is contained in a card source must receive the card of interest as input. When operations are implemented in traditional methods, this kind of data flow is not an issue: input is passed in as argument to a method, and output can be returned to the calling context through return statements. In the VISITOR pattern, this is not possible. To support a general and extensible mechanism for defining operations on an object graph, the pattern requires that no assumption be made about the nature of the input and output of operations.

Data flow for VISITOR-based operations is thus implemented differently, by storing data within a visitor object. Input values can be provided when constructing a new visitor object and made accessible to the visit methods. Output values can be stored internally by visit methods during the traversal of the object graph, and made accessible to client code through a getter method. Let us consider each case in turn, starting with output values. To exemplify the process, we implement a visitor to count the total number of cards in the source. This version assumes that the abstract visitor class defined above is available:

```java
public class CountingVisitor extends AbstractCardSourceVisitor
{
  private int aCount = 0;

  public void visitDeck(Deck pDeck)
  {
    for( Card card : pDeck) { aCount++; }
  }

  public void visitCardSequence(CardSequence pCardSequence)
  { aCount += pCardSequence.size(); }

  public int getCount() { return aCount; }
}
```

To use this operation, it would be necessary to store a reference to the constructed visitor in a variable so that that the count can later be retrieved:

```java
CountingVisitor visitor = new CountingVisitor();
root.accept(visitor);
int result = visitor.getCount();
```

As our final example, we define a visitor that implements an operation to check whether a card source structure contains a certain card. Such an operation requires both input and output.

```java
public class ChecksContainmentVisitor
  extends AbstractCardSourceVisitor
{
  private final Card aCard;
  private boolean aResult = false;

  public ChecksContainmentVisitor(Card pCard)
  { aCard = pCard; }

  public void visitDeck(Deck pDeck)
  {
    for( Card card : pDeck)
    {
      if( card.equals(aCard))
      {
        aResult = true;
        break;
      }
    }
  }
}
```

```
public void visitCardSequence(CardSequence pCardSequence)
{
  for( int i = 0; i < pCardSequence.size(); i++ )
  {
    if( pCardSequence.get(i).equals(aCard))
    {
      aResult = true;
      break;
    }
  }
}

public boolean contains()
{ return aResult; }
}
```

Although this implementation works, it is not as efficient as it should be because aggregate nodes are traversed even when a card has already been found. Fortunately, the structure of the VISITOR allows us to eliminate this source of inefficiency with very little impact on the overall design: all we need to do is to provide an implementation for `visitCompositeCardSource` that only triggers the traversal if the card has not already been found.

```
public void visitCompositeCardSource(
  CompositeCardSource pCompositeCardSource)
{
  if( !aResult )
  { super.visitCompositeCardSource(pCompositeCardSource); }
}
```

Insights

This chapter introduced inversion of control as a way to separate the management of stateful information from the viewing of this information. Inversion of control is the principle behind the OBSERVER pattern which, in turn, is the key mechanism that enables the development of graphical user interface frameworks.

- Avoid PAIRWISE DEPENDENCIES† to keep state synchronized between objects;
- Consider separating the code responsible for storing data from the code responsible for viewing this data from the code responsible for changing the data (the Model–View–Controller decomposition);
- To decrease the coupling between views and model, consider using the OBSERVER pattern, which promotes inversion of control for updating views;
- With an application of the OBSERVER, the model class can be used without any observer, and generally does not depend on the specific types of any observer that observes it;
- In the OBSERVER, the model aggregates a number of abstract observers. The abstract observer is an interface that is implemented by the concrete observers;

- The abstract observer interface should define one or more callback methods that map to state-changing events in the model;
- The model needs to notify observers when it changes its state, but when to issue that notification is a design decision;
- There are two strategies for exchanging data between a model and its observers: push or pull;
- Callback methods can be thought of as "events" to support a type of "event-based programming". In this case, models are the event source and observers are the event handlers;
- An abstract observer can define multiple callbacks. Abstract observer interfaces can also be split up in smaller observer interfaces to afford more flexibility in defining how observers can respond to events;
- If it is often the case that observers implement callbacks by doing nothing, consider using adapter classes;
- A GUI application is built by instantiating an application skeleton provided by the GUI framework. Application code to extend and customize the framework can be separated into two categories: component graph construction and event handling;
- It can be useful to think of the GUI component graph from four different perspectives: user experience, logical, source code, and run-time;
- The component graph must be instantiated before the user interface becomes visible. In JavaFX this instantiation is triggered in the `start` method of the application class;
- You can inherit from component classes of the GUI framework to create custom graphical components that can be added to an application's GUI component graph;
- To make a GUI application interactive, it is necessary to define handlers for GUI events that originate from different objects in the component graph. Handlers are defined as observers of objects in the component graph;
- Handlers can be defined as function objects, or the handling can be delegated to objects of the component graph.
- Consider using the VISITOR pattern to allow extending an object structure with an open-ended set of operations, without requiring modification to the interface of the classes that define this object structure.

Code Exploration

In addition to the LuckyNumber application, all three example projects for this book are GUI applications that provide many opportunities for exploring GUI design in more depth. The following pointers will help you get started.

LuckyNumber

Most of the design of this application is explained in this chapter, and the entire source code can be found on the book website. The only insight about the design of LuckyNumber not covered in the chapter concerns the `SliderPanel`. In contrast to the `IntegerPanel` discussed in the main part of the chapter, the `SliderPanel` does not register a handler directly with the `Slider` component it aggregates. Instead, it registers a handler with a *property* of the `Slider`, as such:

```
aSlider.valueProperty().addListener(new ChangeListener<Number>()
{
  public void changed(ObservableValue<? extends Number> pValue,
    Number pOld, Number pNew)
  { aModel.setNumber(pNew.intValue()); }
});
```

Properties are somewhat of an advanced concept that is not covered explicitly in this book. However, the basic logic of the code above can be understood as a direct application of the OBSERVER, with the difference that instead of registering an observer with a user interface component, we are registering this observer directly with a wrapper for the value we wish to observe (the current value of the slider).

Minesweeper

The entire GUI code for Minesweeper is located in its application class, `Minesweeper`. Method `createScene` instantiates the basic component graph and stores the root in an instance variable of the application class `aGrid`. Method `refresh()` re-builds the grid that corresponds to the minefield from scratch every time it is called. The three helper methods `create*Tile` create the leaves of the component graph, which are actually small square buttons. These methods also define and register handlers for clicks to tiles. The handlers in this case are defined as lambda expressions.

Solitaire

The GUI code for Solitaire is located in the ...`solitaire.gui` package. The application class is `Solitaire`. With the exception of the application class, `CardDragHandler` and `CardTransfer`, each remaining class in the package defines a graphical component panel that specializes in viewing a specific part of the data of the `GameModel`. For example, `DiscardPileView` is a subclass of the framework class `Hbox` that is also a `GameModelListener`. Whenever the game model changes, this component responds to the event (`gameStateChanged()`) and shows an image of the card at the top of the discard pile. As usual, the component graph is constructed in the application's `start` method.

The design of the Solitaire application relies on a GUI feature called drag-and-drop. Although the design of drag-and-drop functionality was not covered explicitly in the chapter, its operation is also based on the OBSERVER pattern. The basic idea is that images of cards are objects in the component graph, and it is possible to register a handler for an event that corresponds to a drag gesture being detected on this component.

JetUML

The user interface of JetUML is not simple, but it makes use of a wide variety of GUI framework features (menus, tabs, dialog boxes, persistent properties), so studying its code should have a high return on investment for readers interested in learning GUI programming in more depth.

The application class is `UMLEditor`, but most of the heavy lifting is accomplished by class `EditorFrame`, which is responsible for creating the top window of the application. Reading through the code of `EditorFrame` will expose most of the main design decisions that underlie the user interface code, including how tabs are managed, how menus are created, and how we create dialog boxes.

Further Reading

As for the other patterns, the Gang of Four book [6] has the original treatment of the OBSERVER and VISITOR patterns.

In the book *Patterns of Enterprise Application Architecture* [4], Fowler provides a description of the Model–View–Controller as a web presentation pattern. The book *Pattern-Oriented Software Architecture Volume 4: A Pattern Language for Distributed Computing* [2] presents it as a pattern for software architecture, and integrates it into a general system of patterns for designing distributed applications.

It is possible to find extensive additional information on the JavaFX framework on the websites of Java technology providers, and in particular Oracle and OpenJDK.

Chapter 9
Functional Design

This chapter covers:

Concepts and Principles: Behavior parameterization, first-class functions, higher-order functions, functional programming;
Programming Mechanisms: Functional interfaces, lambda expressions, method references, streams;
Design Techniques: Behavior composition, functions as data sources, interface segregation with first-class functions, pipelining, map–reduce;
Patterns and Antipatterns: STRATEGY, COMMAND.

Object-oriented design offers many valuable principles and techniques for structuring data and computation. However, alternative ways to structure software can also be leveraged when designing applications. This chapter provides an introduction to a style of design that uses the function as its primary building block. With functional-style design, structuring the code is achieved through the use of higher-order functions, that is, functions that take other functions as argument. To use higher-order functions requires the programming language to provide support for functions as a first-class program entity. This chapter provides an overview of the Java mechanisms that support functional-style programming and how to use them to integrate elements of functional style into the design of an overall application.

Design Context

The design problems considered in this chapter mostly focus on the processing of collections of objects to represent playing cards. Problems include sorting a collection of cards, comparing cards, filtering cards, and computing various aggregate values (e.g., cardinality) on a collection of cards. To accommodate contexts where design patterns can be applied, the running examples also include realizing a Model–

© Springer Nature Switzerland AG 2019
M. P. Robillard, *Introduction to Software Design with Java*,
https://doi.org/10.1007/978-3-030-24094-3_9

View separation between an object that stores cards and an object that displays a card, and defining commands on an instance that represents a deck of cards.

9.1 First-Class Functions

Up to now, we have applied most software design principles by organizing data and computation in terms of classes and objects, and interactions between them. This is consistent with the object-oriented programming paradigm. There are, however, situations where the use of objects to realize a design solution seems a bit contrived. We have already seen an example of such a situation in Section 3.4, which introduced the idea of function objects. For example, to sort a list of cards, the library method `Collections.sort(...)` requires as input an argument of type `Comparator<Card>` whose sole purpose is to provide an implementation of the method `compare(Card, Card)`.[1] We can provide this argument by creating a function object that is an instance of an anonymous class:

```
List<Card> cards = ...;
Collections.sort(cards, new Comparator<Card>()
{
  public int compare(Card pCard1, Card pCard2)
  { return pCard1.getRank().compareTo(pCard2.getRank()); }
});
```

The reason the code above is a bit contrived is that, strictly from a software design point of view, what the `sort` method needs is only the desired comparison behavior for cards, yet what we actually supply is a reference to an object, something generally understood as an assembly of data and methods to operate on this data. There is thus a conceptual mismatch between the design goal and the programming mechanism employed to fulfill it. The design goal is to *parameterize the behavior* of the `sort` method, and the mechanism we use to do this is to *pass a reference to an object*. What would be a better fit, would be for the `sort` method to take in as input the desired sorting function directly.

Providing functions as input to other functions, however, requires the programming language to allow this by supporting *first-class functions*. This essentially means treating functions as values that can be passed as argument, stored in variables, and returned by other functions.

Since version 8, Java supports a syntax which, in practice, emulates first-class functions. For example, we could define a function in class `Card` that compares two cards by rank:

```
public class Card
{
  private static int compareByRank(Card pCard1, Card pCard2)
  { return pCard1.getRank().compareTo(pCard2.getRank()); }
}
```

---

[1] In this chapter, the term "function" is used as a general abstraction of computation. In Java, the term would refer to both static and instance methods.

and supply a reference to this function as the second argument to method `sort`:

```
Collections.sort(cards, Card::compareByRank);
```

This code, which compiles and does what we want, is actually syntactic sugar that gives the illusion of first-class functions but actually converts the method reference `Card::compare` into an instance of `Comparator<Card>`. The syntax and detailed behavior of the code above is described in Section 9.2. The implications of being able to design with first-class functions is significant. They are a major design tool which, in some cases, allows us to consider design solutions that make the intent behind the solution clearer, reduce clutter in the code, and help reuse code more effectively.

With first-class functions, it becomes possible to design functions that take other functions as arguments. Such functions are called *higher-order functions*. In a way, when considering the above code from a functional point of view, we can say that `Collections.sort` is a higher-order function. In some contexts, it is possible to build entire applications from the principled use of higher-order functions. In such cases, we would say that the application is designed in the *functional programming paradigm*. Using higher-order functions does not, by itself, mean that an application's entire design becomes "functional". Functional programming is a much more comprehensive paradigm whereby computation is organized by transforming data, ideally without mutating state.

Functional programming, even in the limited context of the Java language, is a major topic whose detailed treatment is outside the scope of this book. There are good references available for learning about the ins and outs of functional programming features in Java and beyond (see Further Reading). The goal of this chapter is to provide enough of an introduction to basic functional programming features to allow the integration of functional elements into an otherwise object-oriented design. First-class functions support a whole new level of versatility for exploring the design space, realizing design principles, and applying design patterns. For this reason, it is important to know about functional-*style* programming even if we are not building an application strictly in the functional paradigm. This being said, the last part of the chapter introduces the map–reduce programming model, which will take us as close to full-fledged functional programming as we will get in this book.

9.2 Functional Interfaces, Lambda Expressions, and Method References

The three mechanisms that enable first-class functions in Java are functional interfaces, lambda expressions, and method references. Let us introduce these in turn.

Functional Interfaces

In Java, a *functional interface* is an interface type that declares a single abstract method. For example, we could define an interface to represent "filtering" behavior for a collection of cards:

```
public interface Filter
{ boolean accept(Card pCard); }
```

There is nothing special about functional interfaces: they are just like any other interface. We can declare classes to implement them as usual. For example, we can use an anonymous class to define a filter that only accepts cards with a black suit (spades or clubs);

```
Filter blackCardFilter = new Filter()
{
  public boolean accept(Card pCard)
  { return pCard.getSuit().getColor() == Suit.Color.BLACK; }
};
```

This example shows how the functional interface `Filter` defines a small slice of behavior, an idea introduced in Section 3.2. In the context of functional-style programming, functional interfaces serve another important purpose, though: they define a *function type*. The idea of a function type basically goes as follows. If we forget about the implicit parameter for a second, we can consider method `accept` of interface `Filter` to be a function that takes as parameter a `Card` instance and returns a **boolean**. Thus, we have a function of type `Card` → **boolean**. Now, because our `Filter` interface only defines a single abstract method, implementing this interface amounts to supplying the implementation for this single function. With a bit of imagination, we can consider that obtaining an instance of `Filter` is equivalent to obtaining an implementation of a method that takes as argument a reference to a `Card` instance and returns a **boolean**. Hence, functional interfaces can play the role of function types.

The use of the word *abstract* in the definition of a functional interface is important. Starting with version 8 of the language, interfaces in Java can define static and default methods. Because an implementation for such methods is provided directly in the interface, implementing types are not required to provide one. Static and default methods are thus, by definition, not abstract. This means that an interface can define multiple methods, and still qualify as a functional interface if only one of them is abstract. A good example of such an interface is `Comparator<T>` (see Section 3.4). The `Comparator<T>` interface defines numerous static and default methods, whose purpose is going to become clear later in this chapter. However, the interface defines a single abstract method: **int** `compare(T, T)` (where `T` is a type parameter). For this reason, `Comparator` is a functional interface that defines the function type `(T, T)` → **int**. The implication for functional-style programming is that we are able to treat instances of `Comparator<T>` as first-class functions.

With functional-style programming, Java 8 introduced a library of convenient functional interfaces, located in package `java.util.function`. These interfaces provide the most common function types, such as `Function<T, R>`, a generic type that can represent the type of any unary function between reference types.[2] The interface has a single method `apply`.

To use a library type instead of our custom `Filter` interface, we use the functional interface `Predicate<T>`, which represents the type of a function with a single argument of type `T` and returns a **boolean**.[3] The name of the abstract method for `Predicate<T>` is `test(T)`. We can thus rewrite the code above as follows:

```
Predicate<Card> blackCardFilter = new Predicate<Card>()
  {
    public boolean test(Card pCard)
    { return pCard.getSuit().getColor() == Suit.Color.BLACK; }
  };
```

Because they define function types, functional interfaces serve as the basis for all functional-style design in Java.

Lambda Expressions

With functional interfaces, we get one step closer to being able to program with first-class functions. However, with anonymous classes, specifying the behavior of our example function still has a definite object-oriented look. Recalling our implementation of the "black cards" predicate, above:

```
Predicate<Card> blackCardFilter = new Predicate<Card>() { ... };
```

The use of the **new** keyword in the definition of the behavior of our predicate betrays the fact that we are still creating an object. To more directly express our design in terms of a first-class function, we can define the implementation of a functional interface as a *lambda expression*. Lambda expressions are a compact form of expression of functional behavior whose name is derived from *lambda calculus*, a mathematical system for expressing computation. In Java, lambda expressions are basically anonymous functions. They were briefly introduced in Section 3.4. Now we can take a second look at them in the context of functional-style programming. To convert our example to use a lambda expression, we would write:

```
Predicate<Card> blackCardFilter =
  (Card card) -> card.getSuit().getColor() == Suit.Color.BLACK;
```

The syntax of lambda expressions is detailed below, but for now it is sufficient to know that the function parameter is declared on the left of the arrow (`->`), and the expression on the right of the arrow represents the body of the function. Although this code has the same effect as using an anonymous class, the syntax no longer makes use of the **new** keyword. In addition to being more compact, the code makes it even

---

[2] There are equivalent interfaces to represent functions that involve primitive types, e.g., `IntFunction<R>`.

[3] In contrast to `Function<T, R>`, `Predicate<T>` has a single type parameter because the return type is implied by the interface. The function type that corresponds to `Predicate<T>` is thus $T \to$ **boolean**. We could also specify our filter interface as `Function<Card, Boolean>`, but this option is less efficient because it relies on autoboxing.

more obvious that what we are trying to achieve is to initialize `blackCardFilter` with *behavior* (a function) as opposed to *data* (an object). We can also say that the function is "anonymous" because no function name appears in its declaration. From a design point of view, we do not really care about the actual name of the function because it will get called polymorphically through the name of the method in the functional interface. Because functional interfaces are intended to be reused, the name of the method they define tends to be very general, and so it carries little information about what the method does. In our example, the method in the `Predicate<T>` functional interface is `test(T)`: this says nothing about the actual behavior of our lambda expression (which is to return **true** if the suit of the card is black). Information about the behavior of the lambda expression is typically the code of the lambda expression itself or, at best, an informative variable name (as above). In Java, lambda expressions are not typically documented with a header comment.

The syntax of lambda expressions comprises three parts: a list of parameters, a right arrow (the characters `->`), and a body. In the example above, the list of parameters is `(Card card)`. When the lambda expression requires no parameter, we simply provide an empty set of parentheses `()->`. The body of the lambda expression can take one of two forms:

- a single expression (e.g., `a == 1`).
- a block of one or more statements (e.g., `{`**return** `a == 1;}`).

In the `blackCardFilter` example, the definition of the body of the lambda expression uses the first option. Because, given then functional interface, the return type is expected to be **boolean** and the expression evaluates to a Boolean value, the use of the **return** keyword is superfluous and can simply be assumed to be the result of the evaluation. Using the **return** keyword would turn the expression into a statement, thus breaking the syntax. It is worth noting how expressing the body of a lambda as an expression does not require a semicolon after the expression. In the `blackCardFilter` example, the final semicolon terminates the entire assignment statement, not the lambda expression. Let us rewrite the lambda expression to express the body as a block:

```
Predicate<Card> blackCards =
  (Card card) ->
    { return card.getSuit().getColor() == Suit.Color.BLACK; };
```

This code does exactly the same thing as previously. However, because the body of the lambda expression is no longer a single expression, we need to add curly braces around the block that consists of a single statement, use the **return** keyword to indicate what we are returning, and terminate the statement within the block with a semicolon. As can be seen, the first form (using an expression) is more compact. Normally, when we write lambda expressions, we define them as expressions whenever possible and, when the computation is complex and we need multiple statements, fall back on defining them as a block.

Behind the scenes, lambda expressions are checked by the compiler and turned into function objects through a process of inference. Essentially, when the Java compiler sees a lambda expression, it tries to match it to a functional interface. In the code above, the right-hand side of the assignment is a lambda expression. The compiler will thus look for the type of the variable to which this lambda is assigned to make sure everything matches, namely:

- The type of the variable is a functional interface;
- The parameter types of the lambda expression are compatible with those of the functional interface;
- The type of the value returned by the body of the lambda expression is compatible with the one of the abstract method of the functional interface.

The compiler can actually do a bit more than check the code for correctness: it can also *infer* some information about it. Because the types of the parameters of the function implemented by the lambda expression are already encoded in the definition of the abstract method in the corresponding functional interface, it is not necessary to repeat them in the declaration of the lambda expression. To make our code more compact, we could simply omit the optional declaration of parameter type `Card`:

```
Predicate<Card> blackCardFilter =
   (card) -> card.getSuit().getColor() == Suit.Color.BLACK;
```

In fact, if the function type takes a single parameter, we can even omit the parentheses around the parameter:

```
Predicate<Card> blackCardFilter =
  card -> card.getSuit().getColor() == Suit.Color.BLACK;
```

Whether or not to include parameter types in the declaration of a lambda expression is a matter of style. However, it is good to keep in mind that they can help make the code more readable. When types are provided, a compact variable name becomes more acceptable. For example, we could rewrite the above as:

```
Predicate<Card> blackCardFilter =
   (Card c) -> c.getSuit().getColor() == Suit.Color.BLACK;
```

Essentially, lambda expressions are an idiom used to instantiate functional interfaces, just like anonymous classes. As such, the single method implemented through a lambda expression is called like any other method. For example, to count the number of black cards in an instance of `Deck`, we could do (assuming the `Deck` is iterable):

```
Deck deck = ...
Predicate<Card> blackCardFilter =
  card -> card.getSuit().getColor() == Suit.Color.BLACK;
int total = 0;
for( Card card : deck )
{
  if( blackCardFilter.test(card) )
  { total++; }
}
```

Lambda expressions are also a good match for providing behavior in-place when required by library or application functions. For example, the method `removeIf` of class `ArrayList` takes a single argument of type `Predicate<T>` and removes all elements in the `ArrayList` for which the predicate is true. Given an `ArrayList` of `Card`, we can remove all black cards from the list with a single call:

```
ArrayList<Card> cards = ...
cards.removeIf(
   card -> card.getSuit().getColor() == Suit.Color.BLACK);
```

Method References

Lambda expressions are especially useful when we need to supply custom behavior not defined anywhere else. However, it is also common that one part of the code requires behavior that is already implemented. Let us consider a slight variant of the design of the `Card` class where the class includes the definition of two helper methods:

```
public final class Card
{
   public boolean hasBlackSuit()
   { return aSuit.getColor() == Color.BLACK; }

   public boolean hasRedSuit()
   { return aSuit.getColor() == Color.RED; }
}
```

If, as above, we are writing some code to delete all back cards from an `ArrayList`:

```
ArrayList<Card> cards = ...
cards.removeIf(
   card -> card.getSuit().getColor() == Suit.Color.BLACK);
```

then we are essentially rewriting the code of method `Card.hasBlackSuit`. This does not look so bad here because the code is tiny. However, the reasoning would become more compelling for a larger piece of code (for example, code with a compound condition). In any case, writing a solution we have already coded is an example of DUPLICATED CODE†, which it is a good idea to avoid whenever possible.

What we really want in the present scenario, is simply to reuse our method `has-BlackSuit` as a first-class function. In other words, we want to pass a reference to `hasBlackSuit` as an argument to method `removeIf`. We can do just that with the concept of *method references*. In Java, method references are indicated with a double colon expression `C::m` where `m` refers to the method of interest and `C` the class in which it is defined. Thus, `Card::hasBlackSuit` refers to method `hasBlackSuit` of class `Card`. With this method reference, we can rewrite our code as:

```
cards.removeIf(Card::hasBlackSuit);
```

It hardly gets more compact and explicit than that: the code almost reads like plain English.

Unfortunately, using method references in Java is not as simple as it looks because there are many possible ways to invoke a method using a reference. For example, we could also have the following static method in some utility class:

```
public final class CardUtils
{
  public static boolean hasBlackSuit(Card pCard)
  { return pCard.getSuit().getColor() != Color.BLACK; }
}
```

and use a reference to that method instead:

```
cards.removeIf(CardUtils::hasBlackSuit);
```

Although the method reference looks exactly the same as the instance method, the compiler uses the reference in a different way. In one case (`Card::hasBlackSuit`), the method reference is interpreted as:

```
cards.removeIf(new Predicate<Card>()
{
  public boolean test(Card card)
  { return card.hasBlackSuit(); }
});
```

whereas in the second case (`CardUtils::hasBlackSuit`), the method reference is interpreted as:

```
cards.removeIf(new Predicate<Card>()
{
  public boolean test(Card card)
  { return CardUtils.hasBlackSuit(card); }
});
```

In the first case, the argument of the call to the method of the functional interface is bound to the implicit parameter of the method reference. In the second case, this argument is bound to the explicit parameter of the method reference. How the compiler correctly determines what to do is outside the scope of this book. However, it is important to know that method references support using both static and instance methods as first-class functions, and that the mapping between the reference and the interface method is based on the parameter and return types. In our case, both `Card::hasBlackSuit` and `CardUtils::hasBlackSuit` return a **boolean** and take as input a single parameter of type `Card`. In the case of the instance method, the parameter is the implicit parameter of the method, whereas in the case of the static method, the parameter is the formal parameter of the method. Either way, both implement the function type `Card` $\rightarrow$ **boolean** and can thus be assigned to a variable of type `Predicate<Card>`.

Java also supports supplying a reference to an instance method of a particular object, using the notation `o::m` where `o` is a variable holding a reference to an object and `m` is the method. This language feature is, however, outside the scope of this chapter.

9.3 Using Functions to Compose Behavior

First-class functions make it easy to define small pieces of behavior, such as how to filter or compare objects. Taking this idea a bit further, we can use the principle of divide and conquer to express more complex behavior in terms of simpler behavior. Let us consider the problem of comparing two cards, introduced in Section 3.4. Using a lambda expression, we can define the behavior of the comparison using the Comparator<Card> interface as follows:

```
public class Card
{
  public static Comparator<Card> bySuitComparator()
  {
    return (card1, card2) ->
      card1.getSuit().compareTo(card2.getSuit());
  }
}
```

This design uses a static factory method to return a comparator object that compares two cards in terms of their suit, as defined by the suit ordering in the enumerated type Suit. Because we use a lambda expression, the code expresses the solution more in terms of a first-class function than a function object.

This solution is incomplete because if two cards have the same suit, their relative order is undefined, which is not ideal for many card sorting contexts. To complete the solution, we need to specify a secondary comparison order by rank. One way to do this would be to extend the code of the lambda expression:

```
public static Comparator<Card> bySuitThenRankComparator()
{
  return (card1, card2) ->
  {
    if( card1.getSuit() == card2.getSuit() )
    { return card1.getRank().compareTo(card2.getRank()); }
    else
    { return card1.getSuit().compareTo(card2.getSuit()); }
  };
}
```

This code supports a well-defined total order for cards, at the cost of a more complex lambda expression for which we need to resort to the less compact block form. This code is also less flexible, because if we wish to sort by rank, then suit instead, we need to write an entirely new comparator that repeats most of the code, but with the order of comparison switched. Moreover, if we want to sort in descending order instead of ascending order for either rank or suit, we need to yet again rewrite the code. Ultimately, we have eight options for a basic card comparator: by rank then suit or suit then rank (two options), where either rank or suit can be ascending or descending (times four options). To cover all possibilities with factory methods, we would thus need eight factory methods, and plenty of DUPLICATED CODE†.

To work with finer abstractions, we could start by offering comparison in both relative levels (suit, then rank, and rank, then suit) by creating two factories for single-level comparison (rank or suit) and two additional factories for complete comparisons, where the two complete orders are composed of the single-level comparisons by suit and rank.

```
public static Comparator<Card> byRankComparator()
{ return (card1, card2) ->
    card1.getRank().compareTo(card2.getRank()); }

public static Comparator<Card> bySuitComparator()
{ return (card1, card2) ->
    card1.getSuit().compareTo(card2.getSuit()); }

public static Comparator<Card> byRankThenSuitComparator()
{
  return (card1, card2) ->
  { if( byRankComparator().compare(card1, card2) == 0 )
    { return bySuitComparator().compare(card1, card2 ); }
    else
    { return byRankComparator().compare(card1, card2 ); }
  };
}

public static Comparator<Card> bySuitThenRankComparator()
{
  return (card1, card2) ->
  { if( bySuitComparator().compare(card1, card2) == 0 )
    { return byRankComparator().compare(card1, card2 ); }
    else
    { return bySuitComparator().compare(card1, card2 ); }
  };
}
```

Unfortunately, without extra help, this idea does not really mitigate the complexity of the composite function (and does not even cover the option to reverse the order of either suit- or rank-based ordering). The way out of this situation is the insight that if we want to express a solution in terms of first-class functions, we can also use functions to do the composition. In the case of functions to express comparisons, the Comparator interface provides many static and default methods intended to compose comparison functions out of smaller abstractions. Let us try to rewrite our solution to the problem of supporting the comparison of cards by either rank, then suit, or suit, then rank, in ascending or descending order, using these helper methods. We will proceed bottom up, from the smaller abstractions to the more complex ones.

A first key method is comparing(...). The signature of this method is a bit complex but, essentially, comparing(...) creates a comparator by building on a function that extracts a comparable from its input argument. For example, we could rewrite byRankComparator() as:

```
public static Comparator<Card> byRankComparator()
{ return Comparator.comparing(card -> card.getRank()); }
```

and similarly for `bySuitComparator`. How exactly the method `comparing` works is explained in the next section. For now, it is sufficient to understand the behavior intuitively: the argument to the method is itself a function that extracts the value we want to compare on, and the return value is a comparator structure. The resulting behavior is identical to the original solution using the direct comparison between `Rank` instances.

The second major service available in class `Comparator` is a method to cascade comparisons (for example to compare by suit if the rank is the same, or vice versa). This functionality is provided by the method `thenComparing`. This method is a default method called on a comparator that takes as input another comparator for the same type.[4] With `thenComparing`, we can express our cascaded comparison more directly:

```
public static Comparator<Card> byRankThenSuitComparator()
{ return byRankComparator().thenComparing(bySuitComparator()); }
```

We can observe how this code is already much more explicit about the intent of the computation than the version above, which explicitly does the cascading of comparisons. Inversing the comparison levels then just becomes a question of inversing the order of the comparators in the call chain:

```
public static Comparator<Card> bySuitThenRankComparator()
{ return bySuitComparator().thenComparing(byRankComparator()); }
```

The final step required to complete our solution is to provide a way to reverse the comparison order, from ascending to descending and vice-versa. For example, this would mean going from either ace to king or from king to ace for the rank comparison (assuming ace is the first card in the sequence, called an ace-low sequence). To accomplish this without helper methods, we would need to go back to our basic implementation of comparators and switch the order of the arguments:

```
public static Comparator<Card> byRankComparatorReversed()
{ return (card1, card2) ->
    card2.getRank().compareTo(card1.getRank()); }
```

In the code above, the order of the two parameters in the body of the lambda expression are reversed. Expressing this difference requires a different factory. Fortunately, it is possible to avoid this DUPLICATED CODE† thanks to the helper method `reversed()`, which creates a new comparator that orders elements using the reverse of the order used by the implicit argument of `reversed()`. We can then use `reversed()` to reverse either or both of the comparison levels. For example, to sort by descending suit, then ascending rank, we create a comparator factory as follows

```
public static Comparator<Card> bySuitReversedThenRankComparator()
{ return bySuitComparator()
    .reversed()
    .thenComparing(byRankComparator()); }
```

---

[4] Or a super type, although this eventuality is not covered here.

Similarly, to sort by descending suit, then descending rank:

```
public static Comparator<Card>
  bySuitReversedThenRankReversedComparator()
{ return bySuitComparator()
    .reversed()
    .thenComparing(byRankComparator().reversed()); }
```

At this point, we can express all eight possible comparison orders simply by combining functions with the help of other functions. The resulting code is so straightforward to understand that the abstraction benefit gained by encapsulating comparators in a factory method becomes marginal. In the last code fragment above, the name of the factory method is basically the list of steps directly visible in the function call chain in the body of the method. For this reason, here it would make sense to get rid of the factory methods for the comparators.

Because the only part of the Card interface needed to define the comparison behavior is already available through the getter methods getSuit() and getRank(), the factory methods are not strictly necessary. Removing the comparator factories from the interface of class Card helps mitigate the threats of SPECULATIVE GENERALITY†, namely to provide services that are never used. With the helper methods of Comparator, developers will be able to provide compact and explicit definitions of the desired comparison behavior directly where needed. For example, if a code location requires sorting cards by descending order of suit, then rank, the following code could be used:[5]

```
List<Card> cards = ...
cards.sort(Comparator.comparing((Card card) -> card.getSuit()))
    .reversed()
    .thenComparing(Comparator.comparing(
      (Card card) -> card.getRank()))
        .reversed()));
```

Although this code is already explicit, there are three significant ways in which we can further improve it. First, we can use Java's static import feature to eliminate the need to qualify the static methods:

```
import static java.util.Comparator.comparing;
```

This allows us to remove the qualification of the static method comparing:

```
cards.sort(comparing((Card card) -> card.getSuit())
    .reversed()
    .thenComparing(comparing((Card card) -> card.getRank())
      .reversed()));
```

Second, as explained in Section 9.2, we can use method references to refer to getSuit() and getRank() instead of redefining a lambda expression that simply calls them.

---

[5] In this context the parameter types must be supplied as part of the lambda expression because the compiler does not have enough information to infer them.

```
cards.sort(comparing(Card::getSuit)
    .reversed()
    .thenComparing(comparing(Card::getRank)
      .reversed()));
```

Finally, we can observe that class `Comparator` has an overloaded version of `then-Comparing` that combines the behavior of `comparing` and `thenComparing` by directly taking a function that returns the value of the key we wish to use for comparison. In this case we can move the reversal of the comparison to the final comparator. Our code can thus be reduced to:

```
cards.sort(comparing(Card::getSuit)
  .thenComparing(Card::getRank).reversed());
```

This general principle of leveraging library functions to compose first-class functions can be used in a variety of contexts, so before writing Java code that uses first-class functions as abstractions, it is worthwhile to study the options possible. Most of the functional interfaces provided in package `java.util.function` include some static or default helper methods that can be used to compose other functions. For example, returning to our definition of a `Predicate` for filtering black cards (see Section 9.2):

```
Predicate<Card> blackCardFilter =
  card -> card.getSuit().getColor() == Suit.Color.BLACK;
```

If we want only red cards, we can do simply:[6]

```
Predicate<Card> redCardFilter = blackCardFilter.negate();
```

9.4 Using Functions as Suppliers of Data

The static method `Comparator.comparing`, presented in the previous section, introduces a new idea supported by functional-style design: the use of functions as suppliers of data. Let us look again at how this method works. If we want to build a comparator that compares `Card` objects based on their suit, we do:

```
Comparator<Card> bySuit = Comparator.comparing(Card::getSuit);
```

The argument to `comparing` is neither a reference to a `Card` instance nor a reference to a `Suit` instance. Rather, it is an instance of `Function<Card,Suit>`, a functional interface whose method (`apply`) takes an argument of type `Card` and returns a reference to an object of type `Suit`. This means that that the code that implements method `comparing` will have way to extract an instance of `Suit` from an instance of `Card` whenever necessary in the logic of the method's implementation.

Let us use this idea in a different context. Say we are designing a class `CardViewer` to show a graphical representation of the card at the top of a pile in a card game. The `CardViewer` must be able to show the card of interest whenever necessary by

---

[6] This assumes there are only two colors, which is true in this case and for a standard deck of cards.

calling a method `show()`. Such functionality would typically be used as part of the graphical user interface for an application (see Section 8.5). In addition, one of our requirements is that method `show()` takes no parameter so that instances of `CardViewer` can be used by objects that do not know which card should be shown when they call `show`. Figure 9.1 is a class diagram that shows this design context. In this context, the GUI code holds a reference to a `CardViewer` and may need to call `show()`, for example when a button is clicked. However, because the GUI is not responsible for managing the state of the game, it would not know which card should be shown when it calls `show()`.

Fig. 9.1 Design context for the card viewer problem

An unworkable solution is to set the value of the card when `CardViewer` is initialized:

```
public class CardViewer
{
  private Card aCard;

  public CardViewer(Card pCard) { aCard = pCard; }
}
```

Clearly, we cannot simply store an *instance* of `Card` in the viewer, because the reference to the card would be set *once*, when the `CardViewer` is initialized, and all subsequent calls to `show()` would show the same card. In a game where cards move around, this would not work. Although inadequate, this idea helps make the point that what `CardViewer` needs in this design is not *a card object*, but a *way to get* a card object, and specifically the card object that corresponds to a card that should be shown at a given point in the game.

One way to make sure `CardViewer` gets the card it needs is to define an instance variable of type `Card` in `CardViewer` and to require objects that change the state of the game to "push" the value of the appropriate card into the `CardViewer`. For example, let us say the supplier of the card is an instance of `Deck`, and the GUI needs to periodically show the top of the deck. In this case we would have the scenario illustrated in Figure 9.2. In this sequence, the GUI, which acts as a controller for the state of the game, calls `draw()` on an instance of `Deck`, which causes the deck to pop its top card. Because the state of `Deck` changed, it must notify the `CardViewer` that the card to show is now different. Doing so by directly updating `CardViewer` using a `setCard` method would be a very weak design decision because it would require the `Deck` class to depend on the `CardViewer` class. A slightly better option would be to apply the OBSERVER pattern and make the `CardViewer` an observer of `Deck`. However, this solution requires us to turn the `Deck` class into an observable model, which seems a bit elaborate just to exchange a card object once in a while.

Fig. 9.2 Weak solution to the card viewer problem

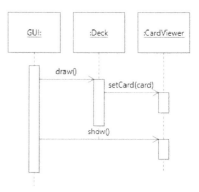

A more promising approach is to use the pull data-flow strategy, where an object that needs data from another object queries this data whenever necessary. This is an idea we already saw in the context of the OBSERVER, in Section 8.3. In the present context, we wish to use the pull strategy to obtain a reference to the correct card to show from within the implementation of method `show()`. To accomplish this goal, we first initialize an instance of `CardViewer` with an object that has the information we need:

```
public class CardViewer
{
  private Deck aDeck;

  public CardViewer(Deck pDeck) { aDeck = pDeck }
}
```

Then, whenever we need to show the card, we call `aDeck.peek()`. With this approach, the code in `CardViewer` only obtains the required `Card` instance when `show()` is called. Naturally, this code assumes that `Deck` has a `peek` method as part of its interface.

Unfortunately, a design weakness remains with the code above. Class `CardViewer` is tightly coupled with `Deck`, which means it cannot be reused with other suppliers of cards (e.g., a different `CardStack` in the Solitaire application). Fortunately, by now we know how to solve this problem: through interfaces and polymorphism. Here we could define a new interface `CardSupplier` with a single method `getCard()`, and make `Deck` implement this interface.[7] Figure 9.3 illustrates that solution.

This last solution achieves the desirable design qualities of loose coupling and reusability. However, it does have a price by requiring the definition of yet a new

---

[7] The interface `CardSource` introduced earlier would not be a good choice, because it defines behavior that can remove cards from a source, whereas here we need to obtain card instances without any side effect.

Fig. 9.3 Interface-based solution for the card viewer problem

interface (`CardSupplier`) and requiring the `Deck` class to implement yet another interface. With functional-style programming, we can pave over these two issues to achieve a flexible design solution with minimal impact. We can transform our object-oriented approach to data pulling into a functional-style solution by implementing the `CardSupplier` interface using a lambda expression or method reference instead of through a class definition. Optionally, we can also use a standard functional interface instead of a user-defined one.

Functions whose purpose is to return a value without considering any argument are a common idiom in functional-style design. So, not surprisingly, the Java library includes a generic type to cover this case. Interface `Supplier<T>` defines a single method `get()` that returns a value of type `T`. Thus, we can avoid defining a new interface for this purpose, and use Java's `Supplier<T>`:

```java
public class CardViewer
{
  private Supplier<Card> aCardSupplier;

  public CardViewer(Supplier<Card> pCardSupplier)
  { aCardSupplier = pCardSupplier; }

  public void show()
  {
    Card card = aCardSupplier.get();
    // Show the card.
  }
}
```

With this code, we can initialize a `CardViewer` with any first-class function that takes no argument and returns a value of type `Card`. In a code context where we want to create an instance of `CardViewer` and we already have an instance of `Deck`, we could initialize the `CardViewer` with its supplier as follows:

```java
Deck deck = ...
CardViewer viewer = new CardViewer( () -> deck.peek() );
```

In this example, the card supplier becomes a closure that can access the specific instance of `Deck` we need to retrieve the required card. Every time method `show()` is called, its code will call the first-class function represented by `aCardSupplier` to obtain a card instance. In the current design, this card will happen to be whatever card is on top of the deck when `show()` is called. Figure 9.4 illustrates the sequence of calls that leads to a card instance being retrieved from a `Deck` instance from the object-oriented perspective. However, in the code, the functional-style design makes it seem like the last two calls in the sequence are abstracted as a single first-class function.

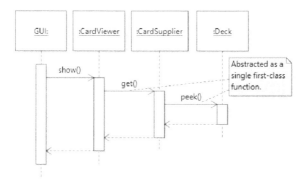

Fig. 9.4 Sequence to access a card in the card viewer design

The card supplier example above illustrates the two main benefits we can achieve when using first-class functions as suppliers of data:

- When passing supplier functions to objects instead of actual data, objects can access the information on-demand instead of storing it as a piece of data they have to manage.
- To narrow the interfaces that objects use to exchange data. Passing supplier functions to objects can take the interface segregation principle to its optimal point, by allowing objects to request precisely the information they need through a set of supplier interfaces, as opposed to aggregating interfaces that may include services they do not need.

In this example of a supplier function, I used the general functional interface `Supplier<T>` to introduce it. However, whether to use a library or user-defined functional interface is a design decision with its usual trade-offs. Generally speaking, user-defined interfaces increase the understandability of a design, whereas library interfaces increase its flexibility. I will revisit this issue in more detail in the next section.

Now that we have seen the concept of a supplier function, we can revisit the implementation of the `comparing` method of class `Comparator`. This method is a bit tricky because it involves two degrees of indirection in the use of first-class functions. The code below is a slightly simplified version of the actual implementation of `comparing` as instantiated for the `Card` and `Suit` type parameters:

```
public static Comparator<Card> comparing(
  Function<Card, Suit> keyExtractor)
{
  return (card1, card2) -> keyExtractor.apply(card1)
    .compareTo(keyExtractor.apply(card2));
}
```

A sample use of this code is as follows:

```
Comparator<Card> comparator =
  comparator.comparing(Card::getSuit());
comparator.compare(card1,card2);
```

When `comparing` is called, it creates a new function object that binds `Card::`
`getSuit` to `keyExtractor`, but without calling either `apply` or its delegate `getSuit`.
This indirection is necessary because `comparing` uses the supplier function as a
building block when creating a new function, as opposed to simply using the supplier (as in our example above). When method `compare` is called, only then is `apply`
called, this time twice, once for each card. Because `apply` redirects to `getSuit`, at
that point the suit value is obtained from the card and used in the comparison. Figure 9.5 illustrates the complete sequence.

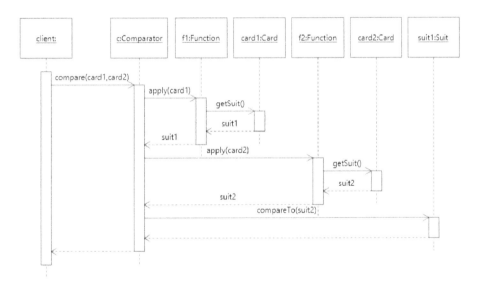

Fig. 9.5 Sequence of calls for comparing two cards using a comparator created with
`Comparator.comparing`

A final note concerning method `comparing` is that, in contrast to the `CardViewer`
example, its "supplier" function `keyExtractor` actually takes an argument. In this
sense, the function is more a data "extractor" than a pure supplier. Notwithstand-
ing this distinction, the mechanism involved is the same: `comparing` will obtain a
reference to a function that it can call whenever it needs some data to work with.

Supplier Functions and the OBSERVER Pattern

When implementing the OBSERVER pattern, supplier functions can offer a flexible
way to support the pull data-flow strategy. As discussed in Section 8.3, one way to
decouple concrete observers from the model is to define some sort of ModelData
interface that only includes getter methods. However, in a design context where
different concrete observers would require very different types of data from the
model, it would be difficult to make this interface a good fit for all observers. With
supplier functions, observers can require exactly the type of data they need. As a
simple example, let us consider that we wish to use the Deck class in an OBSERVER
pattern. One concrete observer needs the size of the deck, one observer needs the
top card, and one observer needs to iterate through all cards in the deck. If we define
an interface DeckData

```java
public interface DeckData extends Iterable<Card>
{
  int size();
  Card peek();
}
```

then all observers will get access to the three pieces of information, even though
they only need one each. Instead, concrete observers can only request what they
need through suppliers. For example, the observer that only needs the size of the
deck could be defined as:

```java
public DeckSizeObserver implements DeckObserver
{
  private IntSupplier aSizeSupplier;

  public DeckSizeObserver(IntSupplier pSizeSupplier)
  { aSizeSupplier = pSizeSupplier; }

  public void deckChanged() /* Callback method */
  {
    int size = aSizeSupplier.get();
    ...
  }
}
```

As expected, the IntSupplier is a functional interface of the Java library that
defines a single **int** get() method. With this design we can thus connect the observer to an instance of Deck stored in a deck variable as such:

```java
DeckSizeObserver observer = new DeckSizeObserver(()->deck.size());
```

With a similar approach to the other observers, we can do away with the impracti-
cal DeckData interface and still use the pull model to extract the desired information
from the model.

9.5 First-Class Functions and Design Patterns

Many design patterns rely on polymorphism to enable variation points in the solution. For example, the STRATEGY pattern relies on polymorphism to allow client code to dispatch the execution of an algorithm to a dynamically selected variant (see Section 3.7). Similarly, the COMMAND pattern uses polymorphism to allow client code to trigger the execution of a command whose exact nature is also determined at run-time (see Section 6.8). In the original object-oriented description of the design patterns, this polymorphism is enabled by extending classes and implementing interfaces.

In functional-style design, first-class functions provide a different perspective on behavior parameterization. Instead of creating objects of different classes and enabling polymorphism through a common supertype, we can define families of functions whose type is compatible and invoke them interchangeably. This is of course possible in any context, but it is interesting to note that first-class functions allow a re-thinking of the implementation of design patterns. By way of illustration, in this section I revisit the implementation of the STRATEGY and COMMAND patterns using a functional style.

Functional-Style STRATEGY

In simple cases where strategies are stateless and their interface boils down to a single method, we can express the abstract strategy as a functional interface and the concrete strategies as lambda expressions. Let us consider a hypothetical context where client code may want to use different strategies for selecting a card in a list. Then, strategies are simply implementations of method `apply` of interface `Function<List<Card>, Card>`, which becomes the abstract strategy. In our case, method `apply` takes as input a list of cards and returns a single card. As an example of a client class for the strategy, we could have:

```
public class AutoPlayer
{
  private Function<List<Card>, Card> aSelectionStrategy;

  public AutoPlayer(Function<List<Card>, Card> pSelectionStrategy)
  { aSelectionStrategy = pSelectionStrategy; }

  public void play()
  {
    Card selected = aSelectionStrategy.apply(getCards());
    ...
  }

  // Gets the cards to supply to the strategy
  private List<Card> getCards() {...}
}
```

In this design, the card selection strategy is provided as an argument to the constructor when the client `AutoPlayer` object is created. Because the strategy is modeled as a first-class function, defining it involves defining the behavior of this function at any convenient point in the code. One option could be to define it on the fly at the location where the instance of `AutoPlayer` is created. For example, a strategy to always select the first card would be:

```
AutoPlayer player = new AutoPlayer(cards -> cards.get(0));
```

For more elaborate strategies, another option could be to define a collection of common strategies in a utility class:

```
public final class CardSelection
{
  private CardSelection() {}

  public static Card lowestBlackCard(List<Card> pCards) { ... }
  public static Card highestFaceCard(List<Card> pCards) { ... }
  ...
}
```

and use method references to select a strategy:

```
AutoPlayer player =
  new AutoPlayer(CardSelection::lowestBlackCard);
```

This implementation style is very compact, and even perhaps too much so. The use of the general `Function` functional interface in this context has two potential limitations. First, it has low documentation effectiveness. Looking at the type `Function<List<Card>, Card>`, all we know is that it can return a `Card` given a list of cards. For this reason, any reference to the card selection strategy in the code needs to be done through well-named variables for the code to remain readable. Here, field `aSelectionStrategy` fulfills the requirement. A second problem is that the single method in the `Function` interface is also very general-purpose, and for this reason cannot include any context-specific information. In our case, we need to determine how to handle the case where the list is empty. One possibility would be to redefine the strategy as `Function<List<Card>, Optional<Card>`, and somehow remember that by convention passing an empty list results in an empty optional object. Another possibility would be to state that the input list must not be empty is a precondition for the strategy. In both cases, it is not clear where one would document this critical piece of information.

For these reasons, defining an additional functional interface to represent the strategy will lead to clearer code and a more self-explicit design. Since the new interface can also be used to locate the standard strategies, the impact on the code base is minimal. The following code shows an implementation of a STRATEGY application for selecting cards that uses design by contract to guard against the case of selecting from an empty list and uses the `Optional` type to guard against the case where a strategy yields no card. Although in this case it would make sense to return `Optional.empty()` if the input list is also empty, both options are included for sake of illustration.

```
public interface CardSelectionStrategy
{
  /**
   * Select an instance of Card from pCards.
   * @param A list of cards to choose from.
   * @pre pCards != null && !pCards.isEmpty()
   * @post If RETURN.isPresent(), pCards.contains(RETURN.get())
   */
  Optional<Card> select(List<Card> pCards);

  public static Optional<Card> first(List<Card> pCards)
  { return Optional.of(pCards.get(0)); }

  public static Optional<Card> lowestBlackCard(List<Card> pCards)
  { ... }

  public static Optional<Card> highestFaceCard(List<Card> pCards)
  { ... }
}
```

Functional-Style COMMAND

Similarly to the STRATEGY pattern, the central idea of the COMMAND pattern is one of behavior parameterization. In the classic implementation of the pattern, the concrete behavior of a command is achieved by defining different classes with a common supertype, where each class represents a type of command (see Section 6.8). With first-class functions, we can parameterize the behavior of a single concrete command class by defining a field that stores a function that is called when executing the command.

Let us consider again the original example of COMMAND introduced in Section 6.8, to support a number of commands to modify the state of a `Deck` object. In this case, we could apply the pattern by designing a *single* command class that serves as both the abstract and concrete command:

```
public class Command
{
  private final Runnable aCommand;

  public Command(Runnable pCommand) { aCommand = pCommand; }
  public void execute() { aCommand.run(); }
}
```

This minimalist application of the pattern uses the library functional interface `Runnable`, which declares a single method `run()` that takes no parameter and returns no value. However, the data required to execute the command can be obtained from the environment in which a new command is created, and bundled into a closure:

```
Deck deck = new Deck();

Command draw = new Command(() -> deck.draw());
Command shuffle = new Command(() -> deck.shuffle());
```

Although workable, this design suffers from limitations caused by the minimalism of the implementation:

- Command objects are not self-documenting. Once a command object is created, we need to rely on external means (such as variable names) to keep track of it;
- The `Runnable` interface is very general: we cannot arbitrarily add constraints to the declaration of its `run()` method, for example to prevent executing commands on an empty deck;
- If some commands require a outflow of data, we need a mechanism to support this data flow.

These three limitations are identical to those of the functional-style implementation of the STRATEGY, and we can address them in a similar way.

First, we can make commands more self-documenting by storing the name of the command in the command object and naming the command class more specifically:

```
public class DeckCommand
{
  private final Runnable aCommand;
  private final String aName;

  public DeckCommand(String pName, Runnable pCommand)
  {
    aName = pName;
    aCommand = pCommand;
  }

  public void execute() { aCommand.run(); }
}
```

Second, we can define our own functional interface and use it instead of `Runnable` to qualify the type of the first-class function that represents the command. However, here because the first-class functions that will represent commands can only be called by being first passed as values to the constructor of `DeckCommand`, we have a more obvious single point for documenting the preconditions for executing the function. It is possible to make our design constraint explicit by appropriately documenting the constructor of the `DeckCommand` class, its `execute()` method, or both.

Finally, the choice of how to support collecting the result of a command is, just as in the object-oriented version of the pattern, an open-ended decision that should be informed by the design context in which the pattern is applied. The more flexible option is to store the result in a data structure accessed through a closure, e.g.,

```
Deck deck = new Deck();
List<Card> drawnCards = new ArrayList<>();
DeckCommand draw = new DeckCommand("draw",
  () -> drawnCards.add(deck.draw()));
```

Another option is to replace `Runnable` with a functional interface that returns a value (e.g., of type `Card`) and stores this value in the command object, as in the original application of the pattern.

9.6 Functional-Style Data Processing

Up to now, the design ideas presented in this chapter involve including functional elements into an otherwise object-oriented design. In some cases, the design context motivates solutions that have a much stronger flavor of functional-style programming. One scenario where functional-style programming shines is to structure code responsible for processing a collection of data. In a way, most of what software does is to process data, so here we can tighten the definition and consider that functional-style programming provides good support for design problems that involve applying transformations to large sequences of data elements. An example of data processing that meets this definition is counting the number of acronyms in a body of text. In this case, the input is a sequence of words, and the transformations are to filter the input for acronyms, and then to compute the total number of instances found.

Functional-style design is a good match for this type of data processing because it naturally calls for the use of behavior parameterization and higher-order functions. Higher-order functions implement the general data-processing strategies, which are then parameterized for a particular context with first-class functions. In the text processing example above, the general strategy is to check whether each input element (a word) matches a certain predicate (acronym or not). Although the general strategy of filtering over a predicate is likely to apply to many different problems, the predicate itself (acronym detection) is specific to the particular design context. In other cases we might want to write code that detects short words, proper nouns, etc. This idiom can be illustrated by the statement:

```
data.higherOrderFunction(firstClassFunction);
```

Applied to our current example, this would mean:

```
listOfWords.filter(isAcronym);
```

Functional-style data processing is a major topic in software design. This section provides a basic overview of the main concepts and techniques that underlie this design style, and how to realize them in Java.

Data as a Stream

The main concept that enables functional-style data processing in Java and similar technologies is that of a *stream*. Simply stated, a stream is a sequence of data elements, a bit like a collection. However, the major conceptual difference between a stream and a collection is that a collection represents a *store* of data whereas a stream represents a *flow* of data. This distinction is similar to the difference between storing music as a file vs. playing music via an on-line streaming service. For software design, the distinction between collections and streams has many practical implications:

- Elements in a collection have to exist before they are added to the collection, but elements in a stream can be computed on-demand.
- Although collections can only store a finite number of elements, streams can technically be infinite. For example, although it is not possible to define a list that contains all the even numbers, it is possible to create a stream that produces this data.
- Collections can be traversed multiple times, but the traversal code is located outside the collection, for example in a `for` loop or iterator class. In contrast, streams can be traversed once: their elements are *consumed* as part of the traversal. However, the traversal code is hidden within the higher-order functions provided by the stream's interface.
- Streams are amenable to being parallelized, mainly because the traversal of their elements is hidden as part of the stream abstraction.

An additional, more pragmatic, difference relates to the evolution of the Java language. Collection classes (`List`, `Set`, etc.) were released before the language had explicit support for first-class functions, so collections provide almost no support for higher-order functions.[8] In contrast, Java 8 provides support for first-class functions (in the form of method references and lambda expressions) and includes a powerful `Stream` API designed to support functional-style design. The remainder of this section shows how to design functional-style data processing in Java using the `Stream` API.

In Java, the simplest way to obtain a stream is to call the `stream()` method on an instance of a collection class. For example, let us modify the design of the `Deck` class illustrated in Figure 9.6 to support streaming cards using an instance of `Deck` as supplier of data.

Fig. 9.6 Initial design of the `Deck` class, which can be modified to add support for streaming `Card` instances from a `Deck` instance

Making an instance of `Deck` able to stream cards simply requires propagating the `Stream` instance obtainable from the list to the interface of `Deck`:

[8] The notable exception is the default method `forEach` available on the `Iterable<T>` interface since Java 8.

```
public class CardStack implements Iterable<Card>
{
  private final List<Card> aCards;
  public Stream<Card>  stream() { return aCards.stream(); }
  ...
}


public class Deck implements CardSource , Iterable<Card>
{
  private CardStack aCards;
  public Stream<Card> stream() { return aCards.stream(); }
  ...
}
```

By themselves, streams already support many useful (non-higher-order) functions. For example, we can easily count the elements in the stream:

```
Stream<Card> cards = new Deck().stream();
long total = cards.count();
```

Streams also support operations that take as input a stream as its implicit parameter and output a different stream, a process known as *pipelining*. For example, the `sorted` method returns the elements of the original stream in sorted order. Because method `sorted()` requires the instances in the stream to be subtypes of `Comparable`, the code below assumes the version of class `Card` used implements `Comparable`:

```
Stream<Card> sortedCards = cards.stream().sorted();
```

Pipelining also makes it easy to combine operations on streams. For example, method `limit(int max)` returns up to `max` elements from the stream. To obtain the first ten cards in sorted order, we can thus write:

```
Stream<Card> sortedCards = cards.stream().sorted().limit(10);
```

It is also possible to combine multiple streams. For example, to assemble all the cards from two decks and sort them, we can do:

```
Stream<Card> cards =
  Stream.concat(new Deck().stream(), new Deck().stream());
```

To revert to a single deck one option is to remove the duplicates using `distinct()`:

```
Stream<Card> withDuplicates =
  Stream.concat(new Deck().stream(), new Deck().stream());
Stream<Card> withoutDuplicates = withDuplicates.distinct();
```

Applying Higher-Order Functions to Streams

The main way that streams support functional-style programming is that they define a number of higher-order functions. The essential higher-order function for streams is `forEach`, which applies an input function to all elements of the stream. For example, to print all cards in a stream in a functional way, we could do the following:

```
new Deck().stream().forEach(card -> System.out.println(card));
```

The method `forEach` takes an argument of type `Consumer<? super T>`, which means we can supply it a reference to a function that defines a single parameter of type `Card` (or any supertype of `Card`). In the example above this reference is supplied in the form of a lambda expression.[9] Because `forEach` is not guaranteed to respect the order in which elements are encountered in the stream, a second version, `forEachOrdered`, can be used if ordering is important. Because it does not return a stream, the outcome of the `forEach` function (either variant) cannot be further transformed as part of a pipeline. Generally speaking, stream functions that do not produce a stream of results that can be further processed as part of a pipeline are called *terminal* operations. Another example of a terminal operation on streams is the `count` function seen above.

Other types of terminal higher-order functions that can be applied to streams include searching functions such as `allMatch`, `anyMatch`, and `noneMatch`, which take as argument a predicate on the stream element type and return a Boolean value that indicates respectively whether all, any, or none of the elements in the stream evaluate the predicate to **true**. For example, to determine if all cards in a list are in the clubs suit, we would do:

```
List<Card> cards = ...;
boolean allClubs = cards.stream()
  .allMatch(card -> card.getSuit() == Suit.CLUBS );
```

Filtering Streams

The `sorted()` stream function, mentioned above, shows how we can define *intermediate* operations to create a pipeline of transformations on a stream. An intermediate operation thus has a stream as an implicit argument, and returns a stream. An important function in this pipelining process is the `filter` method, which takes a `Predicate` and returns a stream that consists of all the elements of the original stream for which the predicate evaluates to true. For example, assuming we want to count the face cards in a list of cards:

```
long numberOfFaceCards = cards.stream()
  .filter(card -> card.getRank().ordinal() >=
    Rank.JACK.ordinal()).count();
```

To leverage the benefits of both object-orientation and functional-style programming, predicates such as the one above are best captured as instance methods:

```
public final class Card
{
  public boolean isFaceCard()
  { return getRank().ordinal() >= Rank.JACK.ordinal(); }
```

---

[9] An equivalent expression would be to pass the method reference `System.out::println` directly, but this uses a reference to a method applied to a specific instance, a technique that is outside the scope of this chapter.

This allows us to use method references and make the functional code self-explanatory:

```
long numberOfFaceCards = cards.stream()
  .filter(Card::isFaceCard)
  .count();
```

At first glance, capturing predicates in dedicated methods may seem like an obstacle to the creation of compound predicates. For example, what if we want to count only face cards in the clubs suit? Do we have to revert to our original lambda expression?

```
long result = cards.stream()
  .filter(card -> card.getRank().ordinal() >= Rank.JACK.ordinal()
    && card.getSuit()==Suit.CLUBS).count();
```

A key insight to avoid ugly code like this is to observe that filters, being an intermediate operation, can also be pipelined:

```
long result = cards.stream()
  .filter(Card::isFaceCard)
  .filter(card -> card.getSuit() == Suit.CLUBS)
  .count();
```

At this point, it should become apparent that our functional-style code is starting to look much more like a set of high-level rules for processing data than a set of instructions telling a program how to operate on inputs. Indeed, one major advantage of writing data processing code in a functional style is that the result is more declarative than imperative, and thus better conveys the intent behind the code. Here, for example, a single glance at the statement shows that we wish to only consider face cards, then further restrict the data to only consider cards in the clubs suit, and then finally count the data elements. It is also worth noting how the code is formatted, with each stream operation indented and prefixed with its period starting the visible part of a line. This coding style is a usual convention for formatting stream operations in Java. Its benefit is that it emphasizes the declarative nature of the code.

Mapping Data Elements

There are often situations in data processing where we need to transform all data elements in a stream into a derived value. In this case, we leverage the idea of *mapping* objects to their desired value. Here, the word "mapping" is employed in the mathematical sense synonymous to a function. For example, consider how the function that computes the square of a number x, usually denoted x^2, simply *maps* a number x to its square $x \cdot x$.

Many programming languages that support some form of functional-style processing provide a mechanism to apply a map (i.e., a function) to every element in a data collection. In Java the `Stream` class defines a `map` method that takes as input a parameter of type Function<? **super** T, ? **extends** R>. In other words, the argument to the map function is another function that takes as input an object of type T and returns an object of type R.[10] This means that the map function will transform a stream of objects of one type into an stream of objects of a different type.

As a simple example, let us consider a function that maps an instance of Card to an instance of an enumerated type Color that represents the color of the card's suit. We can apply this function systematically to all elements in a stream using the map method:

```
cards.stream().map(card -> card.getSuit().getColor() );
```

If this expression is evaluated on a shuffled deck, the resulting stream will be a random interleaving of the values Color.BLACK and Color.RED. Because the result is also a stream, we can pipeline the result of a mapping operation as for any other stream. For example, to count the number of black cards in a collection, we could write:

```
long result = cards.stream()
  .map(card -> card.getSuit().getColor() )
  .filter( color -> color == Color.BLACK )
  .count();
```

Although the same result can achieved more directly by using filter with a lambda expression that retrieves the card's color, the example above illustrates how we can use map to unpack an object and use only the part of the object that is of interest for a given computation.

Mapping, however, can accomplish much more than simply extracting data from an input element. Let us consider a second example, where we want to compute the score that a card represents. In some games, cards are assigned a point value that corresponds to their rank (e.g., three of clubs is worth three points), except for face cards which are all worth ten points. With a mapping process, we can convert a stream of card objects into a stream of integers that correspond to the score of each card in the original stream:

```
cards.stream()
  .map(card -> Math.min(10, card.getRank().ordinal() + 1));
```

The result of this expression will be a stream of Integer objects that represent the score of each card. As usual, whether to encapsulate the score computation in an instance method of class Card is a context-sensitive design decision. If the score value is used in multiple calling contexts, then it would make sense to add a method getScore() to the interface of class Card. Otherwise, the lambda expression will suffice.

When mapping to numerical values, as in this case, it is useful to know that the language provides specialized support for streams of numbers in the form of classes such as IntStream and DoubleStream. These types of streams work just like other streams, but they define additional operations that only make sense when processing numbers, such as summing the elements in the stream. To adapt our scoring example

---

[10] Technically, T or one of its supertypes, and R or one of its subtypes.

to get the total score, the code needs to explicitly map to an `IntStream`, and then call the `sum` terminal operation:

```
int total = cards.stream()
  .mapToInt(card -> Math.min(10, card.getRank().ordinal() + 1))
  .sum();
```

As an alternative and more declarative way to specify this computation, we could also do:

```
int total = cards.stream()
  .map(Card::getRank)
  .mapToInt(Rank::ordinal)
  .map(ordinal -> Math.min(10, ordinal + 1))
  .sum();
```

Reducing Streams

When processing streams of data, a common scenario is that we want not only to inspect each data element, but also do something with the data as a whole. Typically, this means either:

- Aggregating the effect of the operations into a single result. Terminal operations such as `count()` and `sum()` are good examples of data aggregation in that sense;
- Collecting the individual results of the operations into a stored data structure. In Java this would typically mean a `List` or similar collection type.

Although they seem different, both of these alternatives actually have in common that conceptually they represent *reducing* a stream to a single entity. In the second case, the entity may be a collection of many elements, but conceptually it is nevertheless a single, stored structure as opposed to a stream. The advantage of generalizing all types of data aggregation as a single high-level operation, reduction, introduces a clear distinction between intermediate operations, namely mapping,[11] and terminal operations, namely reducing. In fact programming systems where computation is expressed as a series of mapping operations followed by a reduction operation are commonly known as the map–reduce programming model. Although the term "map–reduce" is mostly used in the context of cluster computing, the basic model itself is directly applicable to functional-style programming with streams.

In Java, reduction is supported through various overloaded versions of the `reduce` method available in `Stream` classes. Implementing a reduction from scratch is a bit tricky, and the complete details are outside the scope of this book. However, the general idea is to provide the `reduce` function with an *accumulator* object that can incrementally update the reduced version of the input every time an element is encountered. For example, to implement the `sum` operation on an `IntStream` using the `reduce` method, the following code is used:

---

[11] We can consider that filtering is a type of mapping without loss of generality.

```
IntStream numbers = ...;
int sum = numbers.reduce(0, (a, b) -> a+b);
```

In practice, a summing reduction uses 0 as the base case and accumulates results by iteratively adding elements. The code below shows a simplified mock-up implementation of the reduce method for IntStream

```
public int reduce(int pBase, IntBinaryOperator operator)
{
  int result = pBase;
  Iterator<Integer> iterator = this.iterator();
  while( iterator.hasNext() )
  {
    int number = iterator.next();
    result = operator.applyAsInt(result, number);
  }
  return result;
}
```

Initially, the result of the reduction operation is set to the base provided, in our case 0. Then, for each element in the stream, the binary operator provided as input to reduce is applied using, as argument, the current result and the next element in the stream. In our case the binary operator was specified using the lambda expression (a,b) -> a + b. Thus, for each element in the stream, the value of the current reduction will be assigned to itself plus the value of the next element.

This being said, because most common reduction operations (min, max, count, sum, etc.) are directly supported by the stream classes, it is possible to get started with streams and actually get quite far without mastering the art of writing reductions.

Reductions that serve to accumulate data in a structure are a bit of a special case. Let us say we wish to collect all face cards in a list of cards in a separate list. One quick solution would be to use the forEach method to store the elements of the stream in the target list:

```
List<Card> result = new ArrayList<>();
cards.stream()
   .filter(Card::isFaceCard)
   .forEach(card -> result.add(card));
```

Although workable, this design loses some of the properties of declarative, functional-style expressions of a computation, because the first-class function that simulates the reduction is implemented using explicit list manipulation operations. As an alternative that supports a more functional style, the Java libraries provide helper methods to create a type of reduction called a *collector*. A collector is a reduction that accumulates elements into a collection. With a collector, the code above can be re-written as:

```
List<Card> result = cards.stream()
   .filter(Card::isFaceCard)
   .collect(Collectors.toList());
```

In this last example, the details of the implementation of the accumulation of elements into a list remain hidden, and the code directly expresses the desired intent: to collect the elements of the stream into a list.

Insights

This chapter introduced functional-style design and the programming language mechanisms that support it, and showed how to employ these mechanisms to embed functional elements into an object-oriented design.

- Consider a solution in the functional style for parts of a design that involve parameterizing behavior;
- Lambda expressions should be short and self-documenting: consider reorganizing your code to make them so;
- Favor short lambda expressions where the body is also an expression (as opposed to a sequence of statements);
- To emphasize flexibility and extensibility in your design, use library functional interfaces to define function types; to emphasize design constraints and intent, use application-defined functional interfaces;
- When designing methods, keep in mind how they could be used through references: ensure they are a good match for likely functional interfaces;
- Compose functions using functions, as opposed to imperative statements;
- Use helper methods on library types to compose functionality in intuitive ways;
- Use supplier function types to implement the pull data-flow strategy if the needs of clients are very specific;
- Consider defining strategies in the STRATEGY pattern as functional interfaces;
- Consider the possibility of composing strategies;
- Consider using first-class functions to define commands in the COMMAND pattern;
- Structure data processing code so that it is more declarative than imperative in style;
- Use the mapping abstract operation to convert data elements into the values that are directly used by a computation;
- Use collector objects to accumulate the result of stream operations.

Code Exploration

Event Handlers in Minesweeper

One common usage scenario for lambda expressions is to serve as event handlers (i.e., callbacks) that can be defined directly at the code location where the handler is connected to its event source. As an easy introduction to this idiom, the code of the Minesweeper application only uses a single lambda expression, located in method `createHiddenTile` of class `Minesweeper`. This lambda expression implements the behavior of the functional interface `EventHandler`, which has a single abstract function of type `Event → `**`void`**.

Strategies in Solitaire

The Solitaire application provides an example of behavior composition using first-class functions in the definition of automatic playing strategies. One of the features of the application is to automatically play a move based on some heuristic when a user types the "Enter" key. However, in a game of Solitaire, there are often situations where multiple legal moves are possible. Class `GreedyPlayingStrategy` provides an implementation of the `PlayingStrategy` interface by defining a number of "substrategies" as static methods, where each sub-strategy is one type of move (e.g., to select a card from the deck, to move a card to a foundation pile, etc.). The overall strategy can then be reduced to the order in which substrategies are attempted. The meta-heuristic (high-level operation) implemented by the actual strategy method is to cycle through a collection of first-class functions that represent sub-strategies, apply them, and stop as soon as one strategy is successful (as determined by a non-empty value in the `Optional` return value).

Event Handlers in JetUML

JetUML makes extensive use of lambda expressions to define event handlers in classes of package ...`gui`. One example that really shows the code readability benefits of lambda expressions is the definition of a handler for the URL link in the "About" dialog box, which opens a web browser and displays the license information:

```
link.setOnMouseClicked(e ->
   UMLEditor.openBrowser(RESOURCES.getString("dialog.about.url")));
```

In this case the code shows, in one statement, both the source of the event (`link`) and the behavior of its handler (to open a browser).

Observer Notification in JetUML

Functional-style idioms can also be used to implement observer notification in a compact way. For example, class `UserPreferences` allows the application to manage a global store of user preferences (for example, whether to display the grid or not). The preference store is designed as a model in the OBSERVER pattern, so every time a preference is changed, observers have to be notified. This behavior is implemented using the higher-order function `forEach` and a lambda expression to define the call to the handler:

```
public void setBoolean(BooleanPreference pPreference,
  boolean pValue)
{
  aBooleanPreferences.put(pPreference, pValue);
  Preferences.userNodeForPackage(UMLEditor.class).
    put(pPreference.name(), Boolean.toString(pValue));
  aBooleanPreferenceChangeHandlers.forEach(
    handler -> handler.preferenceChanged(pPreference));
}
```

COMMAND Pattern in JetUML

JetUML implements the COMMAND pattern in a functional style, with only two concrete command classes to represent simple and compound commands, respectively. The abstract command type is `DiagramOperation`, which has an `execute()` and an `undo()` method. It is thus not a functional interface. However, class `Simple-Operation` has two fields `aOperation` and `aReverse`, initializable through the constructor. The fields are of type `Runnable`. Because `Runnable` is a functional interface, what `SimpleOperation` represents is basically a container for two method references. Class `CompoundOperation` then simply implements the COMPOSITE pattern.

Absence of Streaming in JetUML

One of the architectural principles of JetUML, listed on its architectural documentation page, is "No streaming". This may seem like a counter-intuitive principle given that this chapter has been expounding the benefits of stream-based designs. Streams, however, impose a non-negligible shift in an application's design that has repercussions both on the interface of classes (which have to provide and/or accept streams) and on how one thinks about data processing. This overhead has to be worth it. In JetUML, the only real data processing that is done is to inspect collections of diagram elements. This can be done with streams but the benefits, in terms of both run-time performance and design qualities, is marginal. After some experimentation, I determined that implementing some operations using streams would most likely have a negative effect of the overall simplicity of the code, and thus I stuck to non-stream-based operations. Shunning streams, however, does not mean avoiding functional programming. Just by using higher-order functions provided by common library types, it is already possible to achieve a stream-like design without actually having to work with streams explicitly. Consider, for example, the code responsible for painting a diagram on a canvas object so that it becomes visible to the user. This code is located in class `DiagramCanvas`:

```java
public void paintPanel()
{
  ...
  aController.getSelectionModel()
    .forEach( selected -> selected.view()
      .drawSelectionHandles(context));

  aController.getSelectionModel().getRubberband()
    .ifPresent( rubberband -> ToolGraphics
      .drawRubberband(context, rubberband));

  aController.getSelectionModel().getLasso()
    .ifPresent( lasso -> ToolGraphics.drawLasso(context, lasso));
}
```

In JetUML, a `SelectionModel` is a list of diagram elements currently selected by the user. Because it implements `Iterable`, it automatically inherits the default method `forEach`, which can be used to traverse all selected elements (as in a stream) and apply a first-class function to them. The last two statements in the code above show how type `Optional` can be used with first-class functions. The type defines a higher-order function `ifPresent` that takes as input a `Consumer` of the optional type and applies the consumer function if the instance is available. Use of this function can thus turn iterative code that tests a value with an **if** statement into a straightforward invocation of a higher-order function that abstracts away the condition check.

Further Reading

An excellent resource for diving more deeply into functional-style programming in Java is the book *Java 8 in Action* by Urma et al. [16]. The book is for experienced programmers, but it provides an accessible introduction to the topic and a progressive treatment, which allows the reader to go as far as they are comfortable with. In terms of code style, *Effective Java* by Bloch [1] includes a chapter "Lambdas and Streams" which provides additional coaching on using these mechanisms in practice. The advice therein is consistent with the recommendations provided in this chapter, but includes additional discussions and examples.

For a more pragmatic review of the topic, the Java Tutorial [10] has a section on "Lambda Expressions" which also covers method references. The section of the tutorial on collections also covers streams, in a subsection titled "Aggregate Operations".

Appendix A
Important Java Programming Concepts

This appendix provides a brief orientation through the concepts of object-oriented programming in Java that are critical for understanding the material in this book and that are not specifically introduced as part of the main content. It is not intended as a general Java programming primer, but rather as a refresher and orientation through the features of the language that play a major role in the design of software in Java. If necessary, this overview should be complemented by an introductory book on Java programming, or on the relevant sections in the Java Tutorial [10].

A.1 Variables and Types

Variables store values. In Java, variables are typed and the type of the variable must be declared before the name of the variable. Java distinguishes between two major categories of types: *primitive* types and *reference* types. Primitive types are used to represent numbers and Boolean values. Variables of a primitive type store the actual data that represents the value. When the content of a variable of a primitive type is assigned to another variable, a copy of the data stored in the initial variable is created and stored in the destination variable. For example:

```
int original = 10;
int copy = original;
```

In this case variable `original` of the primitive type `int` (short for "integer") is assigned the integer literal value `10`. In the second assignment, a copy of the value 10 is used to initialize the new variable `copy`.

Reference types represent more complex arrangements of data as defined by classes (see Section A.2). The important thing to know about references types is that a variable of a reference type T stores a *reference* to an object of type T. Hence, values of reference types are not the data itself, but a reference to this data. The main implication is that copying a value means sharing a reference. Arrays are also reference types. For example:

© Springer Nature Switzerland AG 2019
M. P. Robillard, *Introduction to Software Design with Java*,
https://doi.org/10.1007/978-3-030-24094-3

```
int[] original = new int[] {1,2};
int[] copy = original;
copy[0] = 3;
int result = original[0]; // result == 3
```

In this case, `copy` is assigned the value stored in `original`. However, because the value stored in `original` is a reference to an object of an array type, the copy also refers to the object created in the first statement. Because, in effect, `copy` is only a different name (or *alias*) for `original`, modifying an element in `copy` also modifies that element in `original`.

A.2 Objects and Classes

Essentially, an *object* is a cohesive group of variables that store pieces of data that correspond to a given abstraction, and methods that apply to this abstraction. For example, an object to represent the abstraction "book" could include, among others, the book's title, author name, and publication year. In Java, the *class* is the compile-time entity that defines how to build objects. For example, the class:

```
class Book
{
  String title;
  String author;
  int year;
}
```

states that objects intended to represent a book will have three *instance variables* named `title`, `author`, and `year` of type `String`, `String`, and `int`, respectively. In addition to serving as a template for creating objects, classes also define a corresponding reference type. Objects are created from classes through a process of instantiation with the **new** keyword:

```
Book book = new Book();
```

The statement above creates a new *instance* (object) of class `Book` and stores a *reference* to this object in variable `book` declared to be of reference type `Book`. Instance variables, also known as *fields*, can be accessed by *dereferencing* a variable that stores a reference to the object. The dereferencing operator is the period (.). For example, to obtain the title of a book stored in a variable `book`, we do:

```
String title = book.title;
```

When discussing software design, it is good to avoid subconsciously using the terms *class* and *object* interchangeably. Objects and classes are different things. A class is a strictly compile-time entity that does not exist in running code. Conversely, objects are strictly run-time entities that do not have any representation in program source code. Mixing them up can lead to ambiguity and confusion.

A.3 Static Fields

Java allows the declaration of *static fields*:

```
class Book
{
  static int MIN_PAGES = 50;
  String title;
  String author;
  int year;
}
```

The effect of declaring a field `static` means that the field is not associated with
any object. Rather, a single copy of the field is created when the corresponding class
is loaded by the Java virtual machine, and the field exists for the duration of the
program's execution. Access to static fields can be restricted to only the code of the
class in which it is declared using the access modifier `private`. If declared to be
`public`, a static field can be accessed by any code in the application, in which case
it effectively constitutes a *global variable*. Because it is generally a bad practice to
modify globally-accessible data, global variables are best defined as *constants*, i.e.,
values not meant to be changed. Globally-accessible constants are declared with the
modifiers `public`, `static`, and `final`, and typically named using uppercase letters
(see Appendix B).

```
class Book
{
  public static final int MIN_PAGES = 50;
  ...
}
```

Static fields are accessed in classes other than the class that declares them by
prefixing their name with the name of their declaring class, followed by a period.
For example:

```
int minNumberOfPages = Book.MIN_PAGES;
```

A.4 Methods

In Java and other object-oriented programming languages, a *method* is the abstraction for a piece of computation. A method definition includes a return type, a name,
a (possibly empty) list of parameters, and a method body. The return type can be replaced by the keyword `void` to indicate that the method does not return a value. The
method body comprises the statements that form the implementation of the method.

Methods correspond to procedures in procedural languages and functions in
functional languages. Java supports two main categories of methods: *static* methods
and *instance* methods. Static methods are essentially procedures, or "non-object-
oriented" methods. Although they are declared in a class for reasons discussed in

Chapter 2, they are not automatically related to any object of the class and must explicitly list all their parameters in their signature. Method `abs(int)`, declared in the library class `java.lang.Math`, is a typical example of a static method. It takes an integer as an input and returns an integer that is the absolute value of the input number: no object is involved in this computation. Static methods are declared with the **static** modifier:

```
static int abs(int a) {...}
```

and called by prefixing the name of the method with the name of the class that declares the method, for example:

```
int absolute = Math.abs(-4);
```

In contrast, instance methods are methods intended to operate on a specific instance of a class. For this reason, instance methods have an *implicit parameter* of the same type as the type of the class they are declared in. An example is the static method `getTitle(Book book)` that simply returns the title of a book. Because this is a static method, it requires all necessary data to be provided as input:

```
class Book
{
  String title;
  ...
  static String getTitle(Book book) { return book.title; }
}
```

Because method `getTitle(Book)` operates on an instance of class `Book`, it makes more sense to declare it as an instance method. In this case, the parameter `book` becomes *implicit*: it must not be declared in the method's list of parameters, and its corresponding value becomes accessible inside the body of the method in a special variable called **this**. The code for `getTitle` written as an instance method is thus:

```
class Book
{
  String title;
  ...
  String getTitle() { return this.title; }
}
```

An instance method gets invoked by dereferencing a variable that stores a reference to an object. The result of the process is that the object referenced becomes the implicit argument to the instance method. In the statement:

```
Book book = ...;
String title = book.getTitle();
```

the object referenced by variable `book` becomes bound to the **this** pseudo-variable within the body of `getTitle()`.

A.5 Packages and Importing

User-defined types such as classes are organized into *packages*. Types declared to be in one package can be referenced from code in a different package using their *fully-qualified name*. A fully-qualified name consists of the name of the type in the package prefixed by the package name. For example, class `Random` of package `java.util` is a pseudo-random number generator. Its fully-qualified name is `java.util.Random`. Declaring a variable using a fully-qualified name can be rather verbose:

```
java.util.Random randomNumberGenerator = new java.util.Random();
```

For this reason, it is possible to *import* types from another package using the `import` statement at the top of a Java source code file:

```
import java.util.Random;
```

This makes it possible to refer to the imported type using its simple name (here `Random`) instead of the fully-qualified name. In Java, the import statement is simply a mechanism to avoid having to refer to various program elements using fully-qualified names. In contrast to other languages, it does not have the effect of making libraries available that were not already available through their fully-qualified name.

In addition to importing types, Java also makes it possible to import static fields and methods. For example, instead of referring to the `abs` method of class `java.util.Math` as `Math.abs`, we can statically import it:

```
import static java.lang.Math.abs;
```

and then just refer to `abs` in the code:

```
int absolute = abs(-4);
```

In the code fragments in this book, all types referenced in the code are assumed to be imported. When necessary, the surrounding text will clarify the source of the imported type.

A.6 Generic Types

In object-oriented programs, it is often the case that a type definition depends on another type. For example, we can consider the following type `OptionalString`, which may hold a `String` (the concept of the optional type is covered in more detail in Section 4.5):

```
public class OptionalString
{
  String object = null;
  OptionalString(String object) { this.object = object; }
  boolean isPresent() { return object != null; }
  String get() { return object; }
}
```

A class such as this one could easily be used to wrap any other kind of reference type. For this reason it is useful to be able to *parameterize* some of the types that a class depends on. This concept is supported in Java through *generic types*. Generic types are type declarations that include one or more *type parameters*. Type parameters are specified in angle brackets after the type name. In the declaration of a type, a type parameter acts as a placeholder for an actual type, which will be supplied when the generic type is used. Class `OptionalString` can be rewritten to work with any reference type by parameterizing the type of the object it holds:

```
class Optional<T>
{
  T object = null;
  Optional(T object) { this.object = object; }
  boolean isPresent() { return object != null; }
  T get() { return object; }
}
```

In the above code, the letter `T` does not represent an actual type, but a parameter (i.e., a placeholder) that is replaced by the actual type when the generic type is used:

```
Optional<String> myString = new Optional<>();
```

The type declaration for variable `myString` includes a *type instance* `String`. The effect of this type parameter instantiation is to replace the type parameter `T` with `String` everywhere in the declaration of `Optional<T>`. In the corresponding constructor call, the argument of the type parameter can be inferred, so an empty set of angle brackets (`<>`) need only be provided. This empty set of angle brackets is also called the *diamond operator*.

Generic types are used extensively in the library implementations of abstract data types (see Section A.7). Other features that involve generic types include generic methods, type bounds, and type wildcards. This book does not delve into the design of generic types because it is a relatively specialized topic. The content occasionally uses generic types to elaborate design solutions, but to the extent possible, these are limited to the basic instantiation of type parameters.

A.7 Collection Classes

Many of the examples in this book use library implementations of abstract data types (list, stack, etc.). In Java, this set of classes is commonly referred to as the *Collections framework*, and located in the package `java.util`. Collection classes are generic (see Section A.6). This means that the type of the elements held in a collection, such as an `ArrayList`, is a parameter that is provided when the collection type is used. For example, the following statement declares and instantiates a list of `String` instances:

```
ArrayList<String> myStrings = new ArrayList<>();
```

A.8 Exception Handling

Java provides a way for methods to indicate when they cannot complete normally through an *exception-handling* mechanism. In Java, exceptions are objects of a type that is a subtype of `Throwable`. To throw an exception, an exception object must be created and thrown using the **throw** keyword:

```java
void setMonth(int month)
{
  if( month < 1 || month > 12) throw new InvalidDateException();
  ...
}
```

Throwing an exception causes the control flow of the executing code to jump to a point in the code where the exception can be handled, unwinding the call stack as it goes. To handle an exception, it is necessary to declare a **try** block with one or more **catch** clauses. A **catch** clauses declares a variable of an exception type. An exception raised in or propagated into a **try** block is *caught* by the block's **catch** clause if the type of the exception can be legally assigned (through subtyping) to the exception variable. In this example:

```java
try
{ calendar.setMonth(13); }
catch( InvalidDateException e)
{ System.out.println(e.getMessage()); }
```

the call to `setMonth` throws an exception of type `InvalidDateException` which is immediately caught by the **catch** clause and bound to the variable `e`, which can then be dereferenced, for example to retrieve the message of the exception. If the type of the **catch** clause had been something else (for example `NumberFormatException`), the exception would not have been caught, and have propagated to the previous enclosing **try** block in the control flow.

Appendix B
Coding Conventions

Coding conventions are guidelines for organizing the presentation of source code. Aspects that fall under coding conventions typically include naming conventions, indentation, use of spaces, and line length. Following a set of coding conventions can help improve the readability of the code and prevent some types of errors. Coding conventions can vary from one organization to another because of cultural or practical reasons (each convention has its advantages and disadvantages).

In this appendix, I highlight of the coding conventions used in this book and in the example projects (see Appendix C). For an extensive discussion of coding conventions and why they matter, see Chapters 2, 4, and 5 of the book *Clean Code: A Handbook of Agile Software Craftmanship* by Robert C. Martin [7].

Medial Capitals for Identifier Names

As is usual in Java, the identifier names use medial capitalization, also known as camel case. With medial capitalization, words in a phrase are in lower case and each new word in the phrase starts with an uppercase letter. Type names start with an uppercase letter (e.g., `ArrayList`, `HashMap`) and method names start with a lowercase letter (e.g., `indexOf`, `replaceAll`). Instance variables (i.e., fields), class variables (i.e., static fields), and local variable names also follow medial capitalization, but with a special convention for fields (see below).

All Capitals for Constants

Constants (i.e., fields declared static and final) are named in all uppercase letters, with an underscore separating words (e.g., `WINDOW_SIZE`).

© Springer Nature Switzerland AG 2019
M. P. Robillard, *Introduction to Software Design with Java*,
https://doi.org/10.1007/978-3-030-24094-3

Variable Name Prefixes

Field names are prefixed with a lowercase `a` (for "attribute", a synonym for field),
e.g., `aData`. Method parameter types are camel-cased and prefixed with a lowercase
`p` (for "parameter"), e.g., `(pData)`. Local variables are camel-cased and start with a
lowercase letter, without a prefix (e.g., `data`). The only exception to these guidelines
is for the names of the parameters in lambda expressions, which are named like local
variables. The advantages of this convention are:

- Within a code block, it is always possible to determine what type of variable a
  name refers to without having to navigate to the declaration of this variable;
- The convention eliminates the risk of having a local variable hide a field by
  reusing the same name;
- The convention eliminates the necessity to use the **this** keyword to disam-
  biguate a field that has the same name as a method or constructor parameter
  (e.g., **this**.`data` = `data;`).

The systematic use of prefixes is one of the rare points where I disagree with the
advice of Robert C. Martin (referenced above). He states:

> Your classes and functions should be small enough that you don't need [prefixes]. And you
> should be using an editing environment that highlights or colorizes members to make them
> distinct. [7, p. 24]

Although desirable, both conditions (small classes and the use of an editor) are
not guaranteed to hold. In particular, viewing code hosted on a website such as
GitHub or reading it in a book means we cannot always rely on dynamic code high-
lighting tools. In a book that makes extensive use of partial code fragments, the
prefixes are also helpful for providing the necessary context for a name.

Indentation

Curly braces, which in Java define a code block, are positioned on their own line
such that corresponding braces are vertically aligned. This convention helps to visualize the scope introduced by the braces. Code statements within a block are indented by one unit (typically four spaces or one tab character) with respect to the
brace introducing the block.

```java
public int getHeight()
{
  return aHeight;
}
```

Use of the `@Override` Annotation

Methods intended to override an inherited method or implement an interface method
are annotated with `@Override`:

```
@Override
public String toString()
{
  return String.format("[w=%d x h=%d]", aWidth, aHeight);
}
```

Code Comments

Classes and interfaces must include a Javadoc [9] header comment, along with the
methods they declare. In-line comments are kept to a minimum.

Ellipses and Adaptations

Code in the example applications follows these coding conventions strictly. However, for code fragments in the chapter content I make various concessions for conciseness.

In particular, **code fragments should not be assumed to constitute complete
implementations**. In most cases, I silently elide parts of the code not essential to
the discussion. When there is a risk of ambiguity, I use an ellipsis (...) to indicate
elision, either in a block of code or in the parameter list of a method signature or the
argument list of a method call.

I also use an indentation tighter than four characters. For one-line methods, I also
inline the statement and both curly braces. If possible, I place the body of the method
on the same line as its signature. I will also typically not include the comments and
`@Override` annotation. The code below is a version of the `toString()` method
above with the three adaptations just discussed:

```
public String toString() { return String.format(...); }
```

Example

The following code is an elided and adapted version of class `Dimension` in the JetUML example project (see Appendix C) that illustrates most of the conventions discussed in this appendix.

```java
/**
 * Represents an immutable pair of width and height.
 */
public class Dimension
{
  public static final Dimension NULL = new Dimension(0, 0);

  private final int aWidth;
  private final int aHeight;

  public Dimension( int pWidth, int pHeight )
  {
    aWidth = pWidth;
    aHeight = pHeight;
  }

  public String toString()
  { return String.format(...); }

  public Dimension include(int pWidth, int pHeight)
  {
    return new Dimension(
      max(aWidth, pWidth), max(aHeight, pHeight) );
  }

  public int getWidth() { return aWidth; }
  public int getHeight() { return aHeight; }

  public int hashCode() {...}

  public boolean equals(Object pObject)
  {
    if(this == pObject) { return true; }
    if(pObject == null) { return false; }
    if(getClass() != pObject.getClass()) { return false; }
    Dimension other = (Dimension) pObject;
    return aHeight == other.aHeight &&
      aWidth == other.aWidth;
  }
}
```

Appendix C
Example Applications

Reading and trying to understand existing code is an essential part of learning software design. The three software projects described below provide sample code in the form of complete working applications. They are all graphical, interactive applications because this type of software introduces many opportunities for interesting design questions in a relatively compact code base. Moreover, because it is possible to interact directly with many aspects of the application, it is straightforward to relate design and implementation decisions to their observable realization.

Each of the example applications was developed following the principles and techniques presented in this book. At the end of each chapter, a Code Exploration section identifies and discusses aspects of the example applications that are related to the chapter topic.

The three applications offer three distinct levels of challenge in code understanding. The complete source code and installation and usage instructions can be found on GitHub at the URLs indicated below.

The first example application, **Minesweeper**, is a five-class program that implements the popular puzzle game of the same name. The idea is to discover mines hidden in a rectangular grid. This application is intended to serve as an accessible first approach to code understanding. It should be possible to understand every single design and implementation detail of this project after some reasonable effort. The code discussed in the book is consistent with **Release 1.0**.

```
https://github.com/prmr/Minesweeper
```

The second application, **Solitaire**, implements the card game of the same name. It realizes more complex requirements and thus its design exhibits additional sophistication and features. It also serves as the context for many of the running examples in the book. It should be possible to understand the general architecture of this project and many of the detailed design and implementation decisions after a few months of study. For some of the discussions in the chapters, knowledge of the game terminology will be useful. Figure C.1 illustrates the layout of a game of Solitaire in progress and includes overlays to indicate important terms. At the top-left is the

© Springer Nature Switzerland AG 2019   285
M. P. Robillard, *Introduction to Software Design with Java*,
https://doi.org/10.1007/978-3-030-24094-3

deck of face-down cards. A user *draws* a card from the deck and places it face up in the *discard pile*. The four piles at the top right of the layout are the *foundation piles* (these can be empty). Finally, the seven piles of cards that fan downwards are jointly called the *tableau* (tableau piles can also be empty). The code discussed in the book is consistent with **Release 1.0**.

```
https://github.com/prmr/Solitaire
```

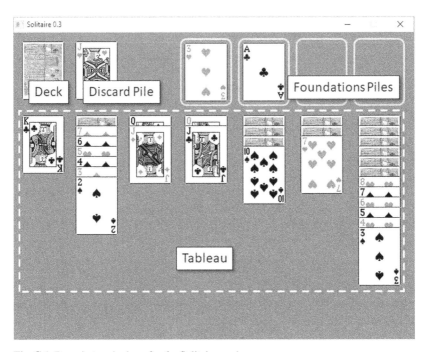

Fig. C.1 Domain terminology for the Solitaire card game

The third application, **JetUML**, is the interactive tool used to create all of the UML diagrams in this book. Although still modest in size compared to most software applications, it can be considered real production code and its design involves decisions that go a bit beyond the material covered in the course. The code discussed in the book is consistent with **Release 2.3**.

```
https://github.com/prmr/JetUML
```

References

1. Joshua Bloch. *Effective Java*. Addison-Wesley, 3rd edition, 2018.
2. Frank Buschmann, Kevin Henney, and Douglas C. Schmidt. *Pattern-Oriented Software Architecture Volume 4: A Pattern Language for Distributed Computing*. Wiley, 2007.
3. Martin Fowler. *Refactoring: Improving the Design of Existing Code*. Addison-Wesley, 1999.
4. Martin Fowler. *Patterns of Enterprise Application Architecture*. Addison-Wesley Professional, 2002.
5. Martin Fowler. *UML Distilled: A Brief Guide to the Standard Object Modeling Language*. Addison-Wesley, 3rd edition, 2004.
6. Erich Gamma, Richard Helm, Ralph Johnson, and John Vlissides. *Design Patterns: Elements of Reusable Object-Oriented Software*. Addison-Wesley Professional, 1994.
7. Robert C. Martin. *Clean Code: A Handbook of Agile Software Craftmanship*. Prentice Hall, 2009.
8. Bertrand Meyer. Applying "design by contract". *Computer*, 25(10):40–51, 1992.
9. Oracle. How to write doc comments for the Javadoc tool. `https://www.oracle.com/technetwork/java/javase/documentation/index-137868.html`. Accessed 17-May-2019.
10. Oracle. The Java tutorials. `https://docs.oracle.com/javase/tutorial/`. Accessed 17-May-2019.
11. David Lorge Parnas. On the criteria to be used in decomposing systems into modules. *Communications of the ACM*, 15(12):1053–1058, 1972.
12. David Lorge Parnas. Software aging. In *Proceedings of the 16th ACM/IEEE International Conference on Software Engineering*, pages 279–287, 1994.
13. Mauro Pezzè and Michal Young. *Software Testing and Analysis: Process, Principles and Techniques*. Wiley, 2007.
14. Martin P. Robillard. Sustainable software design. In *Proceedings of the 24th ACM SIGSOFT International Symposium on the Foundations of Software Engineering*, pages 920–923, 2016.
15. James Rumbaugh, Ivar Jacobson, and Grady Booch. *The Unified Modeling Language Manual*. Addison-Wesley, 2nd edition, 2004.
16. Raoul-Gabriel Urma, Mario Fusco, and Alan Mycroft. *Java 8 in Action*. Manning, 2015.
17. Oliver Vogel, Ingo Arnold, Arif Chughtai, and Timo Kehrer. *Software Architecture: A Comprehensive Framework and Guide for Practitioners*. Springer, 2011.

© Springer Nature Switzerland AG 2019   287
M. P. Robillard, *Introduction to Software Design with Java*,
https://doi.org/10.1007/978-3-030-24094-3

Index

© Springer Nature Switzerland AG 2019
M. P. Robillard, *Introduction to Software Design with Java*,
https://doi.org/10.1007/978-3-030-24094-3